1本就通
小學生
必備單字
2000

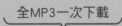

全MP3一次下載

http://www.booknews.com.tw/mp3/9789864543380.htm

全 MP3 一次下載為 zip 壓縮檔，
部分智慧型手機需安裝解壓縮程式方可開啟，iOS 系統請升級至 iOS 13 以上。
此為大型檔案，建議使用 WIFI 連線下載，以免占用流量，並確認連線狀況，以利下載順暢。

Contents

本書使用說明

奠定英文基礎的英文單字學習書！

提升學習動力、效率、效果，
擺脫學習壓力、自然快樂記單字！

主題分類
串聯日常生活主題，創造
英文學習環境！

情境式全圖解
提升學習興趣、看圖就懂，
自然就記住！

教育部頒定常用 2000 字
收錄單字以教育部頒定的常用 2000 字為基準，讓你學到真正用得到的必會
單字，打下紮實英文單字根基！

主題單字詳細剖析

主題內的單字均有詳細解說、發音、例句，並搭配同義字、反義字、小提醒等輔助學習，全面理解單字！

MP3音檔QR碼

外師親錄單字及例句 MP3，搭配書中音標標記，開口說得一口標準英語！

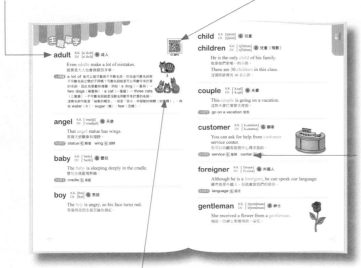

例句單字

例句中的單字一併記住，單字資料庫倍增！

例句插圖

利用生動圖像加深學習印象！

片語格言
輕鬆說

視主題需要補充更多應該知道的片語或格言，讓你除了單字之外，也能增進與主題相關知識。

VOCABULARY
一起看！

除了主題單字外，補充常用單字一起看！

主題句型

視主題需要補充相關知識與句型應用，讓學習更全面。

neighbor 鄰居

man 男人

woman 女人

gentleman 紳士

lady 女士

boy 男孩

queen 皇后

Bookstore

customer 顧客

adult 成人

welcome

king 國王

princess 公主

prince 王子

皇家傳說

kid
孩子

child / children
小孩（們）

girl
女孩

teenager
青少年

angel
天使

giant
巨人

stranger
陌生人

couple
夫婦

baby
嬰兒

foreigner
外國人

guy
男子

01.MP3

adult
KK [ə`dʌlt]
DJ [ə`dʌlt]
名 成人

Even adults make a lot of mistakes.
就算是大人也會做錯很多事。

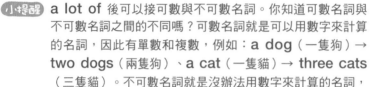

小提醒 **a lot of** 後可以接可數與不可數名詞。你知道可數名詞與不可數名詞之間的不同嗎？可數名詞就是可以用數字來計算的名詞，因此有單數和複數，例如：**a dog**（一隻狗）→ **two dogs**（兩隻狗）、**a cat**（一隻貓）→ **three cats**（三隻貓）。不可數名詞就是沒辦法用數字來計算的名詞，這類名詞可能是「抽象的概念」，或是「很小、非固態的物體（如氣體）」，例如 **water**（水）、**sugar**（糖）、**fear**（恐懼）。

---

angel
KK [`endʒl]
DJ [`eindʒəl]
名 天使

That angel statue has wings.
那個天使雕像有翅膀。

例句單字 statue 名 雕像　wing 名 翅膀

---

baby
KK [`bebɪ]
DJ [`beibi]
名 嬰兒

The baby is sleeping deeply in the cradle.
嬰兒在搖籃裡熟睡。

例句單字 cradle 名 搖籃

---

boy
KK [bɔɪ]
DJ [bɔi]
名 男孩

The boy is angry, so his face turns red.
那個男孩因生氣而臉色發紅。

child
KK [tʃaɪld]
DJ [tʃaild]
名 兒童

children
KK [ˋtʃɪldrən]
DJ [ˋtʃildrən]
名 兒童（複數）

He is the only child of his family.
他是他們家唯一的小孩。

There are 30 children in this class.
這個班級裡有 30 名小孩。

couple
KK [ˋkʌpl̩]
DJ [ˋkʌpl̩]
名 夫妻

This couple is going on a vacation.
這對夫妻打算要去度假。

例句單字 go on a vacation 度假

customer
KK [ˋkʌstəmɚ]
DJ [ˋkʌstəmə]
名 顧客

You can ask for help from the customer service center.
你可以向顧客服務中心尋求協助。

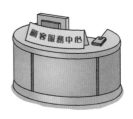

例句單字 service 名 服務　center 名 中心

foreigner
KK [ˋfɔrɪnɚ]
DJ [ˋfɔ:rinə]
名 外國人

Although he is a foreigner, he can speak our language.
雖然他是外國人，但他會說我們的語言。

例句單字 language 名 語言

gentleman
KK [ˋdʒɛntl̩mən]
DJ [ˋdʒɛntl̩mən]
名 紳士

She received a flower from a gentleman.
她從一位紳士那裡得到一朵花。

11

giant
KK [ˈdʒaɪənt]
DJ [ˈdʒaiənt]
名 巨人

The giant lives in a castle on the cloud.
那個巨人住在雲端上的城堡裡。

例句單字 castle 名 城堡

---

girl
KK [gɝl]
DJ [gəːl]
名 女孩

Pink is not just for girls.
粉紅色不是女孩專屬的顏色。

---

guy
KK [gaɪ]
DJ [gai]
名 男子

This guy keeps stepping on my toes.
這名男子一直踩到我的腳趾。

例句單字 step 動 踏；踩

---

kid
KK [kɪd]
DJ [kid]
名 孩子

Teaching a kid is not easy.
教導孩子並不容易。

---

king
KK [kɪŋ]
DJ [kiŋ]
名 國王

Lions are the king of beasts.
獅子是萬獸之王。

例句單字 beast 名 獸；野獸

---

lady
KK [ˈledɪ]
DJ [ˈleidi]
名 女士

It is hard for that old lady to climb the stairs.
對那位老太太而言，爬樓梯很困難。

例句單字 stair 名 （一階）階梯

man
KK [mæn]
DJ [mæn]
名 男人

That old man has a beard.
那位老先生留著鬍子。

例句單字 beard 名 鬍子

---

neighbor
KK [`nebɚ]
DJ [`neibə]
名 鄰居

My neighbor was playing loud music all night yesterday.
我的鄰居昨天一整晚都在大聲的播放音樂。

例句單字 play music 播放音樂

---

person
KK [`pɝsən]
DJ [`pə:sən]
名 人

people
KK [`pipḷ]
DJ [`pi:pḷ]
名 人（複數）

Don't give money to that strange person.
不要給那個奇怪的人錢。

Dogs run faster than people.
狗跑得比人快。

例句單字 faster than 比～快　strange 形 奇怪的

---

prince
KK [prɪns]
DJ [prins]
名 王子

The prince asked the little girl why she was crying.
王子詢問那個小女孩哭的原因。

---

princess
KK [`prɪnsɪs]
DJ [`prin`ses]
名 公主

The princess is wearing a beautiful dress.
公主穿著一件美麗的洋裝。

例句單字 dress 名 洋裝

queen
KK [kwin]
DJ [kwi:n] 名 皇后

The queen made an address on National Day.
女王在國慶日發表了演說。

例句單字 address 名 演說　National Day 名 國慶日

---

stranger
KK [`strendʒɚ]
DJ [`streindʒə] 名 陌生人

He saw a stranger walking around outside his house.
他看見一個陌生人在他家周圍走來走去。

例句單字 walk around （在附近）走來走去

---

teenager
KK [`tin͵edʒɚ]
DJ [`ti:n͵eidʒə] 名 青少年

The TV series is very popular among teenagers.
這部影集在青少年之中非常受歡迎。

例句單字 popular 形 受歡迎的　among 介 在～之中

---

woman
KK [`wʊmən]
DJ [`wumən] 名 女人

The woman who answered the phone spoke French.
接電話的那名女子講法文。

例句單字 answer the phone 接電話

小提醒 除了英文之外，你還知道其他國家的語言的英文是什麼嗎？

法文	French	中文	Chinese
德文	German	義大利文	Italian
西班牙文	Spanish	日文	Japanese
韓文	Korean	俄文	Russian
越南文	Vietnamese	泰文	Thai

I ran into him. 我和他偶然相遇。

　　ran into 裡的 ran 是 **run**（碰撞）的過去式形態，I ran into him. 字面上的意思就是「我碰撞到了他」，但其實就是指「**偶然相遇**」的意思。另外，想要說偶然相遇的話，也可以說「**I bumped into** him.」。如果在路上遇到有人與你打招呼，但是你卻不認識他，我們就可以說「**He's a stranger** to me.」意思是「他對我來說是個陌生人。」。

Vocabulary 一起看！

★certainly [`sɝtənlɪ] 副

　（用於回答）當然；沒問題

★classmate [`klæs͵met] 名 同學

★feeling [`filɪŋ] 名 感覺

★glad [glæd] 形 高興的

★happy [`hæpɪ] 形 快樂的

★honor [`ɑnɚ] 名 榮譽

★meet [mit] 動 認識；遇見

★mutual [`mjutʃuəl] 形 相互的；彼此的

★nice [naɪs] 形 美好的，友好的

★of course 片 當然

★pleasure [`plɛʒɚ] 名 愉快

★ride [raɪd] 動 騎；搭乘

★sure [ʃur] 副 的確，當然

15

Family 家族

live 居住；活著

aunt 姑姑；阿姨

uncle 叔叔；伯伯

marry 結婚

grow 成長

family 家庭

sister 姊妹

brother 兄弟

son 兒子

cousin 堂（表）兄弟姊妹

daughter 女兒

02.MP3

aunt
KK [ænt]
DJ [ɑ:nt]
名 姑姑；阿姨

Adam's aunt has beautiful red hair.
亞當的阿姨有一頭美麗的紅髮。

---

born
KK [bɔrn]
DJ [bɔ:n]
名 出生的

Jesus was born in a stable.
耶穌在馬廄出生。

例句單字 Jesus 名 耶穌　stable 名 馬廄

---

brother
KK [`brʌðə]
DJ [`brʌðə]
名 兄弟

Jeff is my elder brother.
傑夫是我的哥哥。

例句單字 elder 形 年齡較大的

小提醒 在英文裡，brother 和 sister 是沒有區分年齡大小的，
如果想要說哥哥或姐姐、弟弟或妹妹，就要像下面這樣說唷～

| 哥哥 | elder brother | 弟弟 | younger brother |
| 姊姊 | elder sister | 妹妹 | younger sister |

---

cousin
KK [`kʌzən]
DJ [`kʌzən]
名 堂（表）兄弟姊妹

She doesn't like her selfish cousin.
她不喜歡她那位自私的表姊。

例句單字 selfish 形 自私的

---

daughter
KK [`dɔtə]
DJ [`dɔ:tə]
名 女兒

Her daughter is a lawyer.
她的女兒是一位律師。

例句單字 lawyer 名 律師

family
KK [`fæməlɪ]
DJ [`fæmili]
名 家庭；家族

My family is warm and happy.
我的家庭溫暖幸福。

例句單字 warm 形 溫暖的

---

father
KK [`faðɚ]
DJ [`fɑ:ðə]
名 父親

His father suffers from serious illness.
他的父親受到嚴重的疾病所苦。

例句單字 suffer from 受～之苦；受～困擾　illness 名 疾病

---

grandfather
KK [`grænd͵faðɚ]
DJ [`grænd͵fɑ:ðə]
名 祖父；外公

Her grandfather was a soldier.
她的祖父以前是一名軍人。

例句單字 soldier 名 軍人

小提醒 你還知道其他跟軍人有關的單字嗎？

陸軍 **army**　　　海軍 **navy**　　　空軍 **airforce**

---

grandmother
KK [`grænd͵mʌðɚ]
DJ [`grænd͵mʌðə]
名 祖母；外婆

Her grandmother can speak Japanese.
她的祖母會說日文。

例句單字 Japanese 名 日文

---

grow
KK [gro]
DJ [grəu]
動 成長

The sunflower grows toward the sun.
向日葵朝著太陽生長。

例句單字 sunflower 名 向日葵　toward 介 朝；向

husband KK [ˈhʌzbənd] DJ [ˈhʌzbənd] 名 丈夫

Her husband died in a car accident.
她的丈夫在一場車禍中過世。

例句單字 die 動 死亡　accident 名 意外

小提醒 除了車禍之外，你知道其他的事故怎麼說嗎？

車禍	car accident	空難	plane crash
地震	earthquake	海嘯	tsunami
土石流	mudslide	洪水	flood

live KK [lɪv] DJ [lɪv] 動 居住；活著

He lives in a quiet village.
他住在一個安靜的村莊。

You only live once.
人生只有一次。

例句單字 village 名 村莊　once 副 一次

marry KK [ˈmærɪ] DJ [ˈmærɪ] 動 結婚

The freedom to marry should be protected.
婚姻的自由應受到保護。

例句單字 freedom 名 自由　should 助 應該
protect 動 保護

mother KK [ˈmʌðɚ] DJ [ˈmʌðə] 名 母親

Alex's mother is very generous.
艾力克斯的母親非常大方。

例句單字 generous 形 大方的

小提醒 father 和 mother 的中文意思分別是「父親」和「母親」，這兩個字是比較正式的說法，就像我們日常生活當中也不常用「父親」、「母親」來稱呼爸媽，這一點對外國人來說也是一樣的喔！他們通常會用 Dad 代替 father，而用 Mom 來代替 mother，也就是中文的「爸爸」和「媽媽」，下次就這樣說說看吧！

parent
KK [ˋpɛrənt]
DJ [ˋpɛərənt]
名 家長

My parents care about me very much.
我的父母非常關心我。

例句單字 care 動 關心

---

sister
KK [ˋsɪstɚ]
DJ [ˋsɪstə]
名 姊妹

Do you have a twin sister?
你有雙胞胎姊妹嗎？

例句單字 twin 名 雙胞胎

---

son
KK [sʌn]
DJ [sʌn]
名 兒子

He likes to drink coffee with his son.
他喜歡和他的兒子一起喝咖啡。

---

uncle
KK [ˋʌŋkl̩]
DJ [ˋʌŋkl̩]
名 叔叔；伯伯

His uncle is a sports fan.
他的叔叔是個運動迷。

例句單字 fan 名 （運動、電影等）狂熱愛好者

---

wife
KK [waɪf]
DJ [waif]
名 妻子

My uncle's wife is beautiful and nice; she always talks with a smile.
我叔叔的妻子漂亮又和善；她總是帶著微笑說話。

例句單字 beautiful 形 漂亮的　nice 形 和善的　with a smile 帶著微笑

beautiful

漂亮的

blind

眼盲的

cute

可愛的

fat

肥胖的

thin

瘦的

handsome

英俊的

heavy

笨重的

old

年紀大的

young

年輕的

pretty
漂亮的

short tall
矮的 高的

slim
纖瘦的

over-weight
過重的

slender
苗條的

skinny
極瘦的

chubby
胖胖的

nice-looking
好看的

ugly
醜陋的

23

03.MP3

beautiful
KK [`bjutəfəl]
DJ [`bju:təfəl]　形 漂亮的

Exercise will make you more beautiful.
運動會使你更加漂亮。

例句單字 exercise 名 運動

---

blind
KK [blaɪnd]
DJ [blaind]　形 眼盲的

We should let the guide dog stay with the blind man in the restaurant.
我們應該讓導盲犬與視障人士一起待在餐廳裡。

例句單字 guide dog 名 導盲犬

---

cute
KK [kjut]
DJ [kju:t]　形 可愛的

This baby has round cute face.
這個嬰兒有可愛的圓臉。

例句單字 round 形 圓的

小提醒 想要說其他形狀的時候，你知道該怎麼說嗎？
三角形　triangle　　　　正方形　square
長方形　rectangle　　　　菱形　　diamond

---

chubby
KK [`tʃʌbɪ]
DJ [`tʃʌbi]　形 胖胖的

I think Tom is a little chubby.
我認為湯姆有點胖胖的。

---

fat
KK [fæt]
DJ [fæt]　形 肥胖的

Being fat is not good for your health.
肥胖對你的健康不好。

例句單字 good for 對～有效；有幫助

24

handsome
KK [ˋhænsəm]
DJ [ˋhænsəm]
形 英俊的

He is a very handsome actor.
他是一位非常英俊的演員。

例句單字 actor 名 男演員

---

heavy
KK [ˋhɛvɪ]
DJ [ˋhevi]
形 笨重的

This heavy suitcase weighs about 45 kilograms.
這個笨重的行李箱大約有 45 公斤重。

例句單字 suitcase 名 行李箱　weigh 動 稱～的重量

---

nice-looking
KK [ˋnaɪsˋlʊkɪŋ]
DJ [ˋnaɪsˋlukiŋ]
形 好看的

Where did you buy that nice-looking necklace?
你那條好看的項鍊是去哪裡買的？

例句單字 necklace 名 項鍊

小提醒 想要問別人其他飾品要去哪裡買的話，你一定要會底下這些字！

耳環　earrings　　　手環　bracelet
腳鍊　anklet

---

old
KK [old]
DJ [əuld]
形 年紀大的

The old man needs his crutch.
這位老先生需要他的拐杖。

例句單字 crutch 名 拐杖

over-weight
KK [`ovə͵wet]
DJ [`əuvə`wet]
形 過重的

We should not make fun of over-weight people.
我們不應該嘲弄過重的人。

例句單字 make fun of 嘲弄～

---

pretty
KK [`prɪtɪ]
DJ [`priti]
形 漂亮的

Lisa spent a lot of money to keep her hair pretty.
麗莎花了很多錢來維持漂亮的頭髮。

例句單字 spend 動 花費（時間、金錢等） keep 動 維持

---

short
KK [ʃɔrt]
DJ [ʃɔ:t]
形 矮的

Alan is a short and fat boy.
亞倫是個又矮又胖的男孩。

---

skinny
KK [`skɪnɪ]
DJ [`skini]
形 極瘦的

Being too skinny is not only bad-looking, but also unhealthy.
太瘦不只不好看，也不健康。

例句單字 not only A but also B 不只A，也是B bad-looking 形 不好看的

---

slender
KK [`slɛndə]
DJ [`slendə]
形 苗條的

The slender man standing there is my teacher.
那個站在那裡的苗條男子是我的老師。

反義詞 fat 形 肥胖的

slim
KK [slɪm]
DJ [slim]
形 纖瘦的

He used to be very slim.
他曾經非常纖瘦。

例句單字 used to be 曾經

tall
KK [tɔl]
DJ [tɔ:l]
形 高的

Not all tall people have tall parents.
不是所有高的人的父母都很高。

thin
KK [θɪn]
DJ [θin]
形 瘦的

While trying to be thin, you should also care for your health.
在想要變瘦的同時，你應該也要注意你的健康。

ugly
KK [ˋʌglɪ]
DJ [ˋʌgli]
形 醜陋的

That's the ugliest doll that I have ever seen.
那是我看過最醜的洋娃娃。

young
KK [jʌŋ]
DJ [jʌŋ]
形 年輕的

Man can't be young forever.
人不可能永遠年輕。

例句單字 forever 副 永遠地

27

Face & Body 臉 & 身體

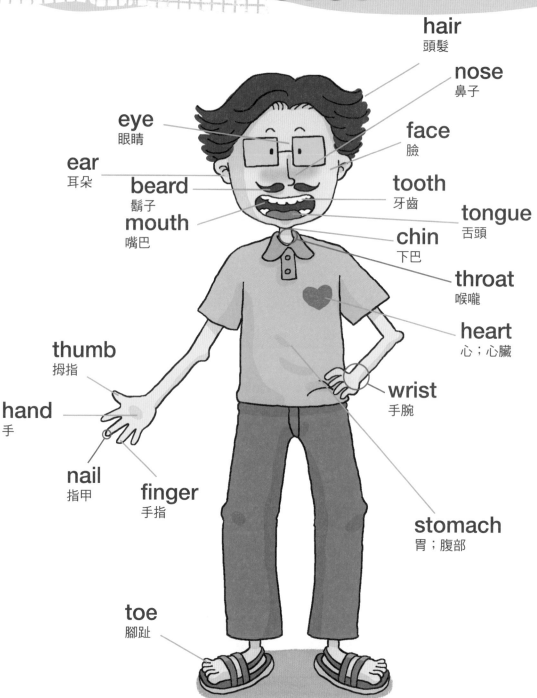

hair
頭髮

nose
鼻子

eye
眼睛

face
臉

ear
耳朵

beard
鬍子

tooth
牙齒

tongue
舌頭

mouth
嘴巴

chin
下巴

throat
喉嚨

heart
心；心臟

thumb
拇指

hand
手

wrist
手腕

nail
指甲

finger
手指

stomach
胃；腹部

toe
腳趾

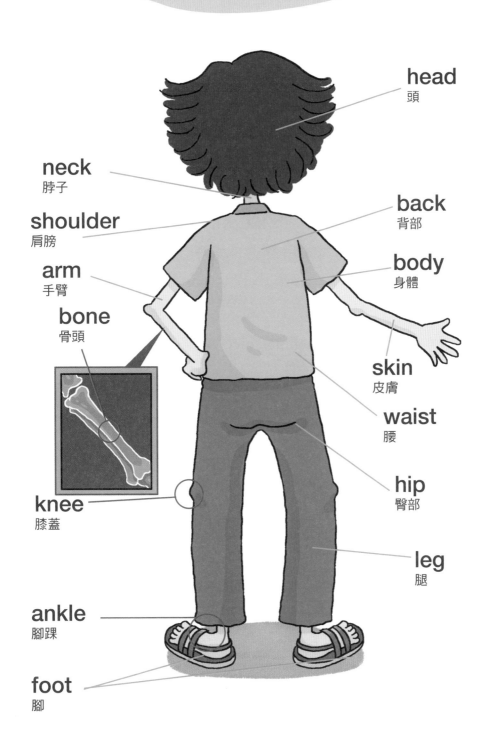

head
頭

neck
脖子

shoulder
肩膀

arm
手臂

bone
骨頭

knee
膝蓋

ankle
腳踝

foot
腳

back
背部

body
身體

skin
皮膚

waist
腰

hip
臀部

leg
腿

04.MP3

ankle
KK [ˋæŋkl̩]
DJ [ˋæŋkəl]
名 腳踝

Amy likes to wear jewels around her ankle.
艾咪喜歡在腳踝上配戴珠寶。

例句單字 jewel 名 珠寶

arm
KK [ɑrm]
DJ [ɑ:m]
名 手臂

Sam has a tattoo on his arm.
山姆在手臂上有刺青。

例句單字 tattoo 名 刺青

back
KK [bæk]
DJ [bæk]
名 背部

Her back has been aching since last night.
她從昨晚開始背就持續疼痛。

例句單字 ache 動 疼痛 since 副 自從

小提醒 你知道身上其他地方痛的話要怎麼說嗎？

胃痛 **stomachache**　　頭痛 **headache**　　牙齒痛 **toothache**

beard
KK [bɪrd]
DJ [biəd]
名 鬍子

How often does a man usually shave his beard?
男人通常多久刮一次鬍子？

例句單字 shave 動 刮除

body
KK [ˋbɑdɪ]
DJ [ˋbɔdi]
名 身體

Everyone's body is unique.
每個人的身體都是獨特的。

例句單字 unique 形 獨特的

bone
KK [bon]
DJ [bəun]
名 骨頭

Our dog buries bones in the garden.
我們的狗將骨頭埋在花園裡。

例句單字 garden 名 花園　bury 動 埋

---

chin
KK [tʃɪn]
DJ [tʃin]
名 下巴

He was bitten by a mosquito on his chin.
蚊子叮了他的下巴。

例句單字 mosquito 名 蚊子

---

ear
KK [ɪr]
DJ [iə]
名 耳朵

He couldn't believe his ears.
他不敢相信他所聽到的。

例句單字 believe 動 相信

小提醒 「不敢相信他所聽到的」可以寫成「不敢相信他的耳朵」，那你就知道「不敢相信所看到的」要怎麼說了吧？

沒錯！就是 **He couldn't believe his eyes.** （他不敢相信他的眼睛。）

---

eye
KK [aɪ]
DJ [ai]
名 眼睛

She is rubbing her eyes.
她正在揉眼睛。

例句單字 rub 動 揉

---

face
KK [fes]
DJ [feis]
名 臉

Her face turned red when she was praised by her teacher.
當她被老師稱讚的時候，她臉紅了。

例句單字 turn 動 變成～　praise 動 稱讚

finger KK [ˋfɪŋɚ] DJ [ˈfiŋgə] 名 手指

He is a pianist with 9 fingers.
他是一位九指鋼琴家。

例句單字 pianist 名 鋼琴家

foot KK [fʊt] DJ [fut] 名 腳
feet KK [fit] DJ [fi:t] 名 腳（複數）

Do you go to school on foot?
你走路去學校嗎？

例句單字 on foot 步行

hair KK [hɛr] DJ [hɛə] 名 頭髮

Her hair is very soft and smooth.
她的頭髮非常柔順。

例句單字 soft 形 柔軟的　smooth 形 滑順的

hand KK [hænd] DJ [hænd] 名 手

Do you have some hand cream?
你有一些護手霜嗎？

例句單字 some 形 一些的

head KK [hɛd] DJ [hed] 名 頭

Tom shook his head.
湯姆搖了搖頭。

例句單字 shake 動 搖晃

關聯片語 nod one's head （某人）點頭

heart
KK [hɑrt]
DJ [hɑ:t]
名 心；心臟

The news gave that old man a heart attack.
這個新聞讓那位老人心臟病發作

例句單字 **heart attack** 名 心臟病

---

hip
KK [hɪp]
DJ [hip]
名 臀部

He shakes his hips while listening to music.
他在聽音樂的時候搖動臀部。

---

knee
KK [ni]
DJ [ni:]
名 膝蓋

Jenny hurt her knees when she fell down.
珍妮摔倒時傷到了膝蓋。

例句單字 **fall down** 摔倒

---

leg
KK [lɛg]
DJ [leg]
名 腿

What happened to your leg?
你的腿怎麼了？

---

mouth
KK [mauθ]
DJ [mauθ]
名 嘴巴

His mouth is full of bread.
他的嘴巴裡都是麵包。

例句單字 **full of** 充滿～

---

nail
KK [nel]
DJ [neil]
名 指甲

She doesn't like men with long nails.
她討厭長指甲的男人。

小提醒 你知道跟指甲相關的單字有哪些嗎？

手指甲	**fingernail**	腳指甲	**toenail**
指甲油	**nail polish**	去光水	**nail polish remover**

neck
KK [nɛk]
DJ [nek]
名 脖子

He is so fat that he has no neck. 他胖到沒有脖子。

例句單字 so~ that~ 太〜以至於〜

nose
KK [noz]
DJ [nəuz]
名 鼻子

This actor is famous for his big nose.
這位演員以他的大鼻子聞名。

例句單字 famous 形 有名的

shoulder
KK [ˈʃoldɚ]
DJ [ˈʃəuldə]
名 肩膀

Mary put her head on Tom's shoulder.
瑪麗將頭放在了湯姆的肩膀上。

skin
KK [skɪn]
DJ [skɪn]
名 皮膚

Her skin is very white. 她的皮膚非常白。

stomach
KK [ˈstʌmək]
DJ [ˈstʌmək]
名 胃；腹部

I laughed so much that my stomach hurts.
我笑得太厲害，肚子都痛了。

例句單字 laugh 動 大笑

throat
KK [θrot]
DJ [θrəut]
名 喉嚨

I forgot to turn off my fan last night, and my throat is sore
now. 我昨天晚上忘記把電風扇關掉，結果現在喉嚨痛。

例句單字 sore 形 疼痛發炎的

thumb
KK [θʌm]
DJ [θʌm]
名 拇指

That baby is sucking her thumb. 那個嬰兒正在吸自己的拇指。

小提醒 你知道要怎麼用英文說其他手指嗎？

食指　index finger　　中指　middle finger

無名指　ring finger　　小指　little finger

toe KK [to] DJ [təu] 名 腳趾

He stepped on my toes.

他踩到了我的腳趾。

例句單字 step 動 踩

tongue KK [tʌŋ] DJ [tʌŋ] 名 舌頭

The soup is so hot that I hurt my tongue.

這湯燙到讓我舌頭受傷了。

例句單字 soup 名 湯

tooth KK [tuθ] DJ [tu:θ] 名 牙齒

teeth KK [tiθ] DJ [ti:θ] 名 牙齒（複數）

I have to let the dentist check my teeth.

我必須去看牙醫檢查牙齒。

例句單字 dentist 名 牙醫

臉 & 身體

Face & Body

waist KK [west] DJ [weist] 名 腰

What is your waist size?

你的腰圍是多少？

wrist KK [rɪst] DJ [rist] 名 手腕

She grabbed my wrist.

她抓住我的手腕。

例句單字 grab 動 抓；握

Personal Characteristics 個人特質

kind
善良的

careless
粗心的

careful
小心謹慎的

generous
大方的

selfish
自私的

nice
好的；和善的

famous
有名的

hard-working
努力的

friendly
友善的

lazy
懶惰的

funny
有趣的

proud
驕傲的

honest
誠實的

poor
窮困的

rich
有錢的

stupid
愚笨的

smart
聰明的

polite
有禮貌的

wise
有智慧的

popular
受歡迎的

lonely
孤單的

lovely
讓人喜愛的

shy
害羞的

successful
成功的

crazy
瘋狂的

05.MP3

careful
KK [`kɛrfəl]
DJ [`kɛəfəl]
形 小心謹慎的

Please be careful.
請小心謹慎。

---

careless
KK [`kɛrlɪs]
DJ [`kɛəlis]
形 粗心的

Jack is a careless person.
傑克是一個粗心的人。

反義詞 careful 形 仔細的　thoughtful 形 細心的
cautious 形 謹慎的

---

crazy
KK [`krezɪ]
DJ [`kreizi]
形 瘋狂的

That crazy man burned down his own house.
那個瘋狂的人燒掉了自己的家。

例句單字 burn 動 燃燒　own 形 自己的

---

famous
KK [`feməs]
DJ [`feiməs]
形 有名的

My uncle is a famous doctor.
我的叔叔是有名的醫生。

例句單字 doctor 名 醫生

---

friendly
KK [`frɛndlɪ]
DJ [`frendli]
形 友善的

Please be friendly to your classmates.
請對你的同學友善。

Personal Characteristics

個人特質

funny
KK [`fʌnɪ]
DJ [`fʌni]
形 有趣的

Her hat looks funny.
她的帽子看起來很有趣。

小提醒 funny 這個字除了「有趣的」這個意思之外，也有「可笑滑稽的」的意思，所以如果我們想要說「某人很有趣」，若用 funny 就會變成說這個人「很可笑滑稽」，除非對方是搞笑藝人，不然可是會惹對方生氣的唷～

---

generous
KK [`dʒɛnərəs]
DJ [`dʒenərəs]
形 大方的

Mary is a generous friend; she often shares nice things with us.
瑪麗是一個大方的朋友，她常與我們分享好東西。

例句單字 share 動 分享

---

hard-working
KK [ˌhɑrd`wɝkɪŋ]
DJ [ˌhɑːd`wəːkiŋ]
形 努力的

He is a hard-working student.
他是一位努力的學生。

---

honest
KK [`ɑnɪst]
DJ [`ɔnist]
形 誠實的

Please be honest with me.
請對我誠實。

小提醒 「誠實」也就是不要說謊的意思，「說謊」的英文是 lie，lie 這個字名詞和動詞長得一模一樣，當名詞的時候就是「謊話」的意思，那你知道要怎麼用英文請對方不要說謊嗎？沒錯，就是 **Please don't lie to me.**

---

kind
KK [kaɪnd]
DJ [kaind]
形 善良的

I think she has a kind heart.
我認為她有一顆善良的心。

lazy
KK [ˋlezɪ]
DJ [ˋleizi]
形 懶惰的

That lazy student doesn't like to go to school.
那個懶惰的學生不喜歡去學校。

反義詞 diligent 形 勤奮的 industrious 形 勤勉的

lonely
KK [ˋlonlɪ]
DJ [ˋləunli]
形 孤單的

When do you feel lonely?
你什麼時候會覺得孤單？

lovely
KK [ˋlʌvlɪ]
DJ [ˋlʌvli]
形 讓人喜愛的

There is a lovely cat in the shop.
這間店裡有一隻讓人喜愛的貓。

nice
KK [naɪs]
DJ [nais]
形 好的；和善的

They are nice kids.
他們是好孩子。

polite
KK [pəˋlaɪt]
DJ [pəˋlait]
形 有禮貌的

He made a polite bow to his teacher.
他向他的老師有禮貌地鞠躬。

例句單字 bow 名 鞠躬

poor
KK [pʊr]
DJ [puə]
形 窮困的

He came from a poor village.
他來自一個窮困的村莊。

例句單字 village 名 村莊

popular
KK [ˋpɑpjələ]
DJ [ˋpɔpjulə]
形 受歡迎的

This handsome Korean actor is popular because of his works.
這位帥氣的韓國演員因他的作品而受到歡迎。

例句單字 drama 名 戲劇

---

proud
KK [praʊd]
DJ [praud]
形 驕傲的

He is a proud kid, so nobody likes him.
他是個驕傲的孩子，所以沒人喜歡他。

小提醒 proud 這個字除了用來形容人很驕傲之外，也可以用 be proud of 的方式來表達「以～為傲」的意思，如：
His parents are proud of him. 他的父母以他為傲。

---

rich
KK [rɪtʃ]
DJ [ritʃ]
形 有錢的

That rich man owns an airplane.
那個有錢人擁有一架飛機。

例句單字 airplane 名 飛機

---

selfish
KK [ˋsɛlfɪʃ]
DJ [ˋselfiʃ]
形 自私的

He made a selfish choice.
他做了一個自私的選擇。

例句單字 choice 名 選擇
反義詞 selfless 形 無私的　unselfish 形 無私的

---

shy
KK [ʃaɪ]
DJ [ʃai]
形 害羞的

Alice is so shy that she can't speak in public.
愛麗絲太過害羞，以至於無法公開發言。

例句單字 speak 動 說話　in public 公開地

smart
KK [smɑrt]
DJ [smɑ:t] 形 聰明的

That smart student does very well on tests.
那個聰明的學生考試考很好。

---

stupid
KK [`stjupɪd]
DJ [`stju:pid] 形 愚笨的

Will you stop asking stupid questions?
你可以停止問笨問題嗎？

例句單字 stop 動 停止　ask 動 詢問

小提醒 你知道 stop 後面接不同形態的動詞代表不同的意思嗎？

如果後面接現在分詞（動詞＋ing），就像上面的例句那樣，那就表示停止「現在正在做的這件事」；而後面若接不定詞（to＋動詞），意思則是停下「原本正在做的事，而去做後面所提到的事」。看以下例句會更清楚唷！

He stops talking. 他停止說話。

He stops to talk. 他停下了動作而開始說話。

---

successful
KK [sək`sɛsfəl]
DJ [sək`sesfəl] 形 成功的

Jane is a successful businesswoman.
珍是一位成功的女企業家。

例句單字 businesswoman 名 女企業家

---

wise
KK [waɪz]
DJ [waiz] 形 有智慧的

Are you wise enough to make the right choice?
你有足夠智慧做出正確的選擇嗎？

例句單字 enough 形 足夠的　right 形 正確的

Health 健康

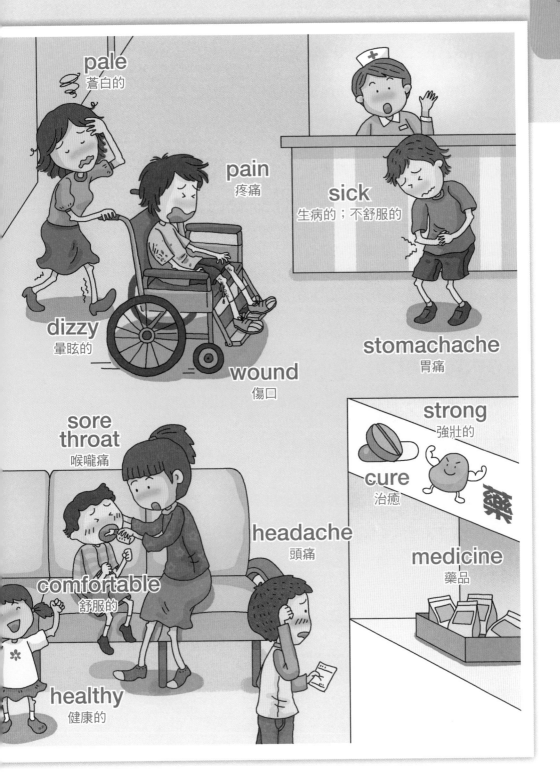

06.MP3

cancer
KK [`kænsɚ]
DJ [`kænsə]　名 癌症

He recovered from cancer.
他從癌症中恢復。

---

cold
KK [kold]
DJ [kəuld]　名 感冒

I had a cold yesterday, so I couldn't go to school .
我昨天因感冒而沒辦法上學。

例句單字 yesterday 名 昨天

小提醒 cold 除了感冒的意思之外，當形容詞的時候是「寒冷的」意思，在記憶的時候可以用：「因為變冷（cold）了，所以得了感冒（cold）」，這樣就可以一次把兩個用法都記下來了唷～

---

comfortable
KK [`kʌmfɚtəbl]
DJ [`kʌmfətəbl]　形 舒服的

The baby is covered with a comfortable blanket.
這個嬰兒被蓋上了一條舒服的毯子。

例句單字 cover 動 覆蓋　blanket 名 毯子

---

cough
KK [kɔf]
DJ [kɔf]　名 咳嗽

That old lady can't stop coughing.
那位老太太咳嗽咳個不停。

---

cure
KK [kjʊr]
DJ [kjuə]　動 治癒

Can this doctor cure his illness?
這位醫生能治癒他的疾病嗎？

例句單字 illness 名 疾病

46

death KK [dɛθ] DJ [deθ] 名 死亡

Tom blames himself for his wife's death.
湯姆為妻子的死而責怪自己。

例句單字 blame A for B 因 B 責怪 A

小提醒 跟死亡相關的單字還有哪些呢？

| 葬禮 | funeral | 棺木 | coffin |
| 花束 | bouquet | 哀悼 | mourn |

dizzy KK [ˋdɪzɪ] DJ [ˋdizi] 形 暈眩的

He feels dizzy, so he can't stand up.
他覺得暈眩而站不起來。

例句單字 stand up 站起來

fever KK [ˋfivɚ] DJ [ˋfiːvə] 名 發燒

This baby stays in the hospital because he has a high fever.
這個嬰兒因發高燒而住院。

例句單字 hospital 名 醫院

flu KK [flu] DJ [fluː] 名 流行性感冒

It is flu season now.
現在是流行性感冒的季節。

headache KK [ˋhɛdˌek] DJ [ˋhedeik] 名 頭痛

I have a headache today.
我今天頭痛。

health
KK [hɛlθ]
DJ [helθ]
名 健康

You should care about your health.
你應該關心自己的健康。

例句單字 care 動 關心

---

healthy
KK [`hɛlθɪ]
DJ [`helθi]
形 健康的

Mary lives a healthy life.
瑪麗過著健康的生活。

例句單字 keep 動 維持

小提醒 你知道健康的生活要維持什麼習慣嗎？這些習慣要怎麼用英文說呢？

吃蔬菜 eat vegetables　　不要熬夜 don't stay up late

喝水 drink water　　運動 exercise

---

ill
KK [ɪl]
DJ [il]
形 疾病的

He is very ill.
他病得很嚴重。

---

life
KK [laɪf]
DJ [laif]
名 生命

Life is short, so live a life with no regrets.
人生很短，不要留下遺憾。

---

medicine
KK [`mɛdəsn̩]
DJ [`medisin]
名 藥品

Do you see my medicine?
你有看到我的藥嗎？

小提醒 只要是藥都可以叫做 medicine，但我們常吃的藥有各種不同的形式，你知道要怎麼說嗎？

藥粉 powder　　藥錠 tablet　　藥水 drop

藥丸；藥片 pill　　膠囊 capsule

pain
KK [pen]
DJ [pein]
名 疼痛

This pill can heal your pain.
這顆藥可以治癒你的疼痛。

例句單字 pill 名 藥丸；藥片

---

pale
KK [pel]
DJ [peil]
形 蒼白的

That patient looks very pale.
那位病人看起來很蒼白。

---

recover
KK [rɪ`kʌvə]
DJ [ri`kʌvə]
動 恢復

He recovered from disappointment quickly.
他從失望中恢復得很快。

例句單字 disappointment 名 失望

---

runny nose
KK [`rʌnɪ] [noz]
DJ [`rʌnɪ] [nəuz]
名 流鼻水

He has a runny nose.
他正在流鼻水。

---

sick
KK [sɪk]
DJ [sik]
形 生病的；不舒服的

She was so sick that she stayed at home for four days.
她病得太嚴重，以致於她在家待了四天。

---

sore throat
KK [sor] [θrot]
DJ [sɔ:] [θrəut]
名 喉嚨痛

I have a sore throat because of my cold.
我因為感冒而喉嚨痛。

例句單字 because of 因為～

because 和 because of 在中文裡都是「因為」的意思，但它們在用法上卻不太一樣喔！

because 是連接詞，被用來連接完整句子（有主詞與動詞的句子），所以當我們看到 because 的時候，它的後面一定會是個有主詞和動詞的句子，就像底下這句：

I came to the party because I promised her.
我去參加了派對，因為我答應了她。

because of 和 because 的最大差別就是後面的 of，而在 of 後面只能接名詞或動名詞，如同底下的例句：

Because of my crazy teacher, I have a lot of homework to do.
因為我那瘋狂的老師，我有一大堆功課要做。

現在知道 because 和 because of 要怎麼用了嗎？

---

stomachache
KK [`stʌmək͵ek]
DJ [`stʌməkeik]
名 胃痛

This medicine is for stomachaches.
這個藥是治胃痛的。

---

strong
KK [strɔŋ]
DJ [strɔŋ]
形 強壯的

Are you strong enough to lift this desk?
你強壯到足以抬起這張書桌嗎？

例句單字 lift 動 抬起

---

tired
KK [taɪrd]
DJ [`taiəd]
形 疲倦的

She stayed up late last night, so she is tired now.
她昨天熬夜熬到很晚，所以她現在很疲倦。

例句單字 stay up late 熬夜熬到很晚

50

toothache
KK [ˋtuθˌek]
DJ [ˈtuːθeik]
名 牙痛

She went to the dentist because she had a toothache.
她去看了牙醫，因為她牙痛。

例句單字 dentist 名 牙醫

---

weak
KK [wik]
DJ [wiːk]
形 虛弱的

Tom is too weak to get up.
湯姆太虛弱而爬不起床。

例句單字 get up 起床

反義詞 strong 形 強壯的　tough 形 堅強的　healthy 形 健康的

---

well
KK [wɛl]
DJ [wel]
副 良好地 形 健康的

He doesn't feel well.
他覺得不舒服。

小提醒 doesn't feel well 是很常用來表示身體不舒服的一種說法唷！尤其是那種說不出來哪裡不對勁，例如有點噁心、倦怠，但又不知道到底是怎麼了的時候，你就可以說：I don't feel well. 來表示自己的身體不舒服。

---

wound
KK [wund]
DJ [wuːnd]
名 傷口

That dog is licking the wound on its paw.
那隻狗正在舔自己腳掌上的傷口。

例句單字 lick 動 舔舐

Time 時間

midnight
午夜

night
夜晚

evening
傍晚

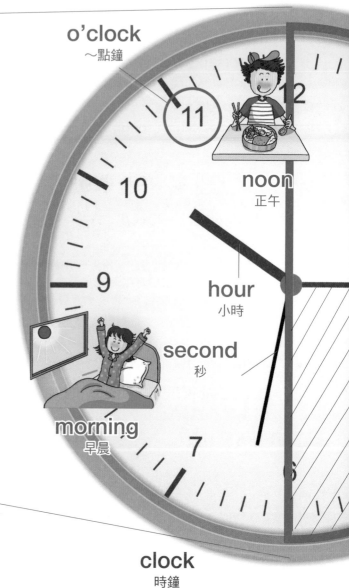

o'clock
～點鐘

noon
正午

hour
小時

second
秒

morning
早晨

clock
時鐘

half
一半的

afternoon
下午

watch
手錶

2

minute
分鐘

3

quarter
15分鐘（1/4小時）

dusk
黃昏

stop watch
碼表

4

dawn
黎明

alarm clock
鬧鐘

07.MP3

afternoon
KK [ˋæftɚˋnun]
DJ [ˋɑːftəˋnuːn]　名　下午

She likes to drink tea in the afternoon.
她喜歡在下午喝茶。

---

alarm clock
KK [əˋlarm] [klɑk]
DJ [əˋlɑːm] [klɔk]　名　鬧鐘

I have to remember to set the alarm clock, or I will be late tomorrow.
我必須記得設定鬧鐘，不然我明天會遲到。

例句單字　set 動 設定　late 形 延遲的

---

evening
KK [ˋivnɪŋ]
DJ [ˋiːvniŋ]　名　傍晚

What did you do this evening?
你今天傍晚做了什麼？

---

clock
KK [klɑk]
DJ [klɔk]　名　時鐘

This clock is very expensive.
這一個時鐘非常昂貴。

例句單字　expensive 形 昂貴的

小提醒　你知道時鐘的時針、分針與秒針要怎麼用英文說嗎？

時針　**the hour hand**　分針　**the minute hand**

秒針　**the second hand**

---

dawn
KK [dɔn]
DJ [dɔːn]　名　黎明

She got up before dawn.
她在黎明之前就起床了。

例句單字　before 介 在～之前

dusk
KK [dʌsk]
DJ [dʌsk]
名 黃昏

He returned home at dusk.
他在黃昏時回到家。

例句單字 return 動 返回

---

half
KK [hæf]
DJ [hɑ:f]
形 一半的

He gave half of an apple to me.
他給了我一半的蘋果。

---

hour
KK [aʊr]
DJ [auə]
名 小時

I spent 2 hours finishing my math practice sheets.
我花了 2 小時完成我的數學練習卷。

例句單字 spend 動 花費

---

midnight
KK [`mɪd͵naɪt]
DJ [`midnait]
名 午夜

She likes to watch TV at midnight.
她喜歡在午夜看電視。

小提醒 大家在午夜的時候都會做些什麼呢？有些人會為了工作或功課而 burn the midnight oil（挑燈夜戰），而有些人則是肚子餓得受不了，而吃起了 midnight snack（宵夜），不知道你是哪種人呢？不過熬夜對身體不好，大家還是要早點睡喔～

---

minute
KK [`mɪnɪt]
DJ [`minit]
名 分鐘

I need 30 minutes to finish my lunch.
我需要 30 分鐘把午餐吃完。

morning
KK [`mɔrnɪŋ]
DJ [`mɔːnɪŋ]
名 早晨

She likes to drink black coffee in the morning.
她喜歡在早晨喝黑咖啡。

例句單字 black coffee 名 黑咖啡（不加糖和奶精的咖啡）

---

night
KK [naɪt]
DJ [nait]
名 夜晚

She enjoys watching her favorite romantic TV series every night.
她喜歡每天晚上看她最愛的浪漫電視影集。

例句單字 TV series 名 電視影集

---

noon
KK [nun]
DJ [nuːn]
名 正午

Please wait till noon, and the teacher will be back then.
請等到正午，那個時候老師就會回來了。

例句單字 wait 動 等待

小提醒 noon 這個字指的是「正午」，也就是「中午 12 點」的意思，如果是 1 點以後，就要用 afternoon（下午），有看出 afternoon 這個字是由什麼組成的嗎？沒錯！就是「after（在～之後）＋noon（正午）＝在正午之後」，也就是「下午」啦！

---

o'clock
KK [ə`klɑk]
DJ [ə`klɔk]
副 ～點鐘

This meeting starts at 2 o'clock.
這場會議從 2 點開始。

例句單字 meeting 名 會議

小提醒 o'clock 的前面加上數字就是指「整點」的意思，多一分鐘或少一分鐘都不能用 o'clock 喔！例如 7 o'clock 就是指「7 點整」，不會是 7 點 01 分或是 6 點 59 分，所以使用的時候要注意唷！

---

quarter
KK [`kwɔrtɚ]
DJ [`kwɔːtə]
名 15 分鐘（1/4 小時）

It is a quarter to two.
現在是 1 點 45 分。

小提醒 quarter 帶有「1/4」的意思，運用在表達時間上時，就是指 1 小時的 1/4，也就是「15 分鐘」，用 quarter 來表示 15 分和 45 分，就像底下這個例子：

1：15 → a quarter after one（在 1 點之後過了 15 分鐘）

1：30 → 這時不會使用 two quarters，而是會用 one and a half（1 點和半個小時）

1：45 → a quarter to two（再過 15 分鐘到兩點）

---

second KK [`sɛkənd] DJ [`sɛkənd] 名 秒

I can finish the 100-meter dash in twelve seconds.
我可以在 12 秒內跑完 100 公尺。

---

stop watch KK [stɑp] [wɑtʃ] DJ [stɔp] [wɔtʃ] 名 碼表

Where can I buy a stop watch?
我可以去哪裡買到碼表？

---

watch KK [wɑtʃ] DJ [wɔtʃ] 名 手錶

She wears a watch decorated with a lot of jewels.
她戴著一隻裝飾著很多寶石的手錶。

例句單字 jewel 名 寶石

57

Timeline 時間軸

past
過去的

present
現在的

once
曾經

now
現在

moment
時刻

ago
在～之前

already
已經

yesterday
昨天

today
今天

tonight
今晚

last
緊接前面的

future
未來的

next
下一個的

daily
每日的；每日

soon
很快地

early
早的；提早

later
之後的

tomorrow
明天

59

08.MP3

ago KK [ə`go]
DJ [ə`gəu] 副 在～之前

Where were you 3 hours ago?
你 3 小時前在哪裡？

---

already KK [ɔl`rɛdɪ]
DJ [ɔːl`redi] 副 已經

I have already finished my homework.
我已經完成了我的功課。

例句單字 homework 名 功課

---

daily KK [`delɪ]
DJ [`deili] 形 每日的 副 每日

I have milk and toast for breakfast daily.
我每天都喝牛奶吃吐司當作早餐。

---

early KK [`ɝlɪ]
DJ [`əːli] 形 早的 副 提早

We have to get up early tomorrow morning in order to catch the flight.
為了趕飛機，我們明天必須要早起。

例句單字 get up 起床 in order to 為了做～
catch the flight 趕飛機

小提醒 趕飛機的「趕」，用英文來表達是
用 catch 這個字，catch 有「捕
捉；抓住」的意思，所以 catch the
flight 直翻的話就是「抓住那個航
班」，是不是非常的有畫面、很好記
呢～

future
KK [`fjutʃɚ]
DJ [`fju:tʃə]   形 未來的

Lisa wants to buy a house in the future.
麗莎未來想買一間房子。

---

last
KK [læst]
DJ [lɑ:st]   形 緊接前面的

When did you meet her last time?
你上一次跟她見面是什麼時候？

例句單字 **meet** 動 相遇；見面

---

later
KK [`letɚ]
DJ [`leitə]   形 之後的

A few minutes later, the teacher entered the classroom.
幾分鐘之後老師進入了教室。

例句單字 **enter** 動 進入 **classroom** 名 教室

---

moment
KK [`momənt]
DJ [`məumənt]   名 時刻

It is a moment worth remembering.
這是一個值得記住的時刻。

例句單字 **worth** 形 值得～的

---

next
KK [`nɛkst]
DJ [`nekst]   形 下一個的

Maybe he will think about it next time.
也許下次他會考慮這件事。

例句單字 **think about** 考慮

---

now
KK [naʊ]
DJ [nau]   副 現在

What are you holding now?
你現在拿著什麼？

例句單字 **hold** 動 握著；拿著

once KK [wʌns] DJ [wʌns] 副 曾經

They were once together.
他們曾經是戀人。

---

past KK [pæst] DJ [pɑ:st] 形 過去的

Jason doesn't care about his friend's past job.
傑森不介意朋友過去的職業。

---

present KK [ˋprɛzənt] DJ [ˋprezənt] 形 現在的

Focus on the present.
專注於現在。

例句單字 focus 動 專注

小提醒 present 是個意思很多、詞性很多,就連發音都會不一樣的單字,使用上常常會讓人覺得一頭霧水,所以我們在底下列出了它的各種意思:

詞性	發音	字義
形容詞	KK [ˋprɛzənt] DJ [ˋprezənt]	現在的;出席的
動詞	KK [prɪˋzɛnt] DJ [prɪˋzent]	贈送;提出;呈現;出示
名詞	KK [ˋprɛzənt] DJ [ˋprezənt]	禮物

↑像上面這樣列出來,是不是清楚多了呢?

---

today KK [təˋde] DJ [təˋdei] 名 副 今天

Amy wears a skirt today.
艾咪今天穿短裙。

例句單字 wear 動 穿著

tomorrow

KK [tə`moro]
DJ [tə`mɔ:rəu]

名 副 明天

Adam is planning to go to the beach tomorrow.
亞當正在計畫明天去海灘。

例句單字 plan 動 計畫　beach 名 海灘

---

tonight

KK [tə`naɪt]
DJ [tə`nait]

名 副 今晚

Will you go to the party tonight?
你今晚會去派對嗎？

例句單字 party 名 派對

---

soon

KK [sun]
DJ [su:n]

副 很快地

I will meet you again soon.
我們很快會再見面。

例句單字 meet 動 見面　again 副 再一次

---

yesterday

KK [`jɛstɚde]
DJ [`jestədi]

名 副 昨天

My sister took an exam yesterday.
我的妹妹昨天考了個試。

例句單字 exam 名 考試

小提醒 除了昨天、今天、明天，你知道前天和後天該怎麼說嗎？其實前天就是 **the day before yesterday**（昨天之前的那一天），而後天是 **the day after tomorrow**（明天之後的那一天），是不是很好記呢？

Calendar 日曆

week 週	**Sunday** 星期日	**Monday** 星期一	**Tuesday** 星期二 **Wednesday** 星期三
day 日；天	**Thursday** 星期四	**Friday** 星期五	**Saturday** 星期六

spring 春天

summer 夏天

autumn / fall 秋天

winter 冬天

January ① 21st, 2017

Sunday	Monday	Tuesday	Wednesday	Thursday	Friday	Saturday
1 元旦	2 元旦補假	3 初六	4 初七	5 小寒	6 初九	7 初十
8 十一	9 十二	10 十三	11 十四	12 十五	13 十五	14 十七
15 十八	16 十九	17 二十	18 廿一	19 廿二	20 大寒	21 廿四
22 廿五	23 廿六	24 廿七	25 廿八	26 廿九	27 除夕	28 春節
29 初二	30 初三	31 初四				

weekend 週末

lunar calendar 農曆

weekday 星期一～五

month
月

century
世紀

year
年

21st, 2017

January 一月	February 二月	March 三月	April 四月

May 五月	June 六月	July 七月	August 八月

September 九月	October 十月	November 十一月	December 十二月

09.MP3

week KK [wik] DJ [wi:k] 名 週

There are four weeks in a month.
一個月有四週。

---

weekday KK [`wik,de] DJ [`wi:kdei] 名 星期一～五

She has to work on weekdays. 她星期一到五必須上班。

Monday KK [`mʌnde] DJ [`mʌndi] 名 星期一

She has to work in a restaurant every Monday.
她星期一必須在餐廳工作。

例句單字 work 動 工作　restaurant 名 餐廳

Tuesday KK [`tjuzde] DJ [`tju:zdi] 名 星期二

Mary goes to dance class on Tuesdays.
瑪麗在星期二上舞蹈課。

例句單字 dance 動 跳舞

Wednesday KK [`wɛnzde] DJ [`wenzdi] 名 星期三

She likes to play the piano on Wednesdays.
她喜歡在星期三彈鋼琴。

例句單字 piano 名 鋼琴

Thursday

KK [`θɝ͵zde]
DJ [`θəːzdi]
名 星期四

They like to eat dinner together every Thursday.
他們喜歡在星期四一起吃晚飯。

例句單字 dinner 名 晚餐

Friday

KK [`fraɪ͵de]
DJ [`fraidi]
名 星期五

I plan to go to a night club on Friday.
我計畫星期五去夜店。

例句單字 night club 名 夜店

---

weekend

KK [`wik͵ɛnd]
DJ [`wiːkˋend]
名 週末

What do you usually do on the weekend? 你週末通常做什麼？

例句單字 usually 副 通常

Saturday

KK [`sætə͵de]
DJ [`sætədi]
名 星期六

Her favorite talk show is on Saturday.
她最喜歡的脫口秀在星期六播出。

例句單字 favorite 形 最喜歡的　talk show 名 脫口秀

Sunday

KK [`sʌnde]
DJ [`sʌndi]
名 星期日

He makes a habit of going to church every Sunday.
他養成在星期天去教堂的習慣。

例句單字 make a habit of~ 養成～的習慣　church 名 教堂

小提醒 除了會去教堂的 Christianity（基督教）或 Catholicism（天主教），你還知道哪些宗教的英文名字呢？

佛教　Buddhism　　伊斯蘭教　Islam　　印度教　Hinduism

67

month KK [mʌnθ] DJ [mʌnθ] 名 月

He stayed in Japan for 5 months.
他在日本待了 5 個月。

小提醒 month 的複數形態不是依照一般的規則加上 **es**，而是直接加 **s**，這點要特別注意唷！

January KK [ˋdʒænjʊˏɛrɪ] DJ [ˋdʒænjueri] 名 一月

They go skiing in January.
她們在一月時去滑雪。

例句單字 ski 動 滑雪

February KK [ˋfɛbrʊˏɛrɪ] DJ [ˋfebruəri] 名 二月

My birthday is in February.
我的生日在二月。

March KK [mɑrtʃ] DJ [mɑ:tʃ] 名 三月

Weather in March is usually hard to predict.
三月的天氣通常很難預測。

例句單字 usually 副 通常　predict 動 預測

April KK [ˋeprəl] DJ [ˋeiprəl] 名 四月

There are a lot of beautiful cherry blossoms
on this mountain in April.
四月在這座山上有許多漂亮的櫻花。

例句單字 cherry blossom 名 櫻花

May
KK [me]
DJ [mei]
名 五月

They married in May.
他們在五月結婚。

例句單字 **marry** 動 結婚

June
KK [dʒun]
DJ [dʒuːn]
名 六月

This photo was taken in June.
這張照片是在六月拍的。

小提醒 想要表達「拍照」的時候該怎麼說呢？其實不管是自己拍、還是幫別人拍，只要簡單地使用 **take** 這個字就可以了喔！但是要注意，**take** 是不規則變化的動詞，過去式是 **took**、過去分詞是 **taken**。

He took a picture for me. 他幫我拍了一張照片。

I have taken a series of pictures of my dog.
我已經幫我的狗拍了一系列的照片。

July
KK [dʒuˋlaɪ]
DJ [dʒuːˋlai]
名 七月

It is very hot here in July.
這裡七月時非常熱。

August
KK [ɔˋgʌst]
DJ [ɔːˋgʌst]
名 八月

She doesn't have to go to school in August.
她八月時不用去上學。

September
KK [sɛpˋtɛmbɚ]
DJ [sepˋtembə]
名 九月

The new semester begins in September.
新學期在九月開始。

例句單字 **semester** 名 學期   **begin** 動 開始

小提醒 在新學期開始的時候還會遇到什麼呢？

註冊 register   課本 textbook

新生訓練 orientation   制服 uniform

October
KK [ɑk`tobɚ] DJ [ɔk`təubə] 名 十月

They went to Japan in October last year.
他們去年十月時去了日本。

November
KK [no`vɛmbɚ] DJ [nəu`vembə] 名 十一月

Maples turn red in November. 楓樹在十一月變紅。

例句單字 maple 名 楓樹

December
KK [dɪ`sɛmbɚ] DJ [di`sembə] 名 十二月

Christmas is in December.
聖誕節在十二月。

例句單字 Christmas 名 聖誕節

---

year
KK [jɪr] DJ [jiə] 名 年

This actor has been acting for 20 years.
這位演員已經演戲演了 20 年。

例句單字 act 動 演出

---

spring
KK [sprɪŋ] DJ [spriŋ] 名 春天

There are many kinds of flowers in spring.
春天有很多種類的花。

---

summer
KK [`sʌmɚ] DJ [`sʌmə] 名 夏天

People like to go to the beach in summer.
人們在夏天的時候喜歡去海邊。

70

---

autumn
KK [`ɔtəm]
DJ [`ɔ:təm]　名 秋天

fall
KK [fɔl]
DJ [fɔ:l]　名 秋天

It is cool and windy in autumn. 秋天的時候天氣涼爽又有風。

It is the perfect time to eat sweet potatoes in fall.
秋天是吃地瓜的絕佳時機。

例句單字 cool 形 涼爽的　windy 形 颳風的　perfect 形 完美的
sweet potato 名 地瓜

---

winter
KK [`wɪntɚ]
DJ [`wɪntə]　名 冬天

There will be snow in winter. 冬天會下雪。

---

lunar calendar
KK [`lunɚ] [`kæləndɚ]
DJ [`lu:nə] [`kælində]　名 農曆

The lunar calendar is part of traditional culture.
農曆是傳統文化的一部分。

例句單字 traditional 形 傳統的　culture 名 文化

日曆　Calendar

---

day
KK [de]
DJ [dei]　名 日；天

Today is their wedding day.
今天是他們結婚的日子。

例句單字 wedding 名 婚禮

---

century
KK [`sɛntʃʊrɪ]
DJ [`sɛntʃuri]　名 世紀

We are in the 21st century.
我們在 21 世紀。

Special Days 特殊的日子

Chinese New Year
農曆新年

Chinese New Year's Eve
除夕

New Year's Day
新年

Lantern Festival
元宵節

Moon Festival
中秋節

Teacher's Day
教師節

Mother's Day
母親節

Father's Day
父親節

Double Tenth Day
雙十節

Halloween
萬聖夜

Christmas
聖誕節

Valentine's Day
情人節

Dragon-boat Festival

端午節

Thanksgiving

感恩節

Easter

復活節

festival

節慶

holiday

假日

vacation

度假

celebrate

慶祝

culture

文化

tradition

傳統

custom

習俗

memory

回憶

birthday

生日

10.MP3

birthday
KK [ˋbɝˏθ͵de]
DJ [ˋbəːθdei]
名 生日

Today is my birthday.
今天是我的生日。

---

celebrate
KK [ˋsɛləˏbret]
DJ [ˋselibreit]
動 慶祝

Our family always celebrates Christmas together.
我們家總是一起慶祝聖誕節。

例句單字 always 副 總是　together 副 一起

Chinese New Year
KK [ˋtʃaɪˋniz] [nju] [jɪr]
DJ [ˋtʃaiːniːz] [njuː] [jiə]
名 農曆新年

Children receive red envelopes during Chinese New Year.
孩子們會在農曆新年時拿到紅包。

例句單字 red envelope 名 紅包

小提醒 在農曆新年還會遇到些什麼呢？

春聯　spring festival couplets
年畫　New Year paintings
守歲　staying-up
年夜飯　New Year's Eve Dinner
舞龍舞獅　lion and dragon dance
鞭炮　firecracker

Chinese New Year's Eve

KK [`tʃaɪ‚niz] [nju] [jɪrz] [iv]
DJ [`tʃaiˈniːz] [njuː] [jiəz] [iːv]　名 除夕

Her mom cooks every Chinese New Year's Eve.
她媽媽每年除夕都會煮飯。

例句單字 cook 動 烹飪

Christmas　KK [`krɪsməs]　名 聖誕節
　　　　　　　DJ [`krɪsməs]

Do you celebrate Christmas?
你會慶祝聖誕節嗎？

小提醒 聖誕節有許多有趣的英文單字，大家一起來認識它們吧～

聖誕樹	Christmas tree	聖誕襪	Christmas stocking
聖誕大餐	Christmas dinner	平安夜	Christmas Eve
聖誕老人	Santa Claus	麋鹿	reindeer

---

custom　KK [`kʌstəm]　名 習俗
　　　　　　DJ [`kʌstəm]

We have to respect different cultures and customs.
我們必須尊重不同的文化和習俗。

例句單字 respect 動 尊重　different 形 不同的

---

culture　KK [`kʌltʃɚ]　名 文化
　　　　　　DJ [`kʌltʃə]

It's fun to learn about French culture.
了解法國文化很有趣。

例句單字 fun 形 有趣的　learn 動 學習

Double Tenth Day　KK [`dʌbl̩] [tɛnθ] [de]　名 雙十節
　　　　　　　　　　　DJ [`dʌbəl] [tenθ] [dei]

What did you do on Double Tenth Day?
你在雙十節的時候做了什麼？

Dragon-boat Festival

KK [ˈdrægən][bot][ˈfɛstəvl]
DJ [ˈdrægən][bəut][ˈfestəvəl]
名 端午節

There will be dragon boat races on Dragon-boat Festival.
在端午節的時候會有划龍舟比賽。

例句單字 racing 名 比賽

小提醒 在端午節的時候我們會在家門口放置 mugwort（艾草），還會吃 rice dumpling（粽子）、配戴 sachet（香包），打開電視看 dragon boat racing（划龍舟比賽）的轉播，看著選手們一邊打著 drum（鼓）一邊衝過終點線，真是超刺激的！大家是不是也這麼覺得呀？

Easter

KK [ˈistə]
DJ [ˈi:stə]
名 復活節

They hide eggs on Easter.
他們在復活節時藏了蛋。

小提醒 說到復活節就會想到復活節兔子和復活節彩蛋，復活節的習俗活動有慶祝春回大地的涵義，而蛋象徵「初春一切恢復生機」，兔子則象徵「多產和生命力」，在復活節時各地常會進行把彩蛋藏起來，然後讓孩子們去找尋的有趣活動。

Father's Day

KK [ˈfɑðə-z] [de]
DJ [ˈfɑ:ðəz] [dei]
名 父親節

He gave his father a watch on Father's Day.
他在父親節那天給了爸爸一支手錶。

---

festival

KK [ˈfɛstəvl]
DJ [ˈfestəvəl]
名 節慶

Are there any special festivals in your country?
在你的國家有什麼特別的節慶嗎？

Halloween

KK [`hælo`in]
DJ [`hæləu`iːn]

名 萬聖夜

They asked their neighbors for candy on Halloween.
他們在萬聖夜時向鄰居要糖果。

例句單字 neighbor 名 鄰居

---

holiday

KK [`hɑlə‚de]
DJ [`hɔlədi]

名 假日

I will spend my holiday reading comic books all day.
我會看一整天漫畫來度過假日。

例句單字 comic book 名 漫畫書

Lantern Festival

KK [`læntɚn] [`fɛstəv!]
DJ [`læntən] [`festəvəl]

名 元宵節

They eat tangyuans on Lantern Festival.
他們在元宵節時吃湯圓。

例句單字 tangyuan 名 湯圓，元宵

小提醒 雖然中文裡湯圓和元宵不太一樣，但是英文都用 tangyuan 這個字，如果想要描述口味的話，則是會在前面加上如 black sesame（黑芝麻）、meat（肉）等字來說明，下次如果有人問你元宵節要做什麼，你就可以和他說：I will eat delicious tangyuans!（我會吃好吃的湯圓！）。

---

memory

KK [`mɛmərɪ]
DJ [`meməri]

名 回憶

Let's make some happy memories together.
讓我們一起製造一些快樂的回憶。

Moon Festival

KK [mun] [`fɛstəv!]
DJ [muːn] [`festəvəl]

名 中秋節

She ate four moon cakes during Moon Fstival.
她在中秋節期間吃了四個月餅。

例句單字 moon cake 名 月餅

Mother's Day
KK [`mʌðɚz] [de]
DJ [`mʌðəz] [dei]
名 母親節

Mary gave her mother a beautiful bag as a gift on Mother's Day.
瑪麗在母親節給了媽媽一個漂亮的包包當作禮物。

例句單字 gift 名 禮物

New Year's Day
KK [nju] [jɪrz] [de]
DJ [nju:] [jiəz] [dei]
名 新年

They plan to watch the firework display together on New Year's Day.
他們計畫在新年那天要一起看煙火表演。

例句單字 plan 動 計畫

Teacher's Day
KK [`titʃɚz] [de]
DJ [`ti:tʃəz] [dei]
名 教師節

Do you say "Happy Teacher's Day" to your teacher on Teacher's Day?
你在教師節時會跟老師說「教師節快樂」嗎？

Thanksgiving
KK [ˌθæŋks`gɪvɪŋ]
DJ [ˌθæŋks`giviŋ]
名 感恩節

They eat turkey together every Thanksgiving.
他們每年感恩節時會一起吃火雞。

例句單字 turkey 名 火雞

tradition
KK [trə`dɪʃən]
DJ [trə`diʃən]
名 傳統

Having a big meal to celebrate a family member's birthday is one of their family traditions.
在家族成員的生日吃大餐是他們的家族傳統之一。

例句單字 meal 名 餐點　member 名 成員

vacation

KK [veˋkeʃən]
DJ [veiˋkeiʃən]

名 度假

I will go to summer camps during summer vacation.
我會在暑假的時候去夏令營。

例句單字 summer camp 名 夏令營

Valentine's Day

KK [ˋvæləntaınz] |
DJ [ˋvæləntaınz] |

Tommy received a lot of chocolates on Valentine's Day.
湯米在情人節時收到了很多巧克力。

例句單字 receive 動 收到

小提醒 說到情人節你會想到什麼呢？除了 chocolate （巧克力）之外，就是 rose （玫瑰）了吧！如果有喜歡的對象，也有不少人會想要寫一封 love letter （情書）來向對方表達自己的 secret crush （暗戀），你的情人節計畫又是什麼呢？

zero
零

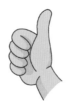

one
一

two
二

three
三

four
四

five
五

six
六

seven
七

eight
八

nine
九

ten
十

eleven
十一

twelve
十二

thirteen
十三

fourteen
十四

fifteen
十五

sixteen
十六

seventeen
十七

eighteen
十八

nineteen
十九

twenty
二十

thirty
三十

forty
四十

fifty
五十

sixty
六十

seventy
七十

eighty
八十

ninety
九十

100

hundred
百

1,000

thousand
千

1,000,000

million
百萬

1,000,000,000

billion
十億

主題單字

11.MP3

zero
KK [`zɪro]
DJ [`zɪərəu]
名 零

Count from 10 down to zero.
從 10 倒數到 0。

例句單字 count 動 數

---

one
KK [wʌn]
DJ [wʌn]
名 一

There is one little boy sitting on the ground.
有一個小男孩坐在地上。

例句單字 ground 名 地面

---

two
KK [tu]
DJ [tu:]
名 二

He is the father of two girls.
他是兩個女孩的爸爸。

---

three
KK [θri]
DJ [θri:]
名 三

They used to keep three dogs.
他們曾經養了三隻狗。

小提醒 飼養寵物的「飼養」，英文要用 keep，而不是 feed（餵養）唷～

---

four
KK [for]
DJ [fɔ:]
名 四

That lady owns four expensive bags.
那位女士擁有四個昂貴的包包。

例句單字 own 動 擁有　expensive 形 昂貴的

85

five
KK [faɪv]
DJ [faiv] 名 五

I have five pairs of shoes.
我有 5 雙鞋子。

小提醒 鞋子都是成雙成對的，所以除非我們要特別指一雙裡的其中一隻鞋，不然一般來說都是用複數的 **shoes**，而鞋子的單位是 **a pair of**（一雙），一雙鞋子就是 **a pair of shoes**，而數量超過一雙之後，記得要在 **pair** 後面加上代表複數的 **s**，所以兩雙鞋就是 **two pairs of shoes** 唷！

six
KK [sɪks]
DJ [siks] 名 六

He has been to six different countries.
他曾去過六個不同的國家。

例句單字 country 名 國家　different 形 不同的

seven
KK [ˋsɛvən]
DJ [ˋsevən] 名 七

It is said that seven is a lucky number.
大家說七是個幸運的數字。

例句單字 lucky 形 幸運的

eight
KK [et]
DJ [eit] 名 八

There are eight people in my group.
我這一組有八個人。

nine
KK [naɪn]
DJ [nain] 名 九

Some people believe that a cat has nine lives.
有些人相信貓有九條命。

例句單字 believe 動 相信

ten KK [tɛn] DJ [ten] 名 十

The little girl is learning how to count from one to ten.
這個小女孩正在學如何從一數到十。

例句單字 learn 動 學習

小提醒 count 是按照順序數，也就是從 1、2、3…數下去，如果我們是從 10、9、8…倒數，就要用 countdown（倒數）這個字，新年時的倒數就叫做 new year countdown 唷～

---

eleven KK [əˋlɛvən] DJ [iˋlevən] 名 十一

That teacher has eleven students.
那位老師有十一位學生。

---

twelve KK [twɛlv] DJ [twelv] 名 十二

I eat lunch at twelve o'clock.
我在十二點吃午餐。

---

thirteen KK [ˋθɝˋtin] DJ [ˋθəːˋtiːn] 名 十三

There are thirteen classes in this school.
這所學校裡有十三個班級。

---

fourteen KK [ˋforˋtin] DJ [ˋfɔːˋtiːn] 名 十四

Her kid is fourteen years old.
她的小孩十四歲。

---

fifteen KK [ˋfifˋtin] DJ [ˋfifˋtiːn] 名 十五

I graduated from junior high school when I was fifteen.
我十五歲時從國中畢業。

例句單字 graduate 動 畢業

sixteen
KK [`sɪks`tin]
DJ [`siks`ti:n]
名 十六

He kissed a girl when he was sixteen.
他在十六歲時親了一個女孩。

---

seventeen
KK [ˌsɛvn`tin]
DJ [ˌsevn`ti:n]
名 十七

I went to Japan when I was seventeen.
我十七歲時去了日本。

---

eighteen
KK [`e`tin]
DJ [`ei`ti:n]
名 十八

This newest cellphone costs eighteen
thousand dollars.
這支新手機要價一萬八。

例句單字 cellphone 名 手機

---

nineteen
KK [`naɪn`tin]
DJ [`nain`ti:n]
名 十九

I took a part-time job in a restaurant when I was nineteen.
我十九歲的時候在一間餐廳裡打工。

例句單字 part-time job 名 打工；兼職

---

twenty
KK [`twɛntɪ]
DJ [`twenti]
名 二十

I got my driver's license when I was twenty.
我在二十歲的時候拿到駕照。

---

thirty
KK [`θɝtɪ]
DJ [`θəːti]
名 三十

They got married when they turned thirty.
他們在滿三十歲那年結了婚。

例句單字 marry 動 結婚

小提醒 想要表達「到了～歲」的時候可以用 turn 這個字，turn 這個字有「變成；轉換」的意思，可以把歲數當成一個**時間點**，turn thirty 就可以想成是**轉換成了三十歲**（到了三十歲這個時間點），因此，用來說明年齡時，就是「到了～歲」的意思唷～

forty
KK [`fɔrtɪ]
DJ [`fɔ:ti] 名 四十

His child is fifteen years old when he is forty.
他四十歲時他的小孩十五歲。

fifty
KK [`fɪftɪ]
DJ [`fifti] 名 五十

My mom gives me fifty dollars as pocket money every month.
媽媽每個月給我五十美元零用錢。

例句單字 pocket money 名 零用錢

sixty
KK [`sɪkstɪ]
DJ [`siksti] 名 六十

My grandfather turns sixty this month.
我的爺爺這個月滿六十歲。

seventy
KK [`sɛvntɪ]
DJ [`sevnti] 名 七十

That old lady is already seventy years old, but she looks young and beautiful.
那位老太太已經七十歲了，但她看起來年輕又漂亮。

eighty
KK [`etɪ]
DJ [`eiti] 名 八十

What do you want to do when you are eighty?
你在八十歲的時候想做什麼？

ninety
KK [`naɪntɪ]
DJ [`nainti]　名 九十

Her brothers and sisters have all lived long lives, and she is now ninety years old.
她的兄弟姊妹都很長壽，而她現在九十歲了。

---

hundred
KK [`hʌndrəd]
DJ [`hʌndrəd]　名 百

I gave Tom one hundred NT dollars and asked him to buy lunch for me.
我給了湯姆一百元，並請他幫我買午餐。

例句單字 ask 動 要求

---

thousand
KK [`θaʊznd]
DJ [`θauzənd]　形 千

My mom paid four thousand NT dollars for my new cell phone. 媽媽花了四千元買我的新手機。

小提醒 除了台灣使用的錢叫做 NTD（New Taiwan Dollar）之外，你知道其他國家的錢的英文是什麼嗎？

美金　USD（United States dollar）
英鎊　pound　日幣　Japanese yen
歐元　Euro

---

million
KK [`mɪljən]
DJ [`miljən]　名 百萬

This house is worth millions of dollars; it is too expensive for me.
這間房子價值好幾百萬美元，對我來說太貴了。

例句單字 worth 形 值～

---

billion
KK [`bɪljən]
DJ [`biljən]　名 十億

He won a billion in the lottery.
他贏得十億的彩券。

例句單字 win 動 贏得（won 是過去式形態）　lottery 名 彩券

Every little bit helps. 小兵立大功。

　　every little bit 直接翻成中文就是「每一個小小的部分」，這裡被拿來當作做動作的主詞，**help** 是「幫助」的意思，所以整句話就是「每一個小小的部分都可以幫助」的意思，也就是中文裡的「小兵立大功」的意思。這麼解釋之後，這句話是不是容易記住了呢？

Vocabulary 一起看！

★abacus [ˋæbəkəs] 图 算盤

★camp [kæmp] 图 露營

★computer [kəmˋpjutɚ] 图 電腦

★difficult [ˋdɪfəˏkəlt] 形 困難的

★friend [frɛnd] 图 朋友

★great [gret] 形 優秀的，極好的

★hard [hɑrd] 形 艱難的；辛苦的

★kid [kɪd] 图 小孩（口語化的說法）

★lesson [ˋlɛsn̩] 图 課程，一節課

★little [ˋlɪtl̩] 形 小的；不多的

★piano [pɪˋæno] 图 鋼琴

★semester [səˋmɛstɚ] 图 半學年；一學期

★term [tɝm] 图 學期

★test [tɛst] 图 測驗，小考

91

Describing Numbers 形容數字

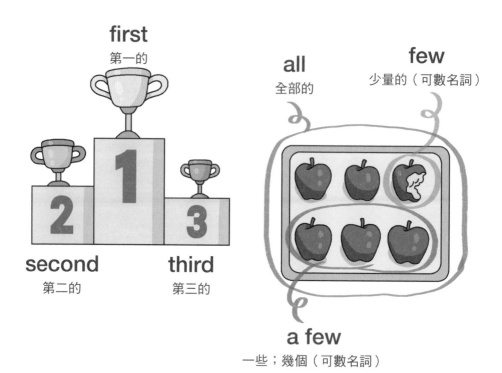

first
第一的

second
第二的

third
第三的

all
全部的

few
少量的（可數名詞）

a few
一些；幾個（可數名詞）

last
最後的

less
較少的

little
少量的
（不可數名詞）

a lot
很多

a little
一些；幾個
（不可數名詞）

both
兩者～都

any
任一的

several
幾個的

some
一些的

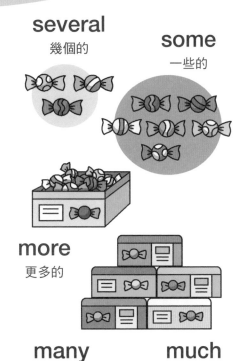

more
更多的

many
很多的
（可數名詞）

much
很多的
（不可數名詞）

add
加

minus
減

number
數字

total
總計的

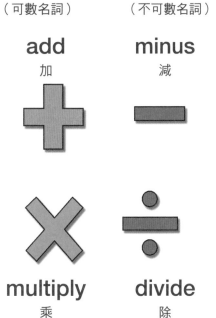

multiply
乘

divide
除

93

12.MP3

all
KK [ɔl]
DJ [ɔ:l]
形 全部的

I want to buy all the beautiful clothes in your store.
我想買你店裡所有的漂亮衣服。

例句單字 clothes 名 衣服

---

add
KK [æd]
DJ [æd]
動 加

If we add 5 to 20, it will be 25.
如果我們把 20 加上 5，那就會是 25。

---

a few
KK [ə\e] [fju]
DJ [ə\ei] [fju:]
形 副 一些；幾個

I have a few books. 我有一些書。

小提醒 a few 只能用在可數名詞上唷～「可數名詞」就是能夠
一個一個拿來數的東西，例如：apple（蘋果）、day
（天）、dog（狗）……等，使用的時候要注意喔！

---

a little
KK [ə\e] [ˋlɪtl]
DJ [ə\ei] [ˋlitəl]
形 副 一些；幾個

I need a little water. 我需要一些水。

小提醒 和 a few 不同，a little 只能用在不可數名詞上，「不可
數名詞」就是沒辦法一個一個數或是抽象的東西，例如：
water（水）、air（空氣）、happiness（快樂）……等。

---

a lot
KK [ə\e] [lɑt]
DJ [ə\ei] [lɔt]
形 副 很多

Denny has a lot of friends. 丹尼有很多朋友。

小提醒 a lot 後面的名詞不論可數不可數都可以，但如果可數就一定是「複數」，因為
a lot 的意思是很多，數量一定會超過一個，當然要用複數囉！

any KK [`ɛnɪ] DJ [`eni] 形 一些的；任一的

Do you have any pets? 你有任何寵物嗎？

例句單字 pet 名 寵物

小提醒 any 這個字一般會用在「否定句」和「疑問句」裡，如果出現在肯定句裡，通常用來加強語氣，表示「任何一個」，例如：**I need a pencil; any pencil is okay.**（我需要一支鉛筆，**任何**鉛筆都可以。），大家在使用的時候要注意這點唷～

both KK [boθ] DJ [bəuθ] 形 兩者～都

They both like to travel. 他們兩人都很喜歡旅行。

例句單字 travel 動 旅行

divide KK [də`vaɪd] DJ [di`vaid] 動 除

15 divided by 5 equals 3. 15 除以 5 等於 3。

few KK [fju] DJ [fju:] 形 少量的

I have few English books. 我有的英文書很少。

小提醒 雖然 few 和 a few 的後面都一樣接可數名詞，但它們的意思不一樣唷～a few 指的是「一些」，而 few 則是「少到幾乎沒有」的意思，就像上面的例句，如果改成：**I have a few English books.**（我有幾本英文書。），意思馬上就不一樣了喔！

first KK [fɝst] DJ [fə:st] 形 第一的

This is the first watch I bought.
這是我買的第一隻手錶。

last KK [læst] DJ [lɑ:st] 形 最後的

He is the last one who came into the classroom.
他是最後進教室的人。

less KK [lɛs] DJ [les] 形 較少的

I have less money than he has.
我有的錢比他少。

---

little KK [ˋlɪtl] DJ [ˋlitəl] 名 少量的

I have little money left. 我剩下一點點錢。

小提醒 little 和 a little 一樣，只能用在「不可數名詞」上喔！

---

many KK [ˋmɛnɪ] DJ [ˋmeni] 形 很多的

There are many books in this library.
這間圖書館裡有很多書。

例句單字 library 名 圖書館

小提醒 many 的後面只能接可數名詞，所以只能用在如 cat（貓）、boy（男孩）……
等單字上，注意 many 後面的名詞要用複數唷～

---

minus KK [ˋmaɪnəs] DJ [ˋmainəs] 動 減

What is 20 minus 3? 20 減 3 是多少？

---

more KK [mor] DJ [mɔ:] 形 更多的

He wants more milk. 他想要更多的牛奶。

---

much KK [mʌtʃ] DJ [mʌtʃ] 形 很多的

Mary drank so much water that she feels like throwing up.
瑪麗喝了太多水，讓她覺得想吐。

例句單字 throw up 嘔吐

小提醒 much 和 many 剛好相反，後面只能接不可數名詞，所以只能用在如
sadness（難過）、wealth（財富）……等單字上，注意 much 後面因為接
的是不可數名詞，所以不會出現加上 s 或 es 的複數形態唷～

multiply
KK [ˋmʌltəplaɪ]
DJ [ˋmʌltiplai]
動 乘

Four multiplied by five is twenty. 4 乘上 5 是 20。

number
KK [ˋnʌmbɚ]
DJ [ˋnʌmbə]
名 數字

This is my cellphone number. 這是我的手機號碼。

second
KK [ˋsɛkənd]
DJ [ˋsekənd]
形 第二的

I will get a second job. 我會找第二份工作。

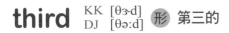 job 名 工作

several
KK [ˋsɛvərəl]
DJ [ˋsevərəl]
形 幾個的

There are several cats in the park. 公園裡有幾隻貓。

some
KK [sʌm]
DJ [sʌm]
形 一些的；某一個的

I have some toys. 我有一些玩具。

小提醒 some 和 any 的中文意思都是「一些」，但是 some 常用在肯定句，另外 some 後面如果接單數名詞，就變成「某一個的」的意思，就像底下例句：

Jennifer is talking with some guy at the door.
珍妮佛正在門口和某人說話。

但如果接的是複數名詞，則是「一些的」的意思，大家在用的時候要記得改變單複數來正確表達自己的意思唷～

third
KK [θɝːd]
DJ [θəːd]
形 第三的

Your room is the third on the right. 你的房間是右邊第三間。

total
KK [ˋtotl]
DJ [ˋtəutl]
形 總計的

The total cost is one hundred dollars.
總共的花費是 100 美元。

Money 金錢

bill
鈔票

cash
現金

coin
硬幣

change
零錢

dollar
元；美元

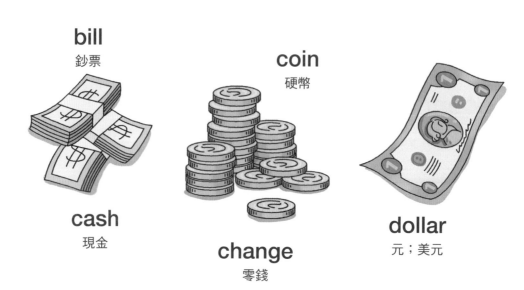

cent
分

borrow
借（入）

lend 借（出）

buy
購買

pay
支付

cost
花費

spend
花費

cheap
便宜的

expensive
昂貴的

price
價格

credit card
信用卡

13.MP3

bill KK [bɪl] DJ [bil] 名 鈔票

I only have a 100-dollar bill.
我只有一張 100 美元的鈔票。

---

borrow KK [`bɑro] DJ [`borəu] 動 借（入）

Can I borrow your book?
我能向你借書嗎？

小提醒 borrow 跟 lend 只看中文字義的話，都是「借」的意思，但它們的意思其實不太一樣唷！**borrow 是「跟別人借」，lend 則是「借給別人」**，例如以下例句：

Tom borrows Mary's book. 湯姆跟瑪麗借書。

Mary lends Tom a book. 瑪麗借了湯姆一本書。

這兩句想表達的都是「瑪麗把自己的書借給了湯姆」，但因為主詞不同，所以就要用不同的動詞唷！

---

buy KK [baɪ] DJ [bai] 動 購買

I want to buy a cellphone.
我想要買一支手機。

---

cash KK [kæʃ] DJ [kæʃ] 名 現金

Can I pay in cash?
我能用現金付錢嗎？

---

cent KK [sɛnt] DJ [sent] 名 分

This toy costs five dollars and 10 cents.
這個玩具 5 塊 10 分錢。

change

KK [tʃendʒ]
DJ [tʃeindʒ]
名 零錢

You can keep the change.
你可以把零錢留著。

小提醒 這句話在外國影集或是電影中常聽到，因為在國外的餐廳或咖啡廳結帳的時候，為了感謝服務人員的辛苦，都會給予一定比例的小費，如果剛好找零的金額和想給的小費數目差不多，就可以和對方說這句話，讓他把零錢留下來當作小費。

---

cheap

KK [tʃip]
DJ [tʃiːp]
形 便宜的

This skirt is very cheap. 這件裙子很便宜。

同義字 inexpensive 形 便宜的
反義詞 expensive 形 昂貴的

---

coin

KK [kɔɪn]
DJ [kɔin]
名 硬幣

I have a lot of coins in my pocket.
我口袋裡有很多硬幣。

---

cost

KK [kɔst]
DJ [kɔst]
動 花費

This scarf cost me 100 dollars. 這條圍巾花了我 100 美金。

例句單字 scarf 名 圍巾

---

credit card

KK [ˈkrɛdɪt] [kɑrd]
DJ [ˈkredit] [kɑːd]
名 信用卡

You are too young to use a credit card.
你要用信用卡還太年輕。

---

dollar

KK [ˈdɑlɚ]
DJ [ˈdɔlə]
名 元；美元

I owe him 100 dollars. 我欠他 100 美元。

例句單字 owe 動 欠（債等）

小提醒 如果沒有特別說是哪個國家的 dollar（元），通常就是指「美元」。

expensive
KK [ɪk`spɛnsɪv]
DJ [iks`pensiv] 形 昂貴的

This necklace is very expensive.
這條項鍊很貴。

例句單字 necklace 名 項鍊

同義字 costly 形 花費高昂的　high-priced 形 高價的

---

lend
KK [lɛnd]
DJ [lend] 動 借（出）

My father lends his car to his friend.
我爸爸把他的車借給朋友。

---

pay
KK [pe]
DJ [pei] 動 支付

My mother paid for my toy.
我媽媽付了我玩具的錢。

---

price
KK [praɪs]
DJ [prais] 名 價格

What is the price of this pen?
這支筆的價格是多少？

---

spend
KK [spɛnd]
DJ [spend] 動 花費

I spent all my pocket money on the
new video game.
我把所有的零用錢都花在新的電玩遊戲上
了。

例句單字 video game 電玩遊戲

小提醒 spend 這個字不只是花「錢」，也可以是花費
「時間」或「精力」。例如：

I spent three days writing my final reports.
我花費了三天來寫期末報告。

反義詞 earn 動 賺取　save 動 儲存；省下（錢等）

Time is money. 時間就是金錢。

　　這句話的意思是指「時間就像是金錢一樣的寶貴。」因為時間一旦過去之後就再也無法找回來，所以我們應該要珍惜地利用時間，所以如果想要勸告別人不要再浪費時間就可以說「Don't **waste** your time.」

　　如果想要勸告別人說不要亂花錢則可以說 You shouldn't **spend** money foolishly.（你不應該亂花錢。）或者說 You shouldn't waste your money.（你不應該浪費錢。）

Vocabulary 一起看！

★allowance [ə`lauəns] 名 津貼；零用錢

★book [buk] 名 書

★candy [`kændɪ] 名 糖果

★change [tʃendʒ] 動 兌換（錢）

★dollar [`dɑlɚ] 名 （美國或加拿大等國的）元

★enough [ə`nʌf] 形 足夠的；充足的

★fishy [`fɪʃɪ] 形 （口語化的說法）可疑的

★joking [dʒokɪŋ] 形 開玩笑的

★lie [laɪ] 名 謊話

★money [`mʌnɪ] 名 錢

★serious [`sɪrɪəs] 形 嚴肅的

★spend [spɛnd] 動 花費；花（錢、時間、精力）

★true [tru] 形 真實的；真的

★truth [truθ] 名 事實

★waste [west] 動 浪費

★weekly [`wiklɪ] 副 每週地

Food 食物

KFG

French fries 薯條

chicken 雞；雞肉

beef 牛肉

meat 肉

pizza 披薩

fast food 速食

hamburger 漢堡

welcome

salad 沙拉

cereal 穀麥片

sandwich 三明治

order 點餐

menu 菜單

ham 火腿

breakfast 早餐

brunch 早午餐

bun 餐包

lunch 午餐

spaghetti 義大利麵

dinner 晚餐

steak 牛排

hot dog 熱狗

soup 湯

seafood 海鮮

fish 魚；魚肉

pork 豬肉

tofu 豆腐

egg 雞蛋

instant noodles 泡麵

bread 麵包

Fresh

dumpling 水餃

meal 一餐

rice 米；飯

noodle 麵

14.MP3

beef KK [bif] DJ [biːf] 名 牛肉

Some people love to eat beef.
有些人喜愛吃牛肉。

---

bread KK [brɛd] DJ [bred] 名 麵包

I eat bread for breakfast every day.
我每天都吃麵包當早餐。

---

breakfast KK [`brɛkfəst] DJ [`brekfəst] 名 早餐

What do you usually eat for breakfast?
你早餐通常吃什麼？

---

brunch KK [brʌntʃ] DJ [brʌntʃ] 名 早午餐

Mary loves to eat brunch.
瑪麗喜愛吃早午餐。

小提醒 brunch 這個字其實就是 breakfast（早餐）和 lunch（午餐）這兩個字混合後產生的，一般是在過了吃早餐的時間，但吃午餐又太早的 10 點～12 點所吃的一餐，你知道通常會出現在早午餐裡的食物有哪些嗎？

水煮蛋 boiled egg	班尼迪克蛋 eggs benedict
可頌麵包 croissant	法式吐司 French toast
香腸 sausage	培根 bacon

---

bun KK [bʌn] DJ [bʌn] 名 小餐包

I don't like to eat buns.
我不喜歡吃小餐包。

chicken
KK [`tʃɪkɪn]
DJ [`tʃikin]
名 雞；雞肉

My mother likes to cook chicken soup for us.
媽媽喜歡為我們煮雞湯。

---

cereal
KK [`sɪrɪəl]
DJ [`siəriəl]
名 穀麥片

There is a lot of sugar in this delicious cereal.
這種好吃的穀麥片裡有很多糖。

---

dumpling
KK [`dʌmplɪŋ]
DJ [`dʌmpliŋ]
名 水餃

He loves eating dumplings so much that he has a photo album of dumplings in his cellphone.
他愛吃水餃愛到手機裡有一本水餃的相簿。

例句單字 **album** 名 相簿

---

dinner
KK [`dɪnɚ]
DJ [`dinə]
名 晚餐

We like to eat dinner together.
我們喜歡一起吃晚餐。

食物 Food

---

egg
KK [ɛg]
DJ [eg]
名 雞蛋

I am really afraid that I will break the eggs.
我真的很害怕會把蛋打破。

小提醒 雞蛋可以做成的料理超多種的，而且每一樣都超好吃！
底下這些蛋料理，你知道幾種呢？

水波蛋	poached egg	炒蛋	scrambled egg
歐姆蛋（煎蛋捲）	omelet	全熟的荷包蛋	over hard egg
半熟的荷包蛋	over easy egg		
單面煎熟的荷包蛋（太陽蛋）	sunny-side-up egg		

fast food

KK [ˋfæstˋfud]
DJ [ˋfɑːstˋfuːd]
名 速食

Fast food is not good for your health.
速食對你的健康不好。

---

fish

KK [fɪʃ]
DJ [fɪʃ]
名 魚；魚肉

There are a lot of fishes in the pond.
池塘裡有很多魚。

He loves to eat fish.
他喜愛吃魚。

小提醒 fish 這個字當作「魚、魚類」的意思時是**可數名詞**，因為我們可以一條、兩條這樣數，但是如果當作「魚肉」的意思時則是**不可數名詞**，因為肉類沒有一個固定可以數的數量，雖然我們可以用 **a piece of**（一塊）來描述，但魚肉的本身仍然是不可數的，大家在使用的時候要注意唷～

French fries

KK [frɛntʃ] [fraɪz]
DJ [frentʃ] [fraiz]
名 薯條

My little brother likes to dip his French fries in ice cream.
我弟弟喜歡拿他的薯條去沾冰淇淋吃。

例句單字 dip 動 沾；浸一下

---

ham

KK [hæm]
DJ [hæm]
名 火腿

Do you like to eat ham?
你喜歡吃火腿嗎？

---

hamburger

KK [ˋhæmbɚˏgɚ]
DJ [ˋhæmbəːgə]
名 漢堡

I ordered two hamburgers.
我點了兩個漢堡。

---

hot dog

KK [hɑt] [dɔg]
DJ [hɔt] [dɔg]
名 熱狗

This small restaurant is famous for its hot dogs.
這間小餐廳以熱狗聞名。

instant noodles

KK [`ɪnstənt] [`nudḷs]
DJ [`instənt] [`nu:dls]
名 泡麵

How many times do you eat instant noodles in a week?
你一個禮拜吃幾次泡麵？

小提醒 instant noodles 裡的 noodle 是「麵」的意思，一般來說我們不會只吃一條麵條，因此 noodle 都會加上**代表複數**的 **s** 喔！

---

lunch

KK [lʌntʃ]
DJ [lʌntʃ]
名 午餐

I don't know where I can eat lunch.
我不知道可以去哪裡吃午餐。

---

meal

KK [mil]
DJ [mi:l]
名 一餐

How much will you spend for a meal?
你願意花多少錢吃一餐？

---

meat

KK [mit]
DJ [mi:t]
名 肉

My favorite meat is <u>beef</u>.
我最愛吃的肉是牛肉。

小提醒 當你想要和別人介紹自己最喜歡吃的肉類的時候，<u>只要把上面例句的 **beef** 換成其他你喜歡的肉類</u>，這樣就可以了喔！大家一起來開口說說看吧～

| 豬肉 **pork** | 雞肉 **chicken** | 鵝肉 **goose** |
| 羊肉 **lamb** | 鴨肉 **duck** | |

---

menu

KK [`mɛnju]
DJ [`menju:]
名 菜單

There are 30 different kinds of spaghetti on this menu.
這份菜單裡有 30 種不同的義大利麵。

noodle KK [`nudl̩] DJ [`nu:dl] 名 麵

I like noodles more than rice.
我喜歡吃麵勝過於吃飯。

---

order KK [`ɔrdɚ] DJ [`ɔ:də] 動 點餐

Can I order my meal now?
我現在可以點餐了嗎？

---

pizza KK [`pitsə] DJ [`pi:tsə] 名 披薩

I can eat a whole pizza by myself.
我可以自己吃掉一整個披薩。

例句單字 whole 形 全部的

---

pork KK [pork] DJ [pɔ:k] 名 豬肉

Some people don't eat pork because of their religion.
有些人因為他們的宗教而不吃豬肉。

例句單字 religion 名 宗教

---

rice KK [raɪs] DJ [rais] 名 米；飯

He can't eat dinner without rice.
他吃晚餐不能沒有飯。

---

salad KK [`sæləd] DJ [`sæləd] 名 沙拉

Salad is good for your health.
沙拉對你的健康好。

小提醒 吃沙拉不能沒有沙拉醬！你知道哪些沙拉醬的英文呢？

| 田園醬 | ranch dressing | 千島醬 | Thousand Island dressing |
| 油醋醬 | vinaigrette | 日式和風醬 | Japanese dressing |

sandwich
KK [`sændwɪtʃ]
DJ [`sændwitʃ]
名 三明治

I want to eat sandwiches for tomorrow's breakfast.
明天早餐我想吃三明治。

---

seafood
KK [`si͵fud]
DJ [`sifu:d]
名 海鮮

Jenny seldom eats seafood.
珍妮很少吃海鮮。

例句單字 seldom 副 很少地

---

soup
KK [sup]
DJ [su:p]
名 湯

We eat soup with a spoon.
我們用湯匙喝湯。

例句單字 spoon 名 湯匙

---

spaghetti
KK [spə`gɛtɪ]
DJ [spə`geti]
名 義大利麵

I don't want to eat spaghetti again tonight.
我今天晚上不想再吃一次義大利麵。

---

steak
KK [stek]
DJ [steik]
名 牛排

Dad cooks steaks for us.
爸爸為我們煮了牛排。

---

tofu
KK [`tofu]
DJ [`təufu:]
名 豆腐

Emily hates tofu.
艾蜜莉討厭豆腐。

例句單字 hate 動 厭惡

thirsty
口渴的

delicious
美味的

hungry
飢餓的

full
飽的

hot
辛辣的

sweet
甜的

yummy
好吃的

bitter
苦的

sour
酸的

113

15.MP3

bitter
KK [`bɪtɚ]
DJ [`bitə]
形 苦的

This medicine is very bitter.
這個藥非常苦。

---

delicious
KK [dɪ`lɪʃəs]
DJ [di`liʃəs]
形 美味的

I had the most delicious meal tonight.
今天晚上我吃到了最好吃的一餐。

反義詞 distasteful 形 不合口味的　tasteless 形 沒味道的

---

full
KK [fʊl]
DJ [ful]
形 飽的

I am so full that I can't walk right now.
我太飽了以致於我現在無法走路。

例句單字 walk 動 走路

---

hot
KK [hɑt]
DJ [hɔt]
形 辛辣的

Some Korean food is very hot.
有些韓國食物非常辣。

例句單字 Korean 形 韓國的

hungry
KK [`hʌŋgrɪ]
DJ [`hʌŋgri]
形 飢餓的

The lion in the zoo seems very hungry.
那隻在動物園裡的獅子似乎非常飢餓。

例句單字 zoo 名 動物園　seem 動 似乎

---

sour
KK [`saʊr]
DJ [`sauə]
形 酸的

This candy is very sour.
這種糖果非常酸。

---

sweet
KK [swit]
DJ [swi:t]
形 甜的

This chocolate pie is too sweet for me.
這個巧克力派對我來說太甜了。

---

thirsty
KK [`θɝstɪ]
DJ [`θə:sti]
形 口渴的

It is really hot outside. I am very thirsty now.
外面真的很熱。我現在非常口渴。

---

yummy
KK [`jʌmɪ]
DJ [`jʌmi]
形 好吃的

My mother makes yummy cookies for me.
我媽媽為我做了一些好吃的餅乾。

Vegetables & Fruits 蔬菜 & 水果

peach 桃子

mango 芒果

bean 豆子

nut 堅果

potato 馬鈴薯

onion 洋蔥

corn 玉米

sweet potato 地瓜

guava 芭樂

19元/斤

watermelon 西瓜

69元/斤

apple 蘋果

15元/斤

grape 葡萄

tangerine 橘子

cabbage 高麗菜

carrot 胡蘿蔔

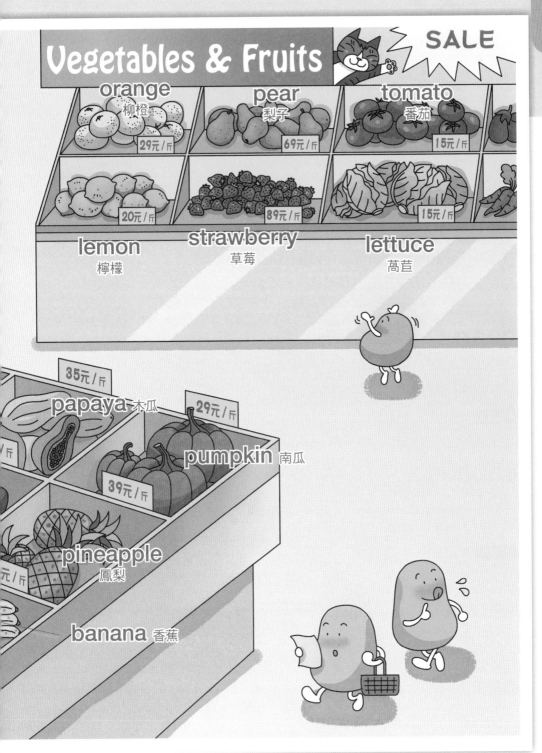

16.MP3

apple
KK [`æpl̩]
DJ [`æpl̩]
名 蘋果

An apple a day keeps the doctor away.
一天一蘋果，醫生遠離我。

小提醒 這句話是一件很常見的俗語，意思就是因為蘋果的營養很豐富，所以如果我們每天都吃一顆蘋果，就可以保持健康，也就不用去看醫生啦！

banana
KK [bə`nænə]
DJ [bə`nɑːnə]
名 香蕉

Taiwan is famous for bananas.
台灣以香蕉聞名。

bean
KK [bin]
DJ [biːn]
名 豆子

I want to plant beans in my garden.
我想在我的花園裡種豆子。

例句單字 plant 動 種植

cabbage
KK [`kæbɪdʒ]
DJ [`kæbɪdʒ]
名 高麗菜

I like to eat vegetables, especially cabbage.
我喜歡吃蔬菜，特別是高麗菜。

例句單字 especially 副 特別

carrot
KK [`kærət]
DJ [`kærət]
名 胡蘿蔔

I feed my rabbit carrots.
我餵我的兔子吃胡蘿蔔。

例句單字 feed 動 餵養

corn
KK [kɔrn]
DJ [kɔːn]
名 玉米

Grilled corn in night markets is really delicious.
夜市裡的烤玉米真的很好吃。

例句單字 grill 動 烤

---

grape
KK [grep]
DJ [greip]
名 葡萄

I want to drink some grape juice after breakfast.
我在早餐後想喝一些葡萄汁。

---

guava
KK [ˋgwɑvə]
DJ [ˋgwɑːvə]
名 芭樂

Guavas are too hard for some old people to eat.
芭樂對於有些老人家來說太硬了而沒辦法吃。

---

lemon
KK [ˋlɛmən]
DJ [ˋlemən]
名 檸檬

It is said that lemon juice is good
for health.
據說檸檬汁對健康很好。

小提醒 說到「檸檬汁」你會想到哪種檸檬汁呢？如果
是直接從檸檬裡面擠出來、不加糖和水的**原
汁**，就是例句裡提到的 **lemon juice**，如果
是我們在外面買的加了水和糖來調味的**檸檬汁
飲料**，則叫做 **lemonade**。不要搞錯了唷～

---

lettuce
KK [ˋlɛtəs]
DJ [ˋletis]
名 萵苣

She likes to put lettuce into her salad.
她喜歡在她的沙拉裡放萵苣。

mango

KK [`mæŋgo]
DJ [`mæŋgəu] 名 芒果

Summer is the season of mangos.
夏天是芒果的季節。

小提醒 mango 這個字的複數加 s 或 es 都可以唷～

---

nut

KK [nʌt]
DJ [nʌt] 名 堅果

I add milk to my nuts and cereal for breakfast every day.
我每天在牛奶中加入堅果和穀麥片當早餐。

---

onion

KK [`ʌnjən]
DJ [`ʌnjən] 名 洋蔥

I always cut onions in tears.
我總是一邊哭一邊切洋蔥。

---

orange

KK [`ɔrɪndʒ]
DJ [`ɔ:rindʒ] 名 柳橙

I prefer apples to oranges.
我喜歡蘋果勝過柳橙。

例句單字 prefer A to B 偏好 A 勝過 B

---

papaya

KK [pə`paɪə]
DJ [pə`pɑiə] 名 木瓜

You can buy papaya milk almost everywhere in Taiwan.
你幾乎可以在台灣的任何地方買到木瓜牛奶。

---

pear

KK [pɛr]
DJ [pɛə] 名 梨子

There are six pears in this beautiful gift box.
這個美麗的禮盒裡有六顆梨子。

例句單字 gift box 名 禮盒

peach

KK [pitʃ]　DJ [pi:tʃ]　名 桃子

I plan to give my teacher some Japanese peaches.
我計畫給我的老師一些日本桃子。

pineapple

KK [`paɪnˏæpl̩]　DJ [`paɪnˏæpəl]　名 鳳梨

How much does a box of pineapples cost?
一箱鳳梨要多少錢？

potato

KK [pə`teto]　DJ [pə`teitəu]　名 馬鈴薯

She doesn't know how to peel the potatoes quickly.
她不知道要如何快速的削馬鈴薯皮。

例句單字 peel 動 削（或剝）皮

pumpkin

KK [`pʌmpkɪn]　DJ [`pʌmpkɪn]　名 南瓜

Cinderella uses a pumpkin carriage to go to the palace.
辛蒂瑞拉坐南瓜馬車去宮殿。

例句單字 carriage 名 馬車　palace 名 宮殿

strawberry

KK [`strɔbɛrɪ]　DJ [`strɔ:bəri]　名 草莓

Strawberry ice cream is Tom's favorite.
草莓冰淇淋是湯姆的最愛。

例句單字 favorite 形 最喜愛的

sweet potato

KK [swit] [pə`teto]
DJ [swi:t] [pə`teitəu]
名 地瓜

You can buy sweet potatoes in convenience stores.
你可以在便利商店買到地瓜。

例句單字 convenience store 名 便利商店

tangerine

KK [`tændʒəˌrin]
DJ [`tændʒəˌri:n]
名 橘子

She likes to eat a lot of tangerines in winter.
她在冬天的時候喜歡吃很多的橘子。

tomato

KK [tə`meto]
DJ [tə`meitəu]
名 番茄

You can make tomato soup tonight.
你今天晚上可以做番茄湯。

watermelon

KK [`wɔtəˌmɛlən]
DJ [`wɔ:təˌmelən]
名 西瓜

Watermelon is the perfect fruit for summer.
西瓜是最好的夏日水果。

I can eat a horse. 我餓到可以吃下一匹馬。

　　我們有時候會說「我餓到可以吃下一頭牛了！」來形容肚子非常餓，中文裡常常用「牛」來形容食量很大；但是在英文裡，如果要形容食量大，可都是以「馬」做比喻喔！例如「I am so hungry, I could eat a horse.」意思就是「我很餓，我餓得可以吃下一匹馬了！」另外，「食量大如牛」可以說「eat like a horse」，很有趣吧！

好餓！
I can eat a horse！

★delicious [dɪ`lɪʃəs] 形 美味的

★dish [dɪʃ] 名 菜餚

★full [fʊl] 形 滿的，充滿的；吃飽的

★handsome [`hænsəm] 形 英俊的

★like [laɪk] 動 喜歡

★picky [`pɪkɪ] 形 挑剔的

★pretty [`prɪtɪ] 形 漂亮的，優美的

★smell [smɛl] 動 嗅，聞；有臭味，有味道

★soup [sup] 名 湯

★tasteless [`testlɪs] 形 沒味道的，味道差的

★tasty [`testɪ] 形 可口的

★thirsty [`θɝstɪ] 形 口渴的

★water [`wɔtɚ] 名 水

★yummy [`jʌmɪ] 形 好吃的；美味的

Drinks & Snacks 飲料＆點心

candy 糖果

milk shake 奶昔

cookie 餅乾

coffee 咖啡

milk 牛奶

water 水

cola 可樂

ice 冰

tea 茶

cake 蛋糕

ice cream 冰淇淋

juice 果汁

chocolate 巧克力

honey 蜂蜜

moon cake
月餅

dessert
甜點

pie 派

新推出！

芝心月餅

toast
吐司

cheese 起士

doughnut
甜甜圈

甜甜烘焙坊

drink
飲料

popcorn
爆米花

soda
汽水

potato
chips
洋芋片

17.MP3

cake
KK [kek]
DJ [keik]
名 蛋糕

She buys a birthday cake for her son every year.
她每年都為兒子買一個生日蛋糕。

小提醒 我們常會聽到有人說：**It is a piece of cake.**，這句話字面上的意思是「這是一塊蛋糕」，但其實這是一個有趣的譬喻說法，意思是這件事「就像吃一塊蛋糕一樣，非常輕鬆簡單」，下次有人拜託你做事，你也可以和他說：**No problem! It's a piece of cake!**（沒問題！小事一樁！）

candy
KK [ˋkændɪ]
DJ [ˋkændi]
名 糖果

Eating too much candy is not good for your teeth.
吃太多糖果對你的牙齒不好。

cheese
KK [tʃiz]
DJ [tʃiːz]
名 起士

I like to eat cheese with bread for an afternoon snack.
我喜歡吃起士配麵包當作下午點心。

chocolate
KK [ˋtʃɑkəlɪt]
DJ [ˋtʃɔkəlit]
名 巧克力

There are many different brands of chocolate.
巧克力有很多不同的品牌。

例句單字 brand 名 品牌

coffee
KK [`kɔfɪ]
DJ [`kɔfi]
名 咖啡

Drinking coffee makes me feel uncomfortable.
喝咖啡讓我覺得不舒服。

例句單字 **uncomfortable** 形 不舒服的

cola
KK [`kolə]
DJ [`kəulə]
名 可樂

I like to drink cola with a lot of ice cubes.
我喜歡喝加了很多冰塊的可樂。

例句單字 **ice cube** 名 冰塊

cookie
KK [`kʊki]
DJ [`kuki]
名 餅乾

She lets her children eat a pack of cookies a day.
她讓她的小孩一天可以吃一包餅乾。

例句單字 **pack** 名 一包

dessert
KK [dɪ`zɝt]
DJ [di`zə:t]
名 甜點

What do you want for dessert?
你甜點想吃什麼？

doughnut
KK [`do͵nʌt]
DJ [`dəunʌt]
名 甜甜圈

This store only sells doughnuts.
這家店只賣甜甜圈。

drink
KK [drɪŋk]
DJ [drɪŋk]
名 飲料

There are many kinds of drinks to choose from in this coffee shop.
在這家咖啡店裡有很多種飲料可以選擇。

小提醒 在咖啡店裡除了咖啡之外，當然還有其他飲料囉！看看你想喝什麼，下次到咖啡店裡點點看唷～

豆漿　**soybean milk**　　烏龍茶　**oolong tea**

蔬菜汁　**vegetable juice**　　紅茶　**black tea**

奶茶　**milk tea**　　綠茶　**green tea**

honey
KK [ˋhʌnɪ]
DJ [ˋhʌni]　名 蜂蜜

Some people like to drink honey water.
有些人喜歡喝蜂蜜水。

ice
KK [aɪs]
DJ [ais]　名 冰

My mom doesn't like me to drink ice tea even in summer.
即使是夏天，媽媽也不喜歡我喝冰紅茶。

小提醒 ice tea 一般來說指的是冰紅茶，但只要是「茶葉沖泡的茶加上冰塊」，就可以被稱為是 ice tea，例如綠茶、烏龍茶等都是，現在也很流行加入不同的香料讓 ice tea 有各種不一樣的風味，下次去飲料店時可以點來喝喝看喔～

ice cream
KK [aɪs] [krim]
DJ [ais] [kri:m]　名 冰淇淋

I want to add some chocolate syrup to my ice cream.
我想加一些巧克力糖漿在我的冰淇淋上。

例句單字 chocolate syrup 名 巧克力糖漿

juice
KK [dʒus]
DJ [dʒu:s]　名 果汁

This cup of juice cost me 5 dollars.
這杯果汁花了我 5 美元。

milk KK [mɪlk] DJ [milk] 名 牛奶

I always add milk to my coffee.
我總是在咖啡裡加牛奶。

milk shake KK [mɪlk] [ʃek] DJ [milk] [ʃeik] 名 奶昔

You can buy milk shakes in fast food restaurants.
你可以在速食店裡買到奶昔。

moon cake KK [mun] [kek] DJ [muːn] [keik] 名 月餅

How many moon cakes have you eaten this year?
你今年吃了幾個月餅？

 每年中秋節在吃的月餅有超多口味的，你知道月餅裡包的餡用英文要怎麼說嗎？

紅豆沙	red bean paste	蓮蓉	lotus seed paste
蛋黃	egg yolk	棗泥	jujube paste
芋泥	taro paste	豆沙	sweet bean paste

pie KK [paɪ] DJ [pai] 名 派

Her mother knows how to make delicious pies.
她媽媽知道如何做出好吃的派。

popcorn KK [ˋpɑpˏkɔrn] DJ [ˋpɔpkɔːn] 名 爆米花

Jane can't watch a movie without popcorn.
珍看電影時不能沒有爆米花。

potato chips

KK [pə`teto] [tʃɪps]
DJ [pə`teitəu] [tʃɪps]
名 洋芋片

Hanson can't live without potato chips.
韓森不能沒有洋芋片。

小提醒 因為通常洋芋片不會只有一片，而是一整包裡有很多片，所以都會加上代表複數的 **s**，寫成 **potato chips**。

---

soda

KK [`sodə]
DJ [`səudə]
名 汽水

Can you buy me a can of soda?
你能買一罐汽水給我嗎？

例句單字 **can** 名 一罐

---

tea

KK [ti]
DJ [ti:]
名 茶

My mother likes to use tea bags because it is convenient.
我的母親喜歡用茶包，因為很方便。

例句單字 **tea bag** 名 茶包

小提醒 除了紅茶、綠茶、烏龍之外，你還知道哪些種類的茶的英文呢？

普洱茶	**pu-erh**	花茶	**scented tea**
大吉嶺茶	**Darjeeling tea**	伯爵茶	**Earl grey tea**

---

toast

KK [tost]
DJ [təust]
名 吐司

I made a lot of chocolate toast for the picnic.
我為了野餐做很多巧克力吐司。

---

water

KK [`wɔtɚ]
DJ [`wɔ:tə]
名 水

I sweat a lot, so I drink a lot of water.
我很會流汗，所以我喝很多水。

Do you want some dessert?

你想吃些甜點嗎？

Do you want some...? (你想吃些…嗎？)

外國人相當享受品嚐甜點的時刻，在一天之中可能會有 morning tea「早茶」，afternoon tea「下午茶」，以及吃完正餐後的 dessert「點心」。國外的媽媽通常會幫孩子帶好一份 lunch box「午餐盒」，除此之外還會幫孩子準備一份在 morning tea 等時刻可以吃的點心，這些點心統稱為「snacks」。

「**Do you want some ~ ?**」意思是「你想吃些～嗎？」，例如說 Do you want some coffee? 是「你想要喝點咖啡嗎？」的意思，相反的可以說「**Can I have** some coffee?」，意思是「我可以喝點咖啡嗎？」

Do you want something to eat?　你想吃點東西嗎？

Do you want some dessert?　你想要吃些甜點嗎？

Would you like to have some dessert?　你想吃些點心嗎？

House 房子

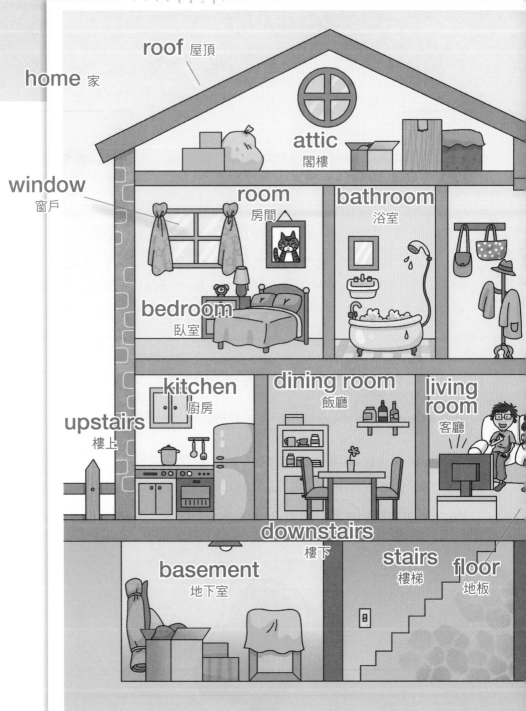

home 家

roof 屋頂

window 窗戶

attic 閣樓

room 房間

bathroom 浴室

bedroom 臥室

kitchen 廚房

dining room 飯廳

living room 客廳

upstairs 樓上

downstairs 樓下

basement 地下室

stairs 樓梯

floor 地板

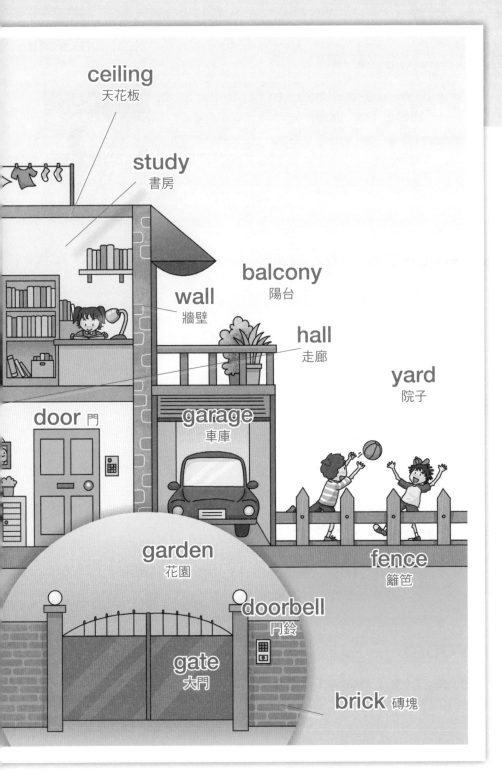

ceiling 天花板

study 書房

balcony 陽台

wall 牆壁

hall 走廊

yard 院子

door 門

garage 車庫

garden 花園

fence 籬笆

doorbell 門鈴

gate 大門

brick 磚塊

18.MP3

attic
KK [`ætɪk]
DJ [`ætik]
名 閣樓

You have to use a ladder to get to the attic.
你必須爬梯子才能到閣樓。

例句單字 ladder 名 梯子

---

balcony
KK [`bælkənɪ]
DJ [`bælkəni]
名 陽台

My mother put some potted plants on the balcony.
我媽媽在陽台放了一些盆栽。

例句單字 potted plant 名 盆栽

---

basement
KK [`besmənt]
DJ [`beismənt]
名 地下室

It's very cold and dark in the basement.
地下室非常寒冷陰暗。

例句單字 dark 形 陰暗的

---

bathroom
KK [`bæθˌrum]
DJ [`bæθrum]
名 浴室

She has a big house; there are 3 bathrooms in it.
她有一間大房子，裡面有三間浴室。

---

bedroom
KK [`bɛdˌrʊm]
DJ [`bedrum]
名 臥室

Jenny likes to put a lot of toys in her bedroom.
珍妮喜歡在她的臥室裡放很多玩具。

brick
KK [brɪk]
DJ [brik]
名 磚塊

My house is made of bricks.
我的房子是用磚塊蓋成的。

例句單字 be made of~ 用～做成的

小提醒 你還知道哪些是蓋房子會用到的材料嗎？

鋼筋 **reinforcing bars**　　水泥 **cement**　　混凝土 **concrete**

---

ceiling
KK [`silɪŋ]
DJ [`si:liŋ]
名 天花板

Can you touch the ceiling?
你能碰到天花板嗎？

例句單字 touch 動 觸碰

---

dining room
KK [`daɪnɪŋ] [rum]
DJ [`dainiŋ] [ru:m]
名 飯廳

Let's eat in the dining room.
我們在飯廳吃飯吧。

---

doorbell
KK [`dor͵bɛl]
DJ [`dɔ:bel]
名 門鈴

The doorbell is ringing.
門鈴正在響。

例句單字 ring 動 （鐘、鈴等）鳴響

---

door
KK [dor]
DJ [dɔ:]
名 門

He put a decoration on his door.
他在他的門上放上了一個裝飾品。

例句單字 decoration 名 裝飾品

downstairs
KK [ˌdaʊnˈstɛrz]
DJ [ˌdaʊnˈstɛəz]　副　樓下

Can you take the kids downstairs for their desserts?
你能帶孩子們到樓下去吃甜點嗎？

---

fence
KK [fɛns]
DJ [fens]　名　籬笆

The fence around our house is very high.
圍繞我家的籬笆非常高。

---

floor
KK [flor]
DJ [flɔ:]　名　地板

My mom wants me to mop the floor.
我媽媽希望我去拖地板。

例句單字　mop　動　用拖把拖

小提醒　除了拖地之外，媽媽還常請你做什麼家事呢？

洗碗　**do dishes**　　　洗衣服　**do laundry**

掃地　**sweep the floor**

摺衣服　**fold clothes**

---

garage
KK [ɡəˈrɑʒ]
DJ [ˈɡærɑ:ʒ]　名　車庫

That house with a garage is so expensive that we can't afford it.
那個附有車庫的房子貴到我們買不起。

例句單字　afford　動　付得起

---

garden
KK [ˈɡɑrdən]
DJ [ˈɡɑ:dən]　名　花園

If you want to enter this famous garden, you have to pay for it.
如果你想進入這座有名的花園，你必須要付錢。

gate KK [get] DJ [geit] 名 大門

Can you tell me how to get to the gate?
你可以告訴我要怎麼去大門嗎？

小提醒 gate 和 door 都有門的意思，但 door 通常是在建築物內，屬於建築物的一部分，就像你臥室的房門就是 door；而 gate 通常遠離建築物且是圍牆的一部分，就像社區的大門口就必須稱作 gate 而不能說 door，在使用的時候要注意它們的差別喔！

---

hall KK [hɔl] DJ [hɔ:l] 名 走廊

Room 108 is at the end of the hall.
第 108 號房間在走廊的盡頭。

例句單字 the end of~ ～的盡頭

房子 House

---

home KK [hom] DJ [həum] 名 家

She decorates her home with ribbons.
她用緞帶裝飾她的家。

例句單字 ribbon 名 緞帶

---

kitchen KK [`kɪtʃɪn] DJ [`kitʃin] 名 廚房

The kitchen is my favorite place in my house.
在我家我最喜歡的地方是廚房。

例句單字 favorite 形 最喜歡的

---

living room KK [`lɪvɪŋ] [rum] DJ [`liviŋ] [ru:m] 名 客廳

She likes to do her homework in the living room.
她喜歡在客廳寫回家功課。

roof
KK [ruf]
DJ [ru:f]
名 屋頂

Can you check the roof for me?
你能幫我檢查屋頂嗎？

---

room
KK [rum]
DJ [ru:m]
名 房間

How many rooms are there in your house?
你的房子裡有幾個房間？

---

stairs
KK [stɛrz]
DJ [steəz]
名 樓梯

She fell down the stairs and hurt her legs.
她從樓梯上摔下來並且傷了她的腿。

小提醒 因為樓梯是由很多的 **stair**（梯級）所組成，所以一定要加上表示複數的 **s**，才是樓梯的意思唷～

stair

---

study
KK [ˈstʌdɪ]
DJ [ˈstʌdi]
名 書房

Stay in the study until you finish your homework.
待在你的書房直到完成回家作業。

例句單字 homework 名 作業

---

upstairs
KK [ˈʌpˈstɛrz]
DJ [ˈʌpˈsteəz]
副 樓上

I took my friends upstairs.
我把我的朋友們帶到樓上。

wall
KK [wɔl]
DJ [wɔ:l]
名 牆壁

I want to paint the walls in my bedroom.
我想粉刷我臥室的牆壁。

例句單字 paint 動 粉刷

---

window
KK [`wɪndo]
DJ [`wɪndəu]
名 窗戶

Can you close the window for me?
你能幫我把窗戶關上嗎？

小提醒 關上窗戶的動詞要用 close，而不能用 turn off，因為 turn off 是「把旋鈕 turn（轉）到 off（關閉）」的意思，通常會用在電器上，例如電視、收音機等，這是因為以前的電器開關都是旋鈕做成的，所以才會這樣說。而窗戶不像電器那樣有旋鈕，自然就不能用 turn off，而要用 close 囉！

House
房子

---

yard
KK [jɑrd]
DJ [jɑ:d]
名 院子

That little boy likes to play in the yard.
那個小男孩喜歡在院子裡玩。

139

light
燈

bookcase
書櫃

air conditioner
冷氣

fan
電風扇

cellphone
手機

video player
放影機

television
電視

towel
毛巾

mirror
鏡子

soap
肥皂

toothbrush
牙刷

mat
地墊

tooth paste
牙膏

bath tub
浴缸

washing machine
洗衣機

basket
籃子

toilet
馬桶

dryer
烘衣機

sofa／couch 沙發

armchair 扶手椅

curtain 窗簾

radio 收音機

trash can 垃圾桶

carpet 地毯

key 鑰匙

telephone 電話

heater 暖氣

dresser 梳妝台

closet 衣櫃

hanger 衣架

blanket 毯子

pillow 枕頭

bed 床

drawer 抽屜

hammer 榔頭

pin 大頭針；圖釘

sheet 床單

printer 印表機

lamp 桌燈

candle 蠟燭

thread 線

needle 針

chair 椅子

rope 繩子

flashlight 手電筒

computer 電腦

desk 書桌

camera 相機

19.MP3

air conditioner
KK [ɛr] [kənˋdɪʃənə]
DJ [ɛə] [kənˋdɪʃənə]
名 冷氣

It is difficult to live without an air conditioner in summer.
夏天時沒有冷氣很難生活。

---

armchair
KK [ˋɑrmˌtʃɛr]
DJ [ˋɑːmˌtʃɛə]
名 扶手椅

My grandmother loves to take a nap in her armchair.
我的祖母喜歡在她的扶手椅上小睡一下。

例句單字 take a nap 打盹

小提醒 take a nap 指的通常是在白天的時候睡午覺或是打個盹，如果想要講晚上開始睡到明天早上，不能用 take a nap，要用 sleep 喔～

---

basket
KK [ˋbæskɪt]
DJ [ˋbɑːskɪt]
名 籃子

What do you want to put in this basket?
你想在這個籃子裡放什麼？

---

bathtub
KK [ˋbæθˌtʌb]
DJ [ˋbɑːθtʌb]
名 浴缸

There is nothing better than bathing in the bathtub.
沒有什麼比在浴缸裡泡澡更好的事了。

例句單字 bath 動 泡澡

小提醒 在泡澡的時候你需要什麼呢？

| 沐浴球 | **bath sponge** | 泡澡劑 | **bath soak** | 橡皮鴨 | **rubber duck** |
| 毛巾 | **towel** | 泡澡錠 | **bath muffin** | 浴帽 | **shower cap** |

bed
KK [bɛd]
DJ [bed]
名 床

You should buy a new bed to replace the old one.
你應該買張新床來取代舊床。

例句單字 replace 動 取代

---

blanket
KK [`blæŋkɪt]
DJ [`blæŋkɪt]
名 毯子

The blanket over there is the baby's favorite.
那邊那條毯子是這個嬰兒最喜歡的毯子。

---

bookcase
KK [`bʊk͵kes]
DJ [`bukkeis]
名 書櫃

How many books are there in your bookcase?
你的書櫃裡有多少書？

---

camera
KK [`kæmərə]
DJ [`kæmərə]
名 相機

I want to buy a new camera with my allowance.
我想用零用錢買一台新相機。

例句單字 allowance 名 零用錢

---

candle
KK [`kændl̩]
DJ [`kændl̩]
名 蠟燭

It's his tenth birthday, so his mother lights
ten candles for him.
這是他的十歲生日，所以他媽媽幫他點了十根蠟燭。

例句單字 light up 點亮

---

carpet
KK [`kɑrpɪt]
DJ [`kɑ:pit]
名 地毯

Movie stars dress beautifully to walk the red carpet.
電影明星穿得很美地走紅毯。

例句單字 red carpet 名 紅毯（頒獎典禮等進場時的紅毯大道）

cellphone KK [ˋsɛlfon] DJ [ˋselfəun] 名 手機

How often do you change your cellphone?
你多久換一次手機？

chair KK [tʃɛr] DJ [tʃɛə] 名 椅子

It is a comfortable chair.
這是一張舒服的椅子。

例句單字 comfortable 形 舒服的

closet KK [ˋklɑzɪt] DJ [ˋklɔzɪt] 名 衣櫃

There is a box of photos in my closet.
我的衣櫃裡有一盒照片。

例句單字 a box of 一盒的～

computer KK [kəmˋpjutɚ] DJ [kəmˋpjuːtə] 名 電腦

I can't work without my computer.
沒有電腦我沒辦法工作。

couch KK [kaʊtʃ] DJ [kaʊtʃ] 名 沙發

I want to buy some cushions and put them on the couch.
我想買一些靠枕放在沙發上。

例句單字 cushion 名 靠枕

curtain KK [ˋkɝtn̩] DJ [ˋkəːtən] 名 窗簾

Jerry is hiding behind the curtain.
傑瑞躲在窗簾的後面。

例句單字 hide 動 躲藏　behind 介 在～的後面

desk
KK [dɛsk]
DJ [desk]
名 書桌

This desk is a gift from my grandfather.
這張書桌是我爺爺送的禮物。

例句單字 gift 名 禮物

---

drawer
KK [`drɔɚ]
DJ [`drɔːə]
名 抽屜

She leaves a lot of snacks in the drawers, so there are a lot of cockroaches.
她放了很多零食在抽屜裡，所以很多蟑螂。

例句單字 cockroach 名 蟑螂

---

dresser
KK [`drɛsɚ]
DJ [`drɛsə]
名 梳妝台

My mom spends a lot of time at her dresser putting on make-up.
媽媽花了很多時間在梳妝台前化妝。

例句單字 make-up 名 化妝

Furniture & Household Objects
家具 & 居家用品

---

dryer
KK [`draɪɚ]
DJ [`draɪə]
名 烘衣機

Can you put the clothes into the dryer for me?
你能幫我把衣服放進烘衣機嗎？

---

fan
KK [fæn]
DJ [fæn]
名 電風扇

She bought a fan at a second-hand shop.
她在二手店買了一台電風扇。

例句單字 second-hand shop 名 二手店

小提醒 fan 除了電風扇之外，還有「仰慕者」的意思，我們常聽到的「粉絲」，其實就是 fan 的複數 fans 喔！

145

flashlight

KK [ˋflæʃ͵laɪt]
DJ [ˋflæʃlait]
名 手電筒

You must have a flashlight in your house in case of emergency.
你家裡應該要有手電筒，以免有緊急情況。

例句單字 emergency 名 緊急情況

---

hammer

KK [ˋhæmɚ]
DJ [ˋhæmə]
名 榔頭

Please don't hurt yourself while you are using the hammer.
當你在使用榔頭的時候，請不要傷到自己。

---

hanger

KK [ˋhæŋɚ]
DJ [ˋhæŋə]
名 衣架

I don't have enough hangers; can you buy some for me?
我沒有足夠的衣架，你能幫我買一些嗎？

---

heater

KK [ˋhitɚ]
DJ [ˋhi:tə]
名 暖氣

Do you use the heater in winter?
你冬天的時候會開暖氣嗎？

---

key

KK [ki]
DJ [ki:]
名 鑰匙

My friend gave me a key chain as my birthday present.
我朋友給我一個鑰匙圈當作生日禮物。

例句單字 key chain 名 鑰匙圈

---

lamp

KK [læmp]
DJ [læmp]
名 桌燈

He can't decide if he should buy a lamp or not.
他無法決定他應不應該買桌燈。

light
KK [laɪt]
DJ [lait]
名 燈

The girl is so afraid of the dark that you must leave a light on for her.
那個女孩非常怕黑，因此你必須留一盞燈給她。

例句單字 afraid 形 害怕的　leave 動 留下

---

mat
KK [mæt]
DJ [mæt]
名 地墊

You can step on the mat to dry your feet.
你可以在地墊上踩一踩把腳弄乾。

例句單字 step 動 踩踏

---

mirror
KK [`mɪrɚ]
DJ [`mirə]
名 鏡子

The queen has a magic mirror.
皇后有一面魔法鏡子。

小提醒 擁有魔法鏡子的皇后出現在 Snow White（白雪公主）的故事裡，你還聽過什麼童話故事呢？

灰姑娘　Cinderella

青蛙王子　The Frog Prince

醜小鴨　The Ugly Duckling

小紅帽　Little Red Riding Hood

---

needle
KK [`nidl]
DJ [`ni:dəl]
名 針

Please be careful with the needle.
在使用針時請小心。

pillow
KK [ˋpɪlo]
DJ [ˋpiləu]
名 枕頭

You can choose the perfect pillow for yourself in that store.
在那家店裡，你可以為你自己選擇最完美的枕頭。

例句單字 choose 動 選擇　perfect 形 完美的

---

pin
KK [pɪn]
DJ [pin]
名 大頭針；圖釘

You can use some push pins to pin up the poster.
你可以用一些圖釘來釘住海報。

例句單字 poster 名 海報

小提醒 pin 這個字在名詞的時候是「大頭針；圖釘」的意思，但它也可以當作動詞，這個時候它的意思就變成了「（用大頭針或圖釘等）別住；釘住」的意思，下次看到一個句子裡面同時出現兩個 pin，你就知道它們的意思不一樣囉～

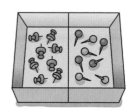

---

printer
KK [ˋprɪntɚ]
DJ [ˋprintə]
名 印表機

Please replace the empty ink cartridge in the printer.
請更換印表機的空墨水匣。

例句單字 replace 動 替換　empty 形 空的　ink 名 墨水　cartridge 名 卡匣

---

radio
KK [ˋredɪˌo]
DJ [ˋreidiəu]
名 收音機

I put the radio beside my bed.
我把那台收音機放在我的床旁邊。

---

rope
KK [rop]
DJ [rəup]
名 繩子

The girl is using curtains to make a rope.
那位女孩正在用窗簾做一條繩子。

sheet KK [ʃit] DJ [ʃi:t] 名 床單

How often do you change your sheets?
你多久換一次床單？

小提醒 除了床單之外，一起來學底下這些跟寢具相關的英文單字吧～

床墊　mattress
棉被　comforter
被套　comforter cover
枕頭　pillow
枕頭套　pillowcase

---

soap KK [sop] DJ [səup] 名 肥皂

She likes to use soap to wash her clothes.
她喜歡用肥皂洗她的衣服。

---

sofa KK [ˋsofə] DJ [ˋsəufə] 名 沙發

My cat likes to sleep on the sofa.
我的貓喜歡在沙發上睡覺。

小提醒 sofa 和前面學過的 couch 中文意思都叫做沙發，不過它們的樣子其實不太一樣唷！sofa 是指靠背較高、兩邊都有扶手，適合多人坐的長沙發，而 couch 則是只有一邊有扶手，最多給兩、三個人靠躺的沙發，在使用的時候要注意它們的不同喔！

---

telephone KK [ˋtɛlə͵fon] DJ [ˋtelifəun] 名 電話

Can someone answer the telephone?
有人能去接一下電話嗎？

television KK [ˋtɛləˏvɪʒən] DJ [ˋteliˏviʒən] 名 電視

Don't sit in front of the television all day.
不要一整天都坐在電視前面。

例句單字 in front of 在～前面

小提醒 television 這個字常常會縮寫成 TV，看到的時候要知道是什麼意思唷～

---

thread KK [θrɛd] DJ [θred] 名 線

My poor eyesight makes it impossible for me to put the thread through the needle.
我糟糕的視力讓我沒辦法把線穿過針。

例句單字 poor 形 糟糕的　eyesight 名 視力

---

toilet KK [ˋtɔɪlɪt] DJ [ˋtɔilit] 名 馬桶

Can you fix the toilet for me?
你能幫我修馬桶嗎？

例句單字 fix 動 修理

---

toothpaste KK [ˋtuθˏpest] DJ [ˋtu:θpeist] 名 牙膏

He squeezed the toothpaste out of the tube.
他把牙膏從管子裡擠了出來。

例句單字 squeeze 動 擠壓　tube 名 管子

小提醒 toothpaste 指的是牙膏膏狀物本身，因為沒辦法一個一個的數，所以是不可數名詞，但是我們可以利用平常在說的「一條」為單位，一條牙膏就是「a tube of toothpaste」、兩條牙膏就是「two tubes of toothpaste」，記得toothpaste 的後面不能加 s 喔！

toothbrush
KK [`tuθ͵brʌʃ]
DJ [`tu:θbrʌʃ]
名 牙刷

You shouldn't run around with a toothbrush in your mouth.
你不應該在嘴裡有牙刷時跑來跑去。

towel
KK [`tauəl]
DJ [`tauəl]
名 毛巾

Mary dries her hair with a towel.
瑪麗用毛巾擦乾自己的頭髮。

例句單字 dry 動 把～弄乾

trash can
KK [træʃ] [kæn]
DJ [træʃ] [kæn]
名 垃圾桶

Please throw your trash into the trash can.
請把你的垃圾丟進垃圾桶。

video player
KK [`vɪdɪ͵o]
DJ [`vidiəu]
名 放影機

Jenny decided to buy a video player for her mom.
珍妮決定要買一台放影機給她媽媽。

washing machine
KK [`waʃɪŋ] [mə`ʃɪn]
DJ [`wɔʃɪŋ] [mə`ʃi:n]
名 洗衣機

The washing machine is broken.
洗衣機壞掉了。

例句單字 broken 形 故障的

In the Kitchen 在廚房裡

ketchup 番茄醬

shelf 架子

vinegar 醋

cup 杯子

faucet 水龍頭

oil 油

bowl 碗

soy-sauce 醬油

can 罐頭

sink 水槽

plate 盤子

pepper 胡椒

salt 鹽

pipe 水管

microwave 微波爐

dish 碟;盤

chopsticks 筷子

fork 叉子

spoon 湯匙

saucer 碟子

sugar 糖

slice 一片

ladle 長柄杓

boil 烹煮；煮沸

cook 煮

pot 鍋子

burn 燃燒

knife 刀

refrigerator 冰箱

bake 烘；烤

stove 瓦斯爐

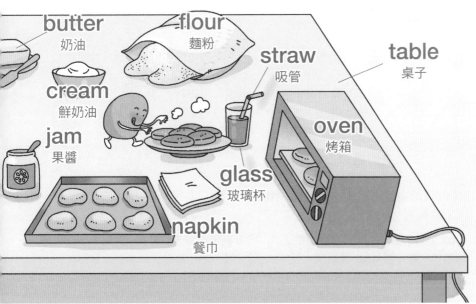

butter 奶油

flour 麵粉

straw 吸管

table 桌子

cream 鮮奶油

jam 果醬

glass 玻璃杯

oven 烤箱

napkin 餐巾

20.MP3

bake
KK [bek]
DJ [beik]
動 烘;烤

Do you know how to bake a cake?
你知道要怎麼烤一個蛋糕嗎？

---

boil
KK [bɔɪl]
DJ [bɔil]
動 烹煮;煮沸

Can you boil some water with this kettle?
你可以用這個茶壺煮一些水嗎？

例句單字 kettle 名 茶壺

---

bowl
KK [bol]
DJ [bəul]
名 碗

She likes to eat a bowl of cereal every morning.
她喜歡每天早上吃一碗穀麥片。

---

burn
KK [bɜn]
DJ [bə:n]
動 燃燒

Adam burns wood to make a pizza.
亞當燒木材來烤披薩。

---

butter
KK [`bʌtɚ]
DJ [`bʌtə]
名 奶油

Let me make you a ham and butter sandwich.
讓我來做一個火腿奶油三明治給你。

---

can
KK [kæn]
DJ [kæn]
名 罐頭

Can you open this can for me?
你能幫我開這個罐頭嗎？

小提醒 can 這個字除了「罐頭」的意思之外，當助動詞時表示「能夠」的意思，像上面的例句，第一個 can 是詢問「能夠」，第二個 can 則是「罐頭」的意思。

chopsticks KK [`tʃɑpˏstɪks] DJ [`tʃɔpstiks] 名 筷子

Learning how to use chopsticks elegantly is very important.
學習如何優雅地使用筷子是很重要的。

例句單字 elegantly 副 優雅地

---

cook KK [kʊk] DJ [kuk] 動 煮

Do you know how to cook fish?
你知道要怎麼煮魚嗎？

---

cream KK [krim] DJ [kri:m] 名 鮮奶油

Eating too much cream will make you fat.
吃太多鮮奶油會讓你變胖。

小提醒 cream 和 butter 雖然都叫做奶油，但它們很不一樣喔！cream 是指鮮奶油，也就是你在蛋糕上看到的那種膏狀奶油，butter 則是固體塊狀的奶油，常會用來塗抹在麵包上或是在煮菜的時候抹在鍋子裡。

---

cup KK [kʌp] DJ [kʌp] 名 杯子

Laura bought a cup in Disneyland as a souvenir.
蘿拉在迪士尼買了一個杯子當作紀念品。

例句單字 souvenir 名 紀念品

---

dish KK [dɪʃ] DJ [diʃ] 名 碟；盤

Cinderella has to wash all the dishes at night.
辛蒂瑞拉晚上的時候必須要洗所有的碗。

小提醒 如果只看 **wash dishes** 的字面意義，洗的只有盤子和碟子，但就和中文「洗碗」一樣，洗的不只是碗，而是包括鍋碗盤碟等全部的餐具。除了 **wash dishes** 之外，也可以說 **do dishes** 喔！

faucet
KK [`fɔsɪt]
DJ [`fɔ:sit]
名 水龍頭

I have to call a plumber to fix the leaky faucet.
我必須打電話給水電工來修漏水的水龍頭。

例句單字 plumber 名 水電工　fix 動 修理　leaking 形 漏水的

flour
KK [flaʊr]
DJ [flauə]
名 麵粉

According to this recipe, you should mix the flour with three eggs.
根據這份食譜，你應該混合麵粉與三顆蛋。

例句單字 according to 根據～　recipe 名 食譜　mix 動 混合

fork
KK [fɔrk]
DJ [fɔ:k]
名 叉子

You should watch your kids when they are using forks.
當你的孩子們在用叉子的時候，你應該看著他們。

glass
KK [glæs]
DJ [glɑ:s]
名 玻璃杯

This glass matches the fine wine.
這個玻璃杯與好酒很相配。

例句單字 match 動 和～相配　fine 形 品質好的

jam
KK [dʒæm]
DJ [dʒæm]
名 果醬

What kind of jam is your favorite?
你最喜歡哪種果醬？

小提醒 果醬有好多口味，你最喜歡哪一種呢？

草莓果醬 strawberry jam　　蘋果果醬 apple jam

藍莓果醬 blueberry jam　　柑橘果醬 marmalade

---

ketchup

KK [ˋkɛtʃəp]
DJ [ˋketʃəp]　名 番茄醬

I don't like to eat French fries with ketchup.
我不喜歡吃薯條配蕃茄醬。

---

knife

KK [naɪf]
DJ [naif]　名 刀

This knife is very sharp.
這把刀很鋒利。

例句單字 sharp 形 鋒利

---

ladle

KK [ˋledl]
DJ [ˋleidl]　名 長柄杓

My mother is holding a ladle with her right hand.
我媽媽的右手正拿著一支長柄杓。

---

microwave

KK [ˋmaɪkroˏwev]
DJ [ˋmaikrəuweiv]　名 微波爐

Microwaves make our lives easier.
微波爐讓我們的生活更便利。

---

napkin

KK [ˋnæpkɪn]
DJ [ˋnæpkɪn]　名 餐巾

After lunch, Jenny used a napkin to wipe her mouth.
在午餐過後，珍妮用了一張餐巾擦嘴巴。

例句單字 wipe 動 擦拭

oil KK [ɔɪl] DJ [ɔil] 名 油

My mom doesn't like to use a lot of oil when she is cooking.
我媽媽在煮菜的時候不喜歡放很多油。

---

oven KK [ˋʌvən] DJ [ˋʌvən] 名 烤箱

He is going to use the oven to bake cookies.
他打算用烤箱來烤餅乾。

---

pepper KK [ˋpɛpɚ] DJ [ˋpepə] 名 胡椒

Susan likes to put some pepper in her soup.
蘇珊喜歡在湯裡加一些胡椒。

---

pipe KK [paɪp] DJ [paip] 名 水管

That pipe burst due to great pressure.
那根水管因強大的壓力而破裂了。

例句單字 burst 動 破裂　due to 因為　pressure 名 壓力

---

plate KK [plet] DJ [pleit] 名 盤子

Eric was so clumsy that he broke some plates when he was washing dishes.
艾瑞克太笨手笨腳了，所以在洗碗時打破了一些盤子。

例句單字 clumsy 形 笨手笨腳的

---

pot KK [pɑt] DJ [pɔt] 名 鍋子

I lifted the lid and looked into the pot.
我把蓋子打開往鍋子裡面看。

refrigerator
KK [rɪ`frɪdʒəˌretə]
DJ [ri`fridʒəˌreitə]
名 冰箱

The refrigerator is not cold enough.
冰箱不夠冷。

---

salt
KK [sɔlt]
DJ [sɔːlt]
名 鹽

Don't forget to add some salt to the dishes.
別忘了在菜裡面加一些鹽巴。

---

saucer
KK [`sɔsə]
DJ [`sɔːsə]
名 碟子

Can you pass that saucer to me?
你能把那個碟子傳過來給我嗎？

例句單字 pass 動 傳遞

---

shelf
KK [ʃɛlf]
DJ [ʃelf]
名 架子

Can you reach the top of the shelf?
妳能碰到架子的上方嗎？

---

sink
KK [sɪŋk]
DJ [siŋk]
名 水槽

Please don't leave your dirty plates in the sink.
請不要把你的髒盤子留在水槽裡。

例句單字 dirty 形 骯髒的

---

slice
KK [slaɪs]
DJ [slais]
名 一片

Amy added a slice of cheese to the sandwich.
艾咪加了一片起司到三明治裡。

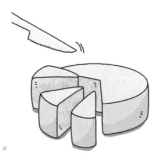

小提醒 slice 也可以變成動詞，當作切片的意思喔～
Dad slices the cake for me. 爸爸幫我把蛋糕切片。

159

soy-sauce
KK [sɔɪ] [sɔs]
DJ [sɔi] [sɔːs]
名 醬油

Don't eat too much soy-sauce because it's not good for your health.
不要吃太多醬油，因為這對你的健康不好。

spoon
KK [spun]
DJ [spuːn]
名 湯匙

Sophie likes to collect silver tea spoons.
蘇菲喜歡搜集銀的茶匙。

例句單字 silver 形 銀的

小提醒 除了銀之外，湯匙還有什麼材質呢？

金 gold　　銅 copper

不鏽鋼 stainless steel

stove
KK [stov]
DJ [stəuv]
名 瓦斯爐

I can't cook without a stove.
我沒有瓦斯爐就無法煮飯。

straw
KK [strɔ]
DJ [strɔː]
名 吸管

Could I have one more straw, please?
我能再要一根吸管嗎？

sugar
KK [ˋʃʊgɚ]
DJ [ˋʃʊgə]
名 糖

She doesn't like to add sugar into her coffee.
她不喜歡在咖啡裡加糖。

table
KK [`tebl]
DJ [`teibl] 名 桌子

The dining table in my house is too small to use.
我家的餐桌太小了不能用。

例句單字 too~ to~ 太～以致於不能～

小提醒 table 和 desk 雖然都是桌子，但 desk 是有抽屜的「書桌」，table 則是沒有抽屜的一般桌子，所以像是茶几（coffee table）、餐桌（dining table），都是用 table 這個字而不是 desk。

---

vinegar
KK [`vɪnɪgɚ]
DJ [`vinigə] 名 醋

Some people like to add some vinegar when eating salad.
有些人在吃沙拉時喜歡加一些醋。

button
釦子

vest
背心

underwear
內衣褲

coat
大衣

jeans
牛仔褲

pants
長褲

50%

clothes
衣服

pocket
口袋

jacket
夾克

trousers
褲子

SA

blouse
（女式）上衣

dress
洋裝

swimsuit
泳裝

skirt
短裙

試衣間　修改室

shirt
襯衫

uniform
制服

suit
西裝；套裝

iron
熨斗

hoodie
連帽衣

sweater
毛衣

T-shirt
T恤

pajamas
睡衣

shorts
短褲

cotton
棉

raincoat
雨衣

21.MP3

blouse
KK [blaʊz]
DJ [blauz]
名 （女式）上衣

Jenny is wearing a silk blouse.
珍妮穿著一件絲質上衣。

例句單字 silk 形 絲的

---

button
KK [ˋbʌtn̩]
DJ [ˋbʌtn̩]
名 鈕扣

This button is loose.
這顆鈕扣鬆掉了。

例句單字 loose 形 鬆掉的

小提醒 鈕扣鬆掉了，就要把扣子縫起來，縫扣子用
英文說就是 sew on a button，下次扣子
要掉了就可以這樣說，請人幫你把扣子縫起
來喔～

---

clothes
KK [kloz]
DJ [kləʊðz]
名 衣服

Mary is working hard so that she can buy beautiful clothes.
瑪麗為了買漂亮的衣服而認真工作。

例句單字 work hard 認真工作

---

coat
KK [kot]
DJ [kəut]
名 大衣

The coats in that store are on sale.
那家店的大衣正在促銷。

例句單字 on sale 促銷；特賣

小提醒 coat 指的是像牛角大衣、風衣等厚重外套，而不
是運動或輕便的外套，如果是像棒球外套的那種，
則可以叫做 jacket（夾克），不要搞錯囉！

cotton

KK [`kɑtn̩]
DJ [`kɔtn̩]　名 棉

My mother likes to buy clothes made of cotton.
我媽媽喜歡買用棉做成的衣服。

---

dress

KK [drɛs]
DJ [dres]　名 洋裝

Amy decided to wear this dress to the ball.
艾咪決定穿這件洋裝去參加舞會。

小提醒 ball 除了「球」的意思之外，還有「舞會」的意思喔！

---

hoodie

KK [`hʊdɪ]
DJ [`hudi]　名 連帽衣

Alex likes to wear the hoodie with his university's name on it.
艾力克斯喜歡穿那件上面有他大學名字的連帽衣。

---

iron

KK [`aɪɚn]
DJ [`aiən]　名 熨斗

I need an iron to iron my clothes.
我需要一個熨斗來燙我的衣服。

小提醒 iron 還可以當**動詞**，這個時候它就變成「熨燙衣服」裡的「**熨燙**」，就像上面的例句，第一個 iron 是名詞、第二個 iron 則是動詞喔！

---

jacket

KK [`dʒækɪt]
DJ [`dʒækit]　名 夾克

My keys are in the pocket of my jacket.
我的鑰匙在我夾克的口袋裡。

jeans

KK [dʒinz]
DJ [dʒiːnz] 名 牛仔褲

You can't wear jeans at work.
你上班的時候不能穿牛仔褲。

小提醒 因為只要是褲子就會有**兩條褲腿**，所以 jeans 和 pants（長褲）之類的褲子一樣，一直都是以複數的樣子出現，而「一條牛仔褲」的「條」，用英文來說就是 ~pair of，用 a pair of jeans（一條牛仔褲）、two pairs of jeans（兩條牛仔褲）…來表示。

pajamas

KK [pəˋdʒæməs]
DJ [pəˋdʒɑːməz] 名 睡衣

I have so many pairs of pajamas that I can wear a different pair every day.
我有好多套睡衣，所以我可以每天都穿不一樣的睡衣。

小提醒 睡覺的時候除了睡衣，有些人還會需要 nightcap（睡帽）來維持自己的髮型，如果怕光線干擾睡眠，就會戴上 eye mask（眼罩），除了這些，你睡覺的時候還需要什麼呢？

pants

KK [pænts]
DJ [pænts] 名 長褲

This pair of pants is too short for me.
這件長褲對我來說太短了。

pocket

KK [ˋpɑkɪt]
DJ [ˋpɔkit] 名 口袋

There is a hole in my pocket, so all my coins are gone.
我的口袋有個洞，所以我的硬幣都不見了。

例句單字 gone 形 不見的

raincoat

KK [ˋrenˌkot]
DJ [ˋreinkəut] 名 雨衣

His mother helped him put on a raincoat.
他媽媽幫他穿上了雨衣。

例句單字 put on 穿上

shirt
KK [ʃɝt]
DJ [ʃəːt]
名 襯衫

Tom put on a new shirt.
湯姆穿上一件新的襯衫。

---

shorts
KK [ʃɔrts]
DJ [ʃɔːts]
名 短褲

That model is wearing a pair of shorts.
那位模特兒穿著一件短褲。

---

skirt
KK [skɝt]
DJ [skəːt]
名 短裙

She doesn't like to wear skirts.
她不喜歡穿短裙。

---

suit
KK [sut]
DJ [suːt]
名 西裝；套裝

Famous actors wear decent suits to walk on the red carpet.
知名演員們穿上體面的西裝走紅毯。

例句單字 decent 形 體面的

---

sweater
KK [`swɛtɚ]
DJ [`swetə]
名 毛衣

It is cold outside, so I put on my sweater.
外面很冷，所以我穿上了毛衣。

---

swimsuit
KK [`swɪmsut]
DJ [`swɪmsjuːt]
名 泳裝

The pop star wore a beautiful swimsuit on the beach.
那位明星在沙灘上穿了件美麗的泳裝。

T-shirt
KK [`ti.ʃɝt]
DJ [`ti:ʃəːt]
名 T 恤

There is a stain on the T-shirt.
這件 T 恤上有塊污漬。

例句單字 stain 名 污漬

---

trousers
KK [`trauzɚ]
DJ [`trauzə]
名 褲子

These trousers are too large for me.
這件褲子對我來說太大了。

小提醒 因為褲子有兩個褲管，所以都被當作複數，因此**不能用單數的** this，而是**要用複數的** these，寫的時候要注意喔～

---

underwear
KK [`ʌndɚ‚wɛr]
DJ [`ʌndəwɛə]
名 內衣褲

He is so fat that it's hard for him to buy underwear.
他太胖了以致於很難買到內衣褲。

---

uniform
KK [`junə‚fɔrm]
DJ [`ju:nifɔ:m]
名 制服

You have to wear a uniform if you want to work in this restaurant.
如果你想在這家餐廳工作，你必須穿制服。

---

vest
KK [vɛst]
DJ [vɛst]
名 背心

The president wears a bullet-proof vest all the time.
總統總是穿著防彈背心。

例句單字 bullet-proof 形 防彈的

Don't judge a book by its cover. 不要以貌取人。

　　如果直接翻譯這句話就是「不要從封面去評斷一本書。」也就是「不要只看外表就下判斷」的意思，換句話說，**Never judge something by its looks.** 意思是「不要看外表評斷某樣東西（某個人）。」當然這句話的另一個涵義就是 **Appearances are deceiving.**（外表是會騙人的。）的意思，所以如果只看一個人的外表或是衣著打扮，就判斷對方是好或是壞，這樣是非常不聰明的喔！

Don't judge a book by its cover.

Vocabulary 一起看！

★appearance [ə`pɪrəns] 名 外貌，外觀；外表

★comedy [`kɑmədɪ] 名 喜劇

★comic book 片 漫畫書

★cover [`kʌvɚ] 名 （書的）封面

★deceiving [dɪ`sivɪŋ] 形 欺騙的

★die [daɪ] 動 死

★fiction [`fɪkʃən] 名 （總稱）小說

★hero [`hɪro] 名 英雄

★judge [dʒʌdʒ] 動 判斷；斷定

★knowledge [`nɑlɪdʒ] 名 知識，學問

★non-fiction [ˌnɑn`fɪkʃən] 名 非小說文學

★one of the best known 片

　　其中最為人所知的，其中最有名的

★picture book 片 繪本；圖畫書

★protect [prə`tɛkt] 動 保護

★reading [`ridɪŋ] 名 閱讀；讀物

★romance [ro`mæns] 名 羅曼史小說

★science [`saɪəns] 名 科學

包包區

配件區

bag 包包

belt 皮帶

hat 帽子　cap 鴨舌帽

glasses 眼鏡

purse 女用皮包

50%

contact lens 隱形眼鏡

wallet 皮夾

necklace 項鍊

diamond 鑽石

ring 戒指

silver 銀

gold 黃金

glove 手套

衣物區

mask 面具

tie 領帶

handkerchief 手帕

umbrella 雨傘

scarf 圍巾

sunglasses 太陽眼鏡

comb 扁梳

sneakers 球鞋

shoe 鞋子

sock 襪子

鞋襪區

首飾區

slipper 室內拖鞋

earring 耳環

bag
KK [bæg]
DJ [bæg] 名 包包

Who left this bag in the park?
誰把這個包包留在公園的？

---

belt
KK [bɛlt]
DJ [belt] 名 皮帶

Lisa gave her boyfriend a belt as his birthday present.
麗莎給男友一條皮帶當作生日禮物。

---

cap
KK [kæp]
DJ [kæp] 名 鴨舌帽

That movie star always wears a cap when he is outside.
那位電影明星外出時都帶著一頂鴨舌帽。

小提醒 hat（帽子）是泛指所有的帽子，不管是什麼款式都可以叫做 hat，而 cap 是 hat 的其中一種，只單指鴨舌帽喔～

---

comb
KK [kom]
DJ [kəum] 名 扁梳

The antique comb is displayed in the museum.
那個古董扁梳被展示在博物館裡。

例句單字 antique 形 骨董的　displayed 形 被展示的　museum 名 博物館

---

contact lens
KK [`kɑntækt] [lɛnz]
DJ [`kɔntækt] [lenz] 名 隱形眼鏡

You shouldn't wear contact lens for more than eight hours a day.
你一天不應該戴隱形眼鏡超過八小時。

小提醒 底下這些跟隱形眼鏡有關的英文單字，你知道嗎？

鏡片　lens

日拋式隱形眼鏡　daily disposable contacts

週拋式隱形眼鏡　weekly disposable contacts

隱形眼鏡保存盒　contact lens case

隱形眼鏡藥水　contact lotion

diamond

KK [`daɪəmənd]
DJ [`daiəmənd]　名 鑽石

That man gave his wife a diamond ring.

那個男人給他老婆一個鑽石戒指。

earring

KK [`daɪəmənd]
DJ [`daiəmənd]　名 耳環

I found the earrings you lost under the sofa.

我在沙發底下找到你弄丟的耳環。

例句單字 lost 形 遺失的

glasses

KK [`glæsɪz]
DJ [`glɑ:siz]　名 眼鏡

He wears glasses every day.

他每天都戴著眼鏡。

小提醒 眼鏡因為有**兩片鏡片**，所以都是以複數的樣子出現，要說「一副眼鏡」的時候用 **a pair of glasses** 來表達，兩副眼鏡的話就是 **two pairs of glasses**，不要用錯囉！

glove

KK [glʌv]
DJ [glʌv]　名 手套

Why aren't you wearing your gloves?

你為什麼不戴著你的手套呢？

gold KK [gold] DJ [gəuld] 名 黃金

This ring is expensive because it is made from pure gold.
這只戒指很貴，因為它是純金做成的。

例句單字 pure 形 純的

---

handkerchief KK [`hæŋkɚ͵tʃɪf] DJ [`hæŋkətʃɪf] 名 手帕

I gave my handkerchief to the crying little girl.
我把我的手帕給了那個正在哭泣的小女孩。

小提醒 handkerchief 這個字的發音比較特別，hand 的 d 是不發出聲音的喔！在唸的時候要注意～

---

hat KK [hæt] DJ [hæt] 名 帽子

Alice likes to wear hats in summer.
愛麗絲夏天的時候喜歡戴帽子。

---

mask KK [mæsk] DJ [mɑːsk] 名 面具

You can wear a mask at this party.
在這場派對中你可以戴著面具。

小提醒 mask 除了面具的意思之外，也有「口罩」的意思。

---

necklace KK [`nɛklɪs] DJ [`neklis] 名 項鍊

The thief broke into her house to steal her necklace.
那個小偷為了要偷她的項鍊闖進她家。

例句單字 thief 名 小偷　steal 動 偷竊

---

purse KK [pɝs] DJ [pəːs] 名 女用皮包

She left her purse at the train station.
她把皮包留在火車站裡了。

ring
KK [rɪŋ]
DJ [riŋ]
名 戒指

Tom proposed to his girlfriend and gave her a diamond ring.
湯姆向他的女朋友求婚並給了她一只鑽戒。

小提醒 propose 動 求婚；提議

---

scarf
KK [skɑrf]
DJ [skɑ:f]
名 圍巾

I put the scarf around my neck.
我在脖子上圍了一條圍巾。

例句單字 注意圍巾的複數形態不是 scarfs，而是 scarves 喔！

---

shoe
KK [ʃu]
DJ [ʃu:]
名 鞋子

Please take off your shoes.
請脫掉你的鞋子。

例句單字 take off 脫下

小提醒 在 take off（脫下）之前，要先學會把鞋子 put on（穿上），並且 lace up your shoes（繫上你的鞋帶），這些跟穿鞋有關的英文，你學會了嗎？

---

silver
KK [ˋsɪlvɚ]
DJ [ˋsilvə]
名 銀

Speech is silver, silence is gold.
雄辯是銀，沈默是金。

例句單字 silence 名 寂靜

---

slipper
KK [ˋslɪpɚ]
DJ [ˋslipə]
名 室內拖鞋

You can wear this pair of slippers.
你可以穿這雙室內拖鞋。

sneakers KK [`snikɚ] DJ [`sni:kə] 名 球鞋

He wants to buy that pair of sneakers.
他想買那雙球鞋。

sock KK [sɑk] DJ [sɔk] 名 襪子

It's getting cold here, so I decided to put on socks before I go to sleep.
這裡變冷了，所以我決定睡覺前去穿襪子。

sunglasses KK [`sʌn͵glæsɪz] DJ [`sʌngla:siz] 名 太陽眼鏡

I wear sunglasses to protect my eyes.
我戴太陽眼鏡來保護眼睛。

例句單字 protect 動 保護

tie KK [taɪ] DJ [tai] 名 領帶

Do you know how to tie a tie?
你知道要如何打領帶嗎？

小提醒 tie 這個字可以當作動詞「**打結；繫上**」的意思，tie a tie 就是「**打領帶**」的意思，除了領帶之外，常看到的還有 bow tie（領結），tie a bow tie 就是「打領結」，是不是很簡單呢？

umbrella KK [ʌm`brɛlə] DJ [ʌm`brelə] 名 雨傘

You can use my umbrella.
你可以用我的雨傘。

wallet KK [`wɑlɪt] DJ [`wɔlit] 名 皮夾

Linda wants to buy a wallet made of leather.
琳達想買一個皮革做成的皮夾。

wear a long face 不高興的拉長著臉

　　如果把這句話翻成中文，就是「穿著一張長長的臉」，形容心情不好而沒有笑容，在中文裡也有用「拉長了臉」來表示不高興的類似說法，是不是很有意思呢！所以我們可以用「**wear a long face**」來表示某人「不高興的拉長著臉」。

　　在這裡我們可以發現 wear 除了「穿戴」的意思之外，也可以用來表示「面帶～」，例如「She was wearing a lovely smile.」就是說「她一直面帶可愛的微笑」。

Please don't wear a long face! Cheer up!

Vocabulary 一起看！

★buckle [ˋbʌkl] 名（皮帶的）環釦

★zip [zɪp] 名 拉鍊

★jumper [ˋdʒʌmpɚ] 名 套頭毛衣

★dressing gown 名 晨袍

★cardigan [ˋkɑrdɪgən] 名 開襟毛衣

★stocking [ˋstɑkɪŋ] 名 長襪

★nightdress [ˋnaɪtˏdrɛs] 名 睡衣

★tights [taɪts] 名 緊身褲

★button hole 名 鈕釦孔

★hair band 名 髮帶

★boot [but] 名 靴子

★hairpin [ˋhɛrˏpɪn] 名 髮夾

black
黑色;黑色的

brown
棕色;棕色的

gray
灰色;灰色的

orange
橘色;橘色的

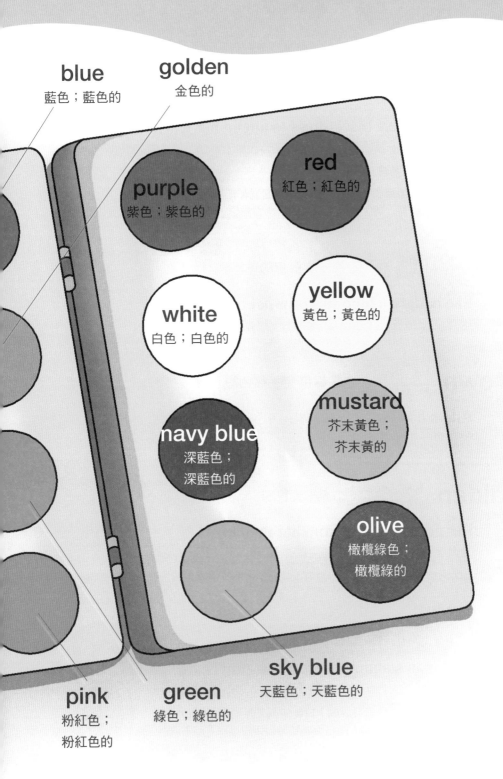

blue
藍色；藍色的

golden
金色的

purple
紫色；紫色的

red
紅色；紅色的

white
白色；白色的

yellow
黃色；黃色的

navy blue
深藍色；
深藍色的

mustard
芥末黃色；
芥末黃的

olive
橄欖綠色；
橄欖綠的

pink
粉紅色；
粉紅色的

green
綠色；綠色的

sky blue
天藍色；天藍色的

23.MP3

black

KK [blæk]
DJ [blæk]

名 黑色　形 黑色的

Laura wore a black dress to attend her teacher's funeral.
蘿拉穿了一件黑色的洋裝去參加她老師的葬禮。

例句單字 funeral 名 葬禮

小提醒 在英文裡，**用來表示顏色的單字通常名詞和形容詞長得一模一樣**，像 black 這個字，同時有「黑色」和「黑色的」兩個意思，大家在使用的時候要注意喔！

---

blue

KK [blu]
DJ [blu:]

名 藍色　形 藍色的

She bought a blue scarf for her best friend.
她買了一條藍色的圍巾給她最好的朋友。

---

brown

KK [braʊn]
DJ [braun]

名 棕色　形 棕色的

Adam has brown eyes.
亞當有著棕色的眼睛。

---

golden

KK [ˋgoldən]
DJ [ˋgəuldən]

形 金色的

Her golden hair is from her mother.
她從她媽媽那邊遺傳了金色的頭髮。

小提醒 golden 的名詞是 gold（金色；黃金），和其他顏色家族成員不一樣喔～

---

gray

KK [gre]
DJ [grei]

名 灰色　形 灰色的

That man standing there has a gray beard.
站在那裡的男子有灰色的鬍子。

小提醒 你知道「白髮」要怎麼說嗎？白髮的英文是 gray hair，而不是 white hair 喔！這是因為當頭髮變白後，混雜著其他維持原來顏色的頭髮，在視覺上會是「灰白色」，而不是單純的白色。

green
KK [grin] DJ [gri:n] 名 綠色 形 綠色的

Every tree turns green in the spring.
所有的樹在春天都變成綠色。

---

mustard
KK [`mʌstəd] DJ [`mʌstəd] 名 芥末黃色 形 芥末黃的

That mustard bag is very special.
那個芥末黃色的包包非常特別。

> **小提醒** mustard 另一個意思是「黃芥末醬」，就是你在吃熱狗時要擠上的黃芥末醬，這裡是藉著黃芥末醬的顏色來衍生出「芥末黃」的意思。

---

navy blue
KK [`nevɪ] [blu] DJ [`neivi] [blu:] 名 深藍色 形 深藍色的

This navy blue jacket is very suitable for you.
這件深藍色夾克很適合你。

> **例句單字** suitable 形 適合的

> **小提醒** navy 的意思是「海軍」，所以 navy blue 也常被稱作「海軍藍」。

---

olive
KK [`ɑlɪv] DJ [`ɔliv] 名 橄欖綠色 形 橄欖綠的

Her dress is olive; it really fits her skin tone.
她的洋裝是橄欖綠的，非常適合她的膚色。

> **例句單字** fit 動 適合 skin tone 名 膚色

> **小提醒** olive 這個字就像 mustard 一樣，都是由原本的「橄欖」衍生出顏色的意思，因此 olive 用來指顏色時就是指橄欖綠色啦！

---

orange
KK [`ɔrɪndʒ] DJ [`ɔ:rindʒ] 名 橘色 形 橘色的

The sky is orange at sunset.
天空在夕陽時呈現橘色。

> **例句單字** sunset 名 夕陽

> **小提醒** orange 也是「柳橙」的意思，柳橙是什麼顏色呢？沒錯，就是「橘色」！

pink
KK [pɪŋk]
DJ [piŋk]
名 粉紅色 形 粉紅色的

Jenny's favorite purse is pink.
珍妮最喜歡的包包是粉紅色的。

---

purple
KK [ˋpɝpl]
DJ [ˋpəːpl]
名 紫色 形 紫色的

If you mix blue and red, you can get purple.
如果你混合藍色跟紅色，你可以得到紫色。

---

red
KK [rɛd]
DJ [red]
名 紅色 形 紅色的

My mom likes red roses.
我的媽媽喜歡紅玫瑰。

---

sky blue
KK [skaɪ] [blu]
DJ [skai] [bluː]
名 天藍色 形 天藍色的

The sky blue balloon is a gift for his daughter.
天藍色的氣球是給他女兒的禮物。

例句單字 balloon 名 氣球

小提醒 sky 是天空的意思，sky blue 指的就是天氣晴朗時天空的顏色。

---

white
KK [hwaɪt]
DJ [hwait]
名 白色 形 白色的

The children are playing with a white dog.
小孩們正在和一隻白狗玩。

---

yellow
KK [ˋjɛlo]
DJ [ˋjeləu]
名 黃色 形 黃色的

The mark of the store is a yellow hat.
那家店的標誌是一頂黃色的帽子。

paint (something) in 把某物畫入圖中

　　「**paint**」這個字可以作為「油漆」的意思，也可以是「上色」的意思。而這句片語是指將某樣物品或人物畫入圖畫裡，例如「She painted the sight in.」意思是「她將景色畫入圖畫中。」

Vocabulary 一起看！

★color [`kʌlə] 名

　　色彩，顏色（作為動詞時則表示「著色」的意思）

★color pen 名 彩色筆

★crayon [`kreən] 名 顏色粉筆；蠟筆

★draw [`drɔ] 動 畫，描繪

★favorite [`fevərɪt] 形 最喜愛的

★left [`lɛft] 形 左方的，左側的

★outline [`aut͵laɪn] 動 畫出…的輪廓

★paint [pent] 動 油漆；繪畫

★pencil [`pɛnsḷ] 名 鉛筆

★prefer [prɪ`fɝ] 動 比起～更喜歡

★right [raɪt] 形 右方的，右側的

★side [saɪd] 名 邊；面；側

★sketch [skɛtʃ] 名 素描；草圖

★use [juz] 動 使用，利用

★wall [wɔl] 名 牆壁

★want [wɑnt] 動 想要

183

24.MP3

badminton
KK [`bædmɪntən]
DJ [`bædmɪntən]
 羽球

My brother teaches badminton.
我的哥哥教羽球。

---

baseball
KK [`bes͵bɔl]
DJ [`beis͵bɔ:l]
名 棒球

Tom and Jerry are on the same baseball team.
湯姆跟傑瑞在同一個棒球隊。

小提醒 你知道棒球各守備位置的英文要怎麼說嗎？

投手	pitcher	一壘手	first baseman
捕手	catcher	二壘手	second baseman
教練	coach	三壘手	third baseman
游擊手	shortstop	外野手	outfielder

---

basketball
KK [`bæskɪt͵bɔl]
DJ [`bæskitbɔ:l]
名 籃球

Jeff wants to join the college basketball team.
傑夫想加入大學的籃球隊。

例句單字 college 名 專科；大學

小提醒 籃球和棒球一樣，每個球員打的位置都有自己的名稱喔！

中鋒	center	大前鋒	power forward
小前鋒	small forward	得分後衛	shoot guard
控球後衛	point guard	第六人（替補）	sixth

---

bowling
KK [`bolɪŋ]
DJ [`bəulɪŋ]
名 保齡球

I like to go bowling with Jenny.
我喜歡跟珍妮一起打保齡球。

cheerleader
KK [`tʃɪrˌlidɚ]
DJ [`tʃiəˌliːdə]
名 啦啦隊員

Lisa always wanted to be a cheerleader.
麗莎一直都想要當啦啦隊員。

---

dodgeball
KK [dɑdʒbɔl]
DJ [dɔdʒbɔːl]
名 躲避球

He hurt his arm when he was playing dodgeball.
他在玩躲避球時傷了手臂。

---

fan
KK [fæn]
DJ [fæn]
名 狂熱愛好者（粉絲）

She is a fan of that popular singer, so she bought
the concert ticket.
她是那位流行歌手的粉絲，所以她買了那場演唱會門票。

例句單字 ticket 名 票

---

football
KK [`fʊtˌbɔl]
DJ [`futbɔːl]
名 美式足球

My father is a professional football
player.
我的父親是一位職業美式足球員。

例句單字 professional 形 職業的

小提醒 football 在美國指的是「美式足球」，但在其
他地區指的都是「足球」，而在美國則稱足球為
「soccer」。

Frisbee
KK [`frɪzbi]
DJ [`frizbiː]
名 飛盤

Alice plays Frisbee with her dogs every day.
愛麗絲每天都跟她的狗玩飛盤。

golf KK [gɑlf] DJ [gɔlf] 名 高爾夫球

You walk a lot when playing golf.
在打高爾夫球時會走很多路。

---

jog KK [dʒɑg] DJ [dʒɔg] 名 慢跑

In order to lose weight, he goes jogging every day.
為了要減肥，他每天都慢跑。

例句單字 in order to 為了～

小提醒 jog 這個字同時可以當作動詞或名詞，但我們平常比較常用 go jogging 這個說法來表示「去慢跑」，下次想要去慢跑的時候，你就可以說：I want to go jogging now.（我現在想要去慢跑。）。

---

lose KK [luz] DJ [lu:z] 動 輸

Sam doesn't want to lose, so he practices very hard.
山姆不想輸，所以非常努力練習。

---

loser KK [`luzɚ] DJ [`lu:zə] 名 輸家

A loser is someone who quits without trying.
輸家是不嘗試就放棄的人。

例句單字 quit 動 放棄

---

player KK [`pleɚ] DJ [`pleiə] 名 球員

Tom is the most valuable player of the year.
湯姆是本年度最有價值球員。

例句單字 valuable 形 有價值的

小提醒 most valuable player 看起來又臭又長，但其實我們很常看到它的縮寫，沒錯，就是 MVP！

prize
KK [praɪz]
DJ [praiz]
名 獎項

She won first prize in the contest.
她在這場比賽中得到第一名。

race
KK [res]
DJ [reis]
名 賽跑

If you win the race, you will get 10,000 dollars.
如果你贏了這場賽跑，你可以得到 1 萬美金。

roller-skating
KK [`rolɚ͵sketɪŋ]
DJ [`rəuləskeitiŋ]
名 溜冰

His mother takes him to the park for roller-skating.
他媽媽帶他去公園溜冰。

小提醒 roller-skating 是來自 roller-skate（用溜冰鞋溜冰）這個字，把 roller-skate 加上個字尾 s，就會變成 roller-skates（溜冰鞋）喔！

running
KK [`rʌnɪŋ]
DJ [`rʌniŋ]
名 跑步

My teacher has us running around the track for twenty minutes in PE class.
我的老師要求我們在體育課繞著跑道跑二十分鐘。

例句單字 PE class 名 體育課

小提醒 running 這個字是由 run（奔跑）而來的，雖然都是「跑」，但它和前面介紹過的 race 不一樣，沒有比賽的意思，只是單純的跑步，但一般來說會比 jog（慢跑）的速度再快一點。

sailing
KK [`selɪŋ]
DJ [`seiliŋ]
名 帆船運動

Sally is looking forward to going sailing with him.
莎莉期待和他一起去玩帆船。

例句單字 looking forward to 期待做～

189

skateboarding
KK [`sket͵bɔrdɪŋ]
DJ [`skeit͵bɔːdiŋ]
名 滑板運動

Skateboarding is really difficult for me.
滑板運動對我來說真的很難。

---

skiing
KK [`skiɪŋ]
DJ [`skiːiŋ]
名 滑雪運動

My dad takes me to go skiing every winter.
我爸爸每年冬天都會帶我去滑雪。

小提醒 跟滑雪有關的單字還有哪些呢？

度假村 **resort** 滑雪場地 **ski site** 滑雪服 **ski suit**

---

soccer
KK [`sɑkɚ]
DJ [`sɔkə]
名 足球

We should watch the soccer game together.
我們應該一起看那場足球比賽。

小提醒 soccer 這個字是美國人為了區別足球和美式足球而使用的字，如果今天到歐洲旅行，想講足球的話記得要說 football 喔！

---

softball
KK [`sɔft͵bɔl]
DJ [`sɔftbɔːl]
名 壘球

He broke his leg playing softball.
他在打壘球時摔斷了腿。

小提醒 break one's leg 是「摔斷某人的腿」的意思，但這其實也是一句常見的慣用語喔！如果今天有人要上台表演，那你可以和他說 Go break your leg!
這邊不是叫他去把腿摔斷，而是**祝他好運**的意思喔！

---

surfing
KK [sɝfɪŋ]
DJ [səfiŋ]
名 衝浪

Adam loves surfing so much that he goes to the beach every week.
亞當愛衝浪愛到每個星期都去海邊。

swimming
KK [`swɪmɪŋ]
DJ [`swimiŋ]
名 游泳

Jane goes swimming every summer vacation.
珍每個暑假都去游泳。

---

table tennis
KK [`tebḷ] [`tɛnɪs]
DJ [`teibḷ] [`tenis]
名 桌球

I can't find a partner to play table tennis with me.
我沒辦法找到夥伴跟我一起打桌球。

---

tennis
KK [`tɛnɪs]
DJ [`tenis]
名 網球

You can't play tennis here.
你不能在這裡打網球。

---

volleyball
KK [`vɑlɪ͵bɔl]
DJ [`vɔli͵bɔːl]
名 排球

You can't play volleyball alone.
你沒辦法自己一個人打排球。

小提醒 就像上面例句說的那樣，自己一個人沒辦法打排球，我們一起來認識一下排球的各個位置吧！

攻擊手	spiker	中間手（攔中）	middle blocker
舉球員	setter	自由人	libero

---

win
KK [wɪn]
DJ [win]
動 贏

Winning this game is very important to that player.
對那名球員來說，贏得這場比賽是非常重要的。

---

winner
KK [`wɪnɚ]
DJ [`winə]
名 贏家

The judges have to decide who will be the winner.
評審們必須決定誰將成為贏家。

例句單字 judge 名 評審

Hobbies 嗜好

barbecue
烤肉（餐會）

camping
露營

hiking
健行

mountain climbing
爬山

cooking
烹飪

dancing
跳舞

drawing
繪畫

picnic
野餐

fishing
釣魚

band 樂團

singing
唱歌

stamp collecting
集郵

trip 旅行

hobby 嗜好

chess 西洋棋

card 紙牌

193

comic 漫畫

computer game
電腦遊戲

doll 洋娃娃

kite 風箏

movie 電影

painting
繪畫（著色）

game 遊戲

toy 玩具

Internet
網路

travel
旅行

cartoon 卡通

drama 戲劇

film 影片

novel 小說

puzzle 拼圖

reading 閱讀

band
KK [bænd]
DJ [bænd]　名 樂團

I have to go to band rehearsal every day.
我必須每天都去樂團的排練。

例句單字　rehearsal 名 排練

---

barbecue
KK [`barbɪkju]
DJ [`baːbikjuː]　名 烤肉（餐會）

They are going to have a barbecue this weekend.
這週末他們打算要辦場烤肉餐會。

---

camping
KK [kæmpɪŋ]
DJ [kæmpiŋ]　名 露營

She loves camping under the stars.
她熱愛在星空下露營。

---

card
KK [kard]
DJ [kaːd]　名 紙牌

Do you like card games?
你喜歡紙牌遊戲嗎？

小提醒　說到紙牌遊戲，大家最熟悉的就是被稱作撲克牌的 **playing cards** 啦！撲克牌的英文照字面翻譯其實是「遊戲紙牌」的意思，但因為常被用來玩撲克遊戲（**poker**），所以被稱為「撲克牌」，你知道撲克牌有哪些花色嗎？

紅心 **heart**　方塊 **diamond**　黑桃 **spade**　梅花 **club**

---

cartoon
KK [kar`tun]
DJ [kaː`tuːn]　名 卡通

You should not watch cartoons all day long.
你不應該看卡通看一整天。

chess
KK [tʃɛs]
DJ [tʃes]
名 西洋棋

I didn't know you could play chess.
我不知道你會玩西洋棋。

---

mountain climbing
KK ['mauntn] ['klaɪmɪŋ]
DJ ['mauntin] ['klaimiŋ]
名 爬山

Sally is good at mountain climbing.
莎莉很擅長爬山。

例句單字 be good at~ 對～擅長

---

comic
KK ['kɑmɪk]
DJ ['kɔmik]
名 漫畫

Adam learns Japanese because he wants to read Japanese comics.
亞當因為想看日文漫畫而學日文。

---

computer game
KK [kəm'pjutɚ] [gem]
DJ [kəm'pju:tə] [geim]
名 電腦遊戲

This computer game is very popular among teenagers.
這款電腦遊戲在青少年之間非常流行。

例句單字 among 介 在～之中

---

cooking
KK ['kʊkɪŋ]
DJ ['kukiŋ]
名 烹飪

I love cooking with my mom.
我熱愛和媽媽一起煮飯。

小提醒 cooking 的動詞是 cook（烹飪），雖然很多動詞的字尾加上 er 就會變成「從事這個動作的人」，但是 cooker 這個字是「鍋具」的意思喔！所以如果你想要和別人說「媽媽很會煮飯」，結果說成 My mom is a nice cooker.，那媽媽就變成一個好鍋子而不是好廚師囉！那「廚師」到底要怎麼說呢？其實 cook 這個字可以直接當作名詞成為廚師的意思，所以只要把上面那句話裡的 cooker 改成 cook 就可以囉！

dancing
KK [`dænsɪŋ]
DJ [`dænsiŋ]
名 跳舞

My parents go dancing when they are free.
我的爸媽會在有空的時候去跳舞。

例句單字 free 形 空閒的

---

doll
KK [dɑl]
DJ [dɔl]
名 洋娃娃

My aunt bought me a doll.
阿姨買了一個洋娃娃給我。

---

drama
KK [`drɑmə]
DJ [`drɑ:mə]
名 戲劇

What is your favorite drama of the year?
你今年最喜歡的戲劇是哪部？

小提醒 你知道各種不同的戲劇類型要怎麼說嗎？

喜劇	comedy	平劇	Peking opera
悲劇	tragedy	歌仔戲	Taiwanese opera
布袋戲	Taiwanese puppet show	歌劇	opera

---

drawing
KK [`drɔɪŋ]
DJ [`drɔ:iŋ]
名 繪畫

Jenny is talented at drawing.
珍妮對繪畫很有天份。

例句單字 talented 形 有天份的

---

film
KK [fɪlm]
DJ [film]
名 影片

She loves to watch films at home.
她喜愛在家看影片。

小提醒 不論影片長度，只要是「影片」都可以叫做 film 喔！

fishing
KK [`fɪʃɪŋ]
DJ [`fiʃiŋ]
名 釣魚

Peter often goes fishing with his high school classmates.
彼得常常和他的高中同學一起去釣魚。

例句單字 often 副 經常　classmate 名 同學

---

game
KK [gem]
DJ [geim]
名 遊戲

Do you want to play a game with me?
你想要和我玩個遊戲嗎？

---

hiking
KK [haɪkɪŋ]
DJ [haikiŋ]
名 健行

Due to the bad weather, we shouldn't go hiking this time.
因為天氣不好，我們應該要取消這次健行。

例句單字 due to 因為～

---

hobby
KK [`hɑbɪ]
DJ [`hɔbi]
名 嗜好

My hobby is taking pictures.
我的嗜好是拍照。

Internet
KK [`ɪntə‚nɛt]
DJ [`intə‚net]
名 網路

I make friends through the Internet.
我透過網路交朋友。

---

kite
KK [kaɪt]
DJ [kait]
名 風箏

The children are flying kites in the park.
小孩們正在公園裡放風箏。

例句單字 fly kite 放風箏

movie
KK [`muvɪ]
DJ [`mu:vi]
名 電影

He wants to take his girlfriend to see the movie.
他想帶女友去看這場電影。

小提醒 電影有很多種類，一起來看看要怎麼用英文說吧！

動作片	action movie	劇情片	drama movie
紀錄片	documentary	科幻片	sci-fi (science-fiction) movie
恐怖片	horror movie	愛情片	romance movie

---

novel
KK [`nɑvl]
DJ [`nɔvəl]
名 小說

Tom wrote three novels.
湯姆寫了三本小說。

---

painting
KK [pentɪŋ]
DJ [peintiŋ]
名 繪畫（著色）

Sarah really enjoys painting with her daughter.
莎拉很享受與她女兒一起著色。

---

picnic
KK [`pɪknɪk]
DJ [`piknik]
名 野餐

It's a wonderful day for a picnic.
這是個適合野餐的好日子。

例句單字 wonderful 形 極好的

小提醒 想要去野餐的話，需要些什麼呢？

野餐墊 mat　紙巾 napkin　野餐籃 basket

---

puzzle
KK [`pʌzl]
DJ [`pʌzəl]
名 拼圖

I completed the puzzle without help.
我自己完成了拼圖。

例句單字 complete 動 完成

reading
KK [`ridɪŋ]
DJ [`ri:dɪŋ]
名 閱讀

I like sitting in a coffee shop and reading.
我喜歡坐在咖啡店裡閱讀。

singing
KK [`sɪŋɪŋ]
DJ [`siŋɪŋ]
名 唱歌

Robert and his friends enjoy singing at Karaoke bars.
羅伯特和他的朋友們很喜歡去卡拉 OK 唱歌。

例句單字 Karaoke 名 卡拉 OK

stamp collecting
KK [`stæmpkə‚lɛktɪŋ]
DJ [`stæmpkə‚lektɪŋ]
名 集郵

His hobby is stamp collecting.
他的嗜好是集郵。

toy
KK [tɔɪ]
DJ [tɔi]
名 玩具

The boy is holding a toy.
那個男孩拿著一個玩具。

travel
KK [`trævl̩]
DJ [`trævəl]
名 旅行

My dad takes me to travel every winter.
我爸每年冬天都會帶我去旅行。

trip
KK [trɪp]
DJ [trɪp]
名 旅行

Terry goes on a field trip every semester.
泰瑞每個學期都會去校外教學。

小提醒 trip 跟 travel 在中文翻譯上都是「旅遊」，但他們其實有一點不一樣喔！trip 指的是「往返一個地點，但是耗費的時間不長」，而 travel 則是「前往某個地點」或「（不論耗費時間長短的）旅遊」，在使用的時候要注意唷！

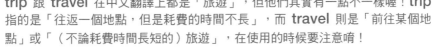

嗜好 Hobbies

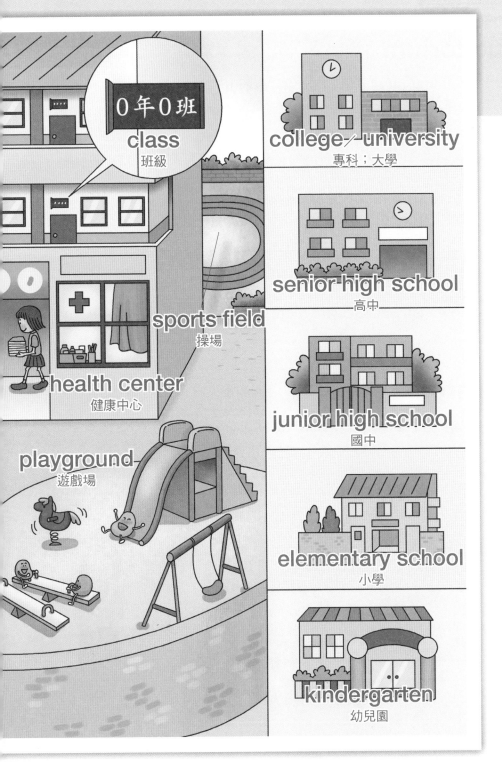

class
班級

college／university
專科；大學

senior high school
高中

sports field
操場

health center
健康中心

junior high school
國中

playground
遊戲場

elementary school
小學

kindergarten
幼兒園

26.MP3

auditorium
KK [ˌɔdəˋtorɪəm]
DJ [ˌɔːdiˋtɔːriəm]
名 禮堂

Can you meet me in the auditorium?
你可以在禮堂跟我見面嗎？

---

campus
KK [ˋkæmpəs]
DJ [ˋkæmpəs]
名 校園

There are a lot of trees on the campus.
校園裡有很多樹。

---

class
KK [klæs]
DJ [klɑːs]
名 班級

How many classes are there in your grade?
你的年級裡有幾個班級？

---

classroom
KK [ˋklæsˌrʊm]
DJ [ˋklɑːsrum]
名 教室

Can you show me where the classroom is?
你能告訴我教室在哪裡嗎？

小提醒 classroom 其實就是「class（班級）＋room（房間）」所組合而成的，也就是「班級待的房間＝教室」，是不是很好記呢？

---

college
KK [ˋkɑlɪdʒ]
DJ [ˋkɔlidʒ]
名 專科；大學

We were roommates in college.
我們是大學室友。

小提醒 college 這個字和我們在後面會說到的 university 一樣都有「大學」的意思，但是 college 指的是學生人數、系所類別規模較小的大學，一般不會提供碩士或博士課程，在台灣指的就是專科學校和技術學院，而 university 指的則是規模較大的綜合大學，除了大學部，通常會設有碩士及博士課程。

elementary school

KK [ˌɛləˋmɛntərɪ][skul]
DJ [ˌeləˋmentəri] [skuːl]

名 小學

His friends from elementary school all live near his house.
他小學的朋友都住他家附近。

---

entrance

KK [ˋɛntrəns]
DJ [ˋentrəns]

名 入口

Please enter the park through the entrance.
請從入口進入這座公園。

例句單字 enter 動 進入

---

guard

KK [gɑrd]
DJ [gɑːd]

名 警衛

The billionaire hired 10 guards to protect his house.
那個億萬富翁雇用了 10 個警衛來保護他的房子。

例句單字 billionaire 名 億萬富翁

---

gym

KK [dʒɪm]
DJ [dʒim]

名 體育館

I am going to the gym for PE class.
我要去體育館上體育課。

小提醒 gym 這個字在前面也有看過，那個時候指的是「健身房」，但其實它也有體育館的意思，gym 這種體育館是讓人做室內運動的，所以如果體育課要上跳馬、跳高之類的時候，老師就會帶你們去 gym 裡上課喔～

---

health center

KK [hɛlθ] [ˋsɛntɚ]
DJ [helθ] [ˋsentə]

名 健康中心

Why are you in the health center?
你為什麼在健康中心裡？

junior high school

KK [`dʒunjɚ] [haɪ][skul]
DJ [`dʒuːnjə] [hai][skuːl]
名 國中

One of his friends from junior high school will get married next month.
他其中一個國中朋友下個月要結婚了。

---

kindergarten

KK [`kɪndɚˌɡɑrtən]
DJ [`kɪndəˌɡaːtən]
名 幼兒園

His grandfather picks him up at kindergarten every afternoon.
他的爺爺每天下午都去幼兒園接他。

例句單字 pick sb. up 接～（某人）

---

library

KK [`laɪˌbrɛrɪ]
DJ [`laibrəri]
名 圖書館

In order to prepare for the test, she stays in the library every night.
為了準備考試，她每天晚上都待在圖書館。

小提醒 在圖書館裡還會用到哪些英文單字呢？

借書證 **library card**　　借書 **borrow**　　還書 **return**

續借 **renew**　　逾期 **overdue**

---

parking lot

KK [`pɑrkɪŋ] [lɑt]
DJ [`paːkiŋ] [lɔt]
名 停車場

Jenny met an old friend in the parking lot.
珍妮在停車場遇見了一位老朋友。

---

playground

KK [`pleˌɡraʊnd]
DJ [`pleiɡraund]
名 遊戲場

Bob takes his child to the playground every afternoon.
鮑伯每天下午都會帶他的小孩去遊戲場。

小提醒 **playground** 指的是設有遊樂設施（翹翹板、溜鞦韆等）的遊戲場所。

principal KK [`prɪnsəpl̩] DJ [`prɪnsəpəl] 名 校長

Our principal is a nice old lady.
我們的校長是一位和藹的老太太。

---

school store KK [skul] [stor] DJ [sku:l] [stɔ:] 名 販賣部

They go to the school store to buy lunch every day.
他們每天都去販賣部買午餐。

---

senior high school KK [`sinjɚ] [haɪ][skul] DJ [`si:njə] [hai] [sku:l] 名 高中

They are going to have a senior high school reunion tomorrow.
他們明天要辦高中同學會。

例句單字 reunion 名 （親友等的）團聚

---

sports field KK [spɔrts] [fild] DJ [spɔ:ts] [fi:ld] 名 操場

Don't throw the ball onto the sports field from the second floor.
不要從二樓把球丟到操場。

小提醒 sports field 指的是有跑道、有球場的戶外運動場，和剛剛前面提到的 gym 剛好相反，sports field 裡通常進行的都是戶外運動，像是田徑、足球等。

---

university KK [ˌjunəˋvɝsətɪ] DJ [ˌju:niˋvə:siti] 名 大學

Adam wants to go to the best university in his country.
亞當想去上他們國家最好的大學。

小提醒 你還知道哪些跟大學有關的英文呢？

學士	bachelor	主修	major
碩士	master	副修	minor
博士	doctor	雙主修	double major

Classroom 教室

- **class schedule** 課表
- **picture** 圖片
- **letter** 字母
- *It's nice to meet you.* 很好的
- **map** 地圖
- **bulletin board** 公布欄
- **screen** 螢幕
- **blackboard** 黑板
- **chalk** 粉筆
- **notebook** 筆記本
- **present** （口頭）報告
- **podium** 講台
- **pencil box** 鉛筆盒
- **workbook** 習作本
- **glue** 膠水

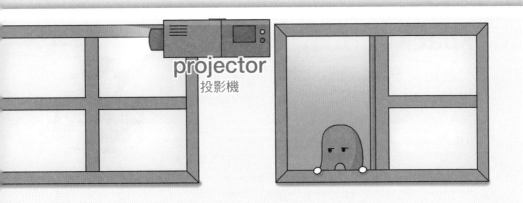

projector 投影機

textbook 教科書

pencil 鉛筆

bookmark 書籤

pen 筆

eraser 橡皮擦

ruler 尺

paper 紙

book 書

envelope 信封

backpack 後背包

dictionary 字典

ink 墨水

page （書本等的）頁

27.MP3

backpack
KK [ˈbækˌpæk]
DJ [ˈbækpæk]
名 後背包

Please put your sandwich in your backpack.
請把三明治放進你的後背包。

小提醒 backpack 是後背包的意思，我們之前有說過，有的時候我們在單字的尾巴加上 er 就會變成和前面單字有關的那個人，那你知道「backpacker ＝背著背包的人」是什麼意思嗎？沒錯，就是「背包客」的意思喔。

---

blackboard
KK [ˈblækˌbord]
DJ [ˈblækbɔːd]
名 黑板

Please write your name on the blackboard.
請把你的名字寫在黑板上。

---

book
KK [bʊk]
DJ [buk]
名 書

I gave him a book as a present.
我給了他一本書當作禮物。

---

bulletin board
KK [ˈbʊlətən] [bord]
DJ [ˈbulitin] [bɔːd]
名 公布欄

There is a poster on the bulletin board.
公布欄上有張海報。

小提醒 bulletin 這個字有「公告」的意思，board 則是「板子」的意思，所以 bulletin board 這個字其實就是「用來貼公告的板子」＝「公布欄」，是不是超好記的！

chalk
KK [tʃɔk]　DJ [tʃɔːk]　名 粉筆

Don't use chalk to draw on the walls of your bedroom.
不要用粉筆畫你房間的牆壁。

---

class schedule
KK [klæs] [ˋskɛdʒʊl]　DJ [klɑːs][ˋskɛdʒul]　名 課表

My teacher gave everyone a class schedule today.
我的老師今天給了大家課表。

教室　Classroom

---

dictionary
KK [ˋdɪkʃənˌɛrɪ]　DJ [ˋdikʃəneri]　名 字典

Why don't you look it up in the dictionary?
你何不查一下字典呢？

例句單字 look sth. up in the dictionary 查字典

小提醒 在字典裡面，你還會看到底下這些英文單字喔！

同義字 **synonym**　　反義字 **antonym**

例句 **example sentence**

---

envelope
KK [ˋɛnvəˌlop]　DJ [ˋenviləup]　名 信封

This envelope is cute and smells good.
這個信封很可愛而且聞起來很香。

例句單字 cute 形 可愛的

---

eraser
KK [ɪˋresɚ]　DJ [iˋreisə]　名 橡皮擦

I borrowed an eraser from the classmate next to me.
我向坐我旁邊的同學借了一個橡皮擦。

glue
KK [glu]
DJ [glu:]
名 膠水

You can use glue to glue the paper together.
你可以用膠水把這些紙黏在一起。

小提醒 glue 也可以當成動詞喔！變成動詞的時候，意思就變成「（用膠水）黏牢」。

---

ink
KK [ɪŋk]
DJ [ɪŋk]
名 墨水

This pen is running out of ink.
這隻筆的墨水快用完了。

例句單字 run out of 用完～

---

letter
KK [ˋlɛtɚ]
DJ [ˋletə]
名 字母

How many letters are there in the word "yellow"?
在「yellow」這個字裡有幾個字母？

小提醒 letter 除了字母之外，也有「信件」的意思，例如：I received a love letter from my boyfriend.（我從男友那邊收到了一封情書。），遇到這個字的時候，要用句意來判斷出 letter 最合理的意思喔！

---

map
KK [mæp]
DJ [mæp]
名 地圖

The spot is not on the map.
這個地點不在地圖上。

---

bookmark
KK [ˋbʊkˌmɑrk]
DJ [bʊkˌmɑ:k]
名 書籤

This bookmark is made of gold so it is very expensive.
這個書籤是用黃金做成的，所以很貴。

notebook
KK [ˋnotˏbʊk]
DJ [ˋnəutbuk]
名 筆記本

Write my words down in your notebook.
把我說的話寫在你的筆記本上。

例句單字 write down 寫下

---

page
KK [pedʒ]
DJ [peidʒ]
名 （書本等的）頁

Please turn the page.
請翻頁。

---

paper
KK [ˋpepɚ]
DJ [ˋpeipə]
名 紙

Draw a line on the paper.
在紙上畫一條線。

小提醒 paper 這個字很常和其他單字組成另一個全新的字，就像底下這些字：

news（新聞）＋paper（紙）→ newspaper（報紙）

toilet（馬桶）＋paper（紙）→ toilet paper（廁所衛生紙）

wall（牆壁）＋paper（紙）→ wallpaper（壁紙）

---

pen
KK [pɛn]
DJ [pen]
名 筆

Can I borrow your pen?
我能跟你借筆嗎？

---

pencil box
KK [ˋpɛnsl] [baks]
DJ [ˋpensəl][bɔks]
名 鉛筆盒

Her birthday present is a pencil box.
她的生日禮物是一個鉛筆盒。

同義字 pencil case 名 鉛筆盒

pencil
KK [ˈpɛnsl̩]
DJ [ˈpensl̩]　名　鉛筆

Sharpen your pencil, please.
請把你的鉛筆削尖。

例句單字 **sharpen** 動 使鋒利

小提醒 除了鉛筆和原子筆之外，還有哪些常用文具呢？

自動鉛筆　**mechanical pencil**

彩色筆　**color pen**　　　　螢光筆　**highlighter**

削鉛筆機　**pencil sharpener**

鋼筆　**fountain pen**　　　　釘書機　**stapler**

---

picture
KK [ˈpɪktʃɚ]
DJ [ˈpɪktʃə]　名　圖片

That is a picture of mountains in Taiwan.
那是一張台灣的山的圖片。

---

podium
KK [ˈpodɪəm]
DJ [ˈpəudɪəm]　名　講台

Our teacher is standing on the podium.
我們的老師正站在講台上。

---

present
KK [prɪˈzɛnt]
DJ [prɪˈzent]　動　（口頭）報告

I am so nervous because I have to present today.
我因為今天要報告而很緊張。

---

projector
KK [prəˈdʒɛktɚ]
DJ [prəˈdʒektə]　名　投影機

Can you teach me how to use the projector?
你能教我怎麼用這台投影機嗎？

ruler
KK [ˋrulɚ]
DJ [ˋruːlə]
名 尺

I want to buy a longer ruler.
我想買一支更長的尺。

小提醒 除了尺之外，底下這些測量工具也是很常用的喔！
三角板 **set square / set triangle**
量角器 **protractor**
圓規 **compass**

screen
KK [skrin]
DJ [skriːn]
名 螢幕

Don't poke the screen.
不要戳螢幕。

例句單字 poke 動 戳

textbook
KK [ˋtɛkstˌbʊk]
DJ [ˋtekstbuk]
名 教科書

The math textbook is too hard for me.
數學教科書對我來說太難了。

workbook
KK [ˋwɝkˌbʊk]
DJ [ˋwəːkbuk]
名 習作本

You need to do your English workbook work.
你應該去寫英文習作本作業。

In the Class 在班上

answer
KK [ˋænsɚ]
DJ [ˋɑːnsə] 動 回答

Please answer my question.
請回答我的問題。

---

ask
KK [æsk]
DJ [ɑːsk] 動 詢問

If you have any questions, just ask me.
如果你有任何疑問就問我。

---

class leader
KK [klæs] [ˋlidɚ]
DJ [klɑːs] [ˋliːdə] 名 班長

She wants to be the class leader.
她想要當班長。

---

classmate
KK [ˋklæsˏmet]
DJ [ˋklɑːsmeit] 名 同學

How many classmates do you have in your class now?
你現在班上有多少同學？

---

exam
KK [ɪgˋzæm]
DJ [igˋzæm] 名 測驗

I have an exam tomorrow so I have to study tonight.
因為明天有測驗，所以我今天晚上必須要念書。

小提醒 exam 這個字指的是比較重要的大考，像是期末考、檢定考等，如果是平時考或隨堂測驗等比較不正式的考試，在英文裡叫做 quiz，而 test（測驗）則不管大考小考，只要是考試，都可以叫做 test，不要用錯囉！

example
KK [ɪgˋzæmpḷ]
DJ [igˋzɑ:mpəl]
名 舉例

Can you give me some examples?
你能舉幾個例嗎？

關聯字　sample 名 樣品　specimen 名 標本　model 名 模型

---

explain
KK [ɪkˋsplen]
DJ [iksˋplein]
動 解釋

Please explain the theory for me.
請解釋這個理論給我聽。

例句單字　theory 名 理論

---

fail
KK [fel]
DJ [feil]
名 不及格

Tom has a fail in math.
湯姆的數學不及格。

---

friend
KK [frɛnd]
DJ [frend]
名 朋友

She is my best friend.
她是我最好的朋友。

關聯字　acquaintance 名 認識（而不熟悉）的人
close friend 名 親密朋友
confidante 名 知己
best friends forever 名 閨蜜（常簡寫成 bff）

---

grade
KK [gred]
DJ [greid]
名 成績

Jenny is good at math; she always gets good grades.
珍妮很擅長數學，她總是拿到好成績。

homework KK [ˋhomˏwɝk] DJ [ˋhəumwəːk] 名 回家功課

Please bring your homework tomorrow.
明天請把回家功課帶來。

---

learn KK [lɝn] DJ [ləːn] 動 學習

People should not stop learning.
人們不應該停止學習。

---

lesson KK [ˋlɛsn] DJ [ˋlesn] 名 課；課程

Today we are going to start from Lesson 15.
今天我們要從第 15 課開始上。

My mom brings me to dance lessons.
媽媽帶我去上舞蹈課。

小提醒 lesson 這個字除了是課本當中的「一課」，或是不同的「課程」，有的時候會
是「教訓」的意思，就像下面這個例句：

Did you learn your lesson? 你學到教訓了嗎？

這邊的 lesson 就是指「因為經歷某事而學習到的道理」，下次你就知道這句話
是什麼意思囉！

---

mark KK [mɑrk] DJ [mɑːk] 動 做記號

You should mark this chapter because it is very important.
你應該把這章做記號，因為很重要。

---

note KK [not] DJ [nəut] 名 筆記

These are my notes taken during
English class.
這些是我上英文課時的筆記。

小提醒 「記筆記」的「記」不是用 write，而是用 take
喔！

pass
KK [pæs]
DJ [pɑːs] 動 及格；通過

He finally passed the bar exam.
他終於通過了律師考試。

例句單字 **bar exam** 名 律師考試

---

question
KK [`kwɛstʃən]
DJ [`kwestʃən] 名 問題

If there are any questions, please let me know.
如果有任何問題，請讓我知道。

---

read
KK [rid]
DJ [riːd] 動 閱讀

I recommend you read this book.
我推薦你閱讀這本書。

例句單字 **recommend** 動 推薦

---

reference book
KK [`rɛfərəns] [bʊk]
DJ [`refərəns][buk] 名 參考書

My mother bought me a bunch of reference books for the new semester.
我媽媽買了很多新學期要用的參考書給我。

例句單字 **a bunch of** 很多的～

---

score
KK [skor]
DJ [skɔː] 名 分數

You should not focus on the scores too much.
你不應該太專注在分數上。

例句單字 **focus** 動 專注

---

sentence
KK [`sɛntəns]
DJ [`sentəns] 名 句子

Can you read this sentence out loud for me?
你能幫我大聲唸出這個句子嗎？

2.24

speak
KK [spik]
DJ [spi:k] 動 說話

How many languages can you speak?
你能說幾種語言呢？

---

spell
KK [spɛl]
DJ [spel] 動 拼字

Could you spell that word, please?
能請你拼出那個字嗎？

小提醒 你知道 **spelling bee** 是什麼嗎？可不是拼字蜜蜂喔！而是我們常在電視上看到的「**拼字競賽**」，參賽者會在不同階段拼出不同難度的單字，只要拼錯就會淘汰，能夠撐到最後的人就是勝利者，這種競賽在歐美十分流行喔～

---

student
KK [`stjudənt]
DJ [`stju:dənt] 名 學生

Most of the students study hard.
大多數的學生很認真學習。

---

teach
KK [titʃ]
DJ [ti:tʃ] 動 教學

Teaching is not an easy task.
教學並不是一項輕鬆的任務。

例句單字 task 名 任務

---

teacher
KK [`titʃɚ]
DJ [`ti:tʃə] 名 老師

Joey's mother is a teacher.
喬伊的媽媽是一位老師。

test sheet

KK [tɛst] [ʃit]
DJ [test] [ʃiːt] 名 考試卷

Please come forward to get your test sheet back.
請到前面來拿回你的考試卷。

---

understand

KK [ˌʌndɚˈstænd]
DJ [ˌʌndəˈstænd] 動 理解

Jenny can't understand the question.
珍妮無法理解這個問題。

小提醒 understand 和 know（知道）有什麼不一樣呢？這兩個字的差異在於 know 是最基礎的「**知道**」，而 understand 是以 know 為基礎來「**理解**」，所以 understand 不只是知道的意思，而是除了知道以外還能理解，看以下例句更清楚喔。

I know Peter, but I don't understand him.
我知道 Peter 這個人，但我不了解他。

---

word

KK [wɝd]
DJ [wəːd] 名 字

I have to memorize all of the Lesson 15 words to prepare for tomorrow's test.
我必須把第 15 課的單字全部記住來準備明天的考試。

---

write

KK [raɪt]
DJ [rait] 動 寫

Adam often writes songs for his girlfriend.
亞當常常寫歌給他的女友。

Subjects 科目

course 課程

art
藝術

Chinese
國文

English
英文

science
科學

music
音樂

history
歷史

geography
地理

physics
物理

PE
(physical
education)
體育

language
語言

biology
生物

math
數學

chemistry
化學

social science
社會科學

health
健康

 主題單字

29.MP3

art
KK [ɑrt]
DJ [a:t]
名 藝術

Lisa is a student of the art department.
麗莎是一位藝術系的學生。

例句單字 department 名 系；部門

---

biology
KK [baɪˋɑlədʒɪ]
DJ [baiˋɔlədʒi]
名 生物

James often cheats on biology examinations.
詹姆士常在生物考試中作弊。

例句單字 cheat 動 作弊
examination 名 測驗（＝exam）

---

chemistry
KK [ˋkɛmɪstrɪ]
DJ [ˋkemistri]
名 化學

My chemistry teacher is a serious and bad-tempered old man.
我的化學老師是個嚴肅且壞脾氣的老先生。

Chinese
KK [ˋtʃaɪˋniz]
DJ [ˋtʃaiˋni:z]
名 國文

Our Chinese teacher is very strict.
我們的國文老師非常嚴格。

例句單字 strict 形 嚴格的

226

course
KK [kors]
DJ [kɔːs]
名 課程

I spend almost all of my free time on yoga courses.
我幾乎將所有的空閒時間花在瑜伽課程上。

例句單字 yoga 名 瑜伽

English
KK [`ɪŋglɪʃ]
DJ [`iŋgliʃ]
名 英文

English class is really boring to me.
英文課對我來說非常無聊。

小提醒 因為歷史演變，英文基本上可以被分成「美式英文」
與「英式英文」兩大類，有些單字的意思或是拼法會
有些不同喔～以下舉幾個例子：

美式	英式	意思
theater	theatre	戲院
color	colour	顏色
tire	tyre	輪胎
check	cheque	支票
gray	grey	灰色

geography
KK [`dʒɪ`ɑgrəfɪ]
DJ [dʒi`ɔgrəfi]
名 地理

Sally loves geography.
莎莉喜愛地理。

health
KK [hɛlθ]
DJ [helθ]
名 健康

My father is worried about my mother's health.
我的父親擔心我母親的健康。

例句單字 be worried about ~ 對～感到擔心

科目
Subjects

history
KK [ˈhɪstərɪ]
DJ [ˈhistəri]
名 歷史

Our history class starts at nine o'clock.
我們的歷史課九點開始。

---

language
KK [ˈlæŋgwɪdʒ]
DJ [ˈlæŋgwidʒ]
名 語言

Amy can speak four languages.
艾咪會說四種語言。

---

math
KK [mæθ]
DJ [mæθ]
名 數學

I am always terrible at math.
我總是很不擅長數學。

例句單字 terrible at~ 對～不擅長

小提醒 math 這個字是 mathematics 的簡寫版，這兩個字的字義有一點點不同，math 強調的加減乘除等數學的**運算與解題**，而 mathematics 更偏向研究**數學的學問**。

---

music
KK [ˈmjuzɪk]
DJ [ˈmjuːzik]
名 音樂

What kind of music do you like?
你喜歡什麼樣的音樂？

小提醒 音樂有很多不同的類型，你知道要怎麼用英文說嗎？

節奏藍調	R&B (Rhythm& Blues)	流行	pop
藍調	blues	搖滾	rock
古典	classical	舞曲	dance

PE (=physical education)

KK [ˈfɪzɪk!][ˌɛdʒʊˈkeʃən]
DJ [ˈfizikəl][ˌedjukeiʃn]　名 體育

She doesn't like her PE teacher.
她不喜歡她的體育老師。

小提醒 PE 是 physical education 的縮寫，physical 是「身體的」、education 是「教育」，所以 physical education 字面上的意思就是「身體的教育」，也就是「體育」的意思。

---

physics
KK [ˈfɪzɪks]
DJ [ˈfiziks]　名 物理

Newton is an authority on physics.
牛頓是物理的權威。

例句單字 authority 名 權威

---

science
KK [ˈsaɪəns]
DJ [ˈsaiəns]　名 科學

Physics is a branch of science.
物理是科學的一個分支。

例句單字 branch 名 分支

---

social science
KK [ˈsoʃəl][ˈsaɪəns]
DJ [ˈsəuʃəl][ˈsaiəns]　名 社會科學

Danny's father is a professor of social science.
丹尼的爸爸是教社會科學的教授。

例句單字 professor 名 教授

church 教堂

shop 商店

flower shop 花店

police station 警察局

museum 博物館

drugstore 藥妝店

gas station 加油站

bus stop 公車站

bank 銀行

zoo 動物園

post office 郵局

郵局

store 商店

BOOK

crosswalk 行人穿越道

castle 城堡

farm 農場

bookstore 書店

place 地點

Let's go!

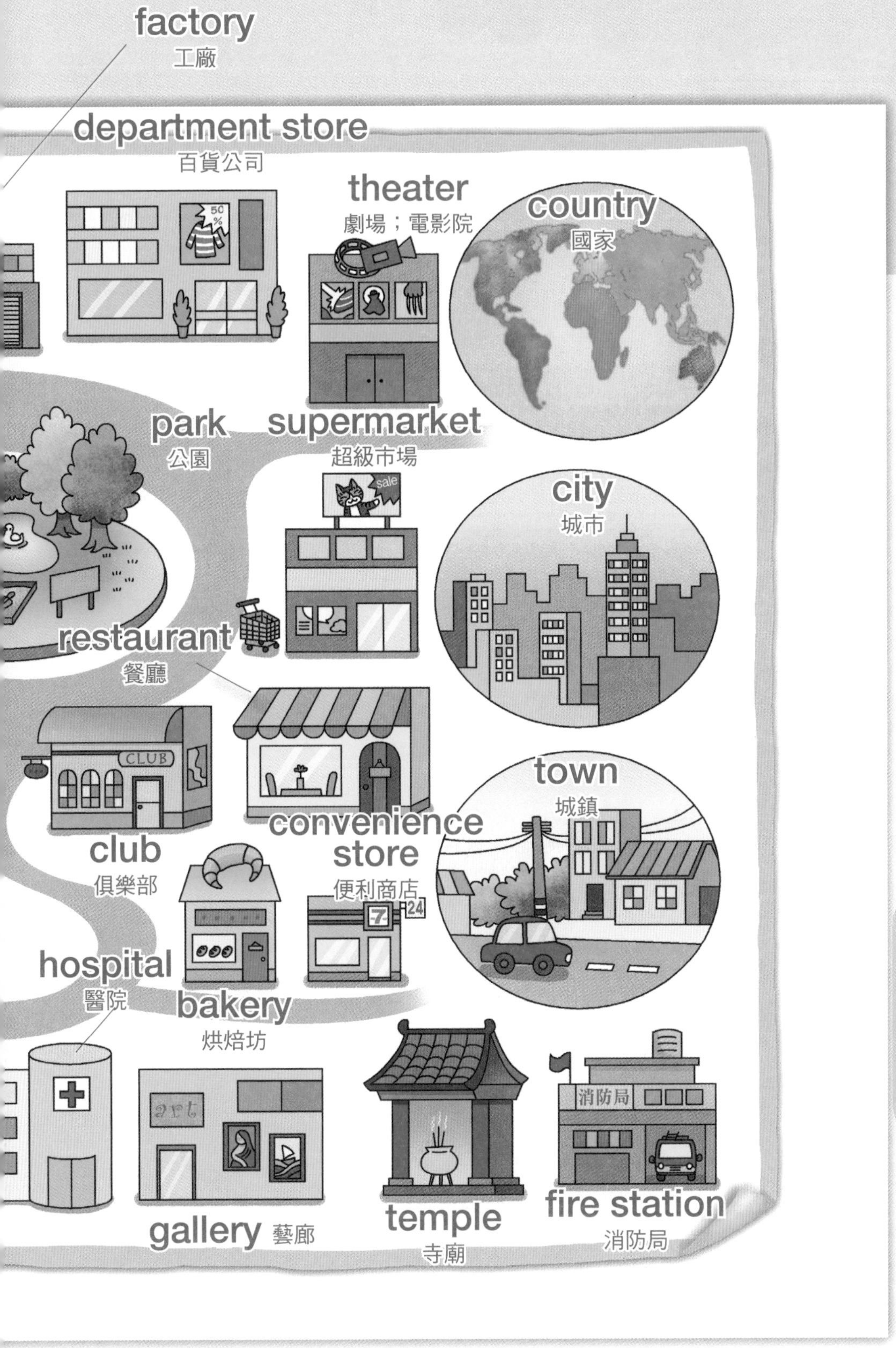
factory
工廠
department store
百貨公司
theater
劇場；電影院
country
國家
park
公園
supermarket
超級市場
city
城市
restaurant
餐廳
CLUB
club
俱樂部
town
城鎮
convenience store
便利商店
hospital
醫院
bakery
烘焙坊
art
gallery 藝廊
temple
寺廟
消防局
fire station
消防局

bakery
KK [`bekərı]
DJ [`beikəri]　 烘焙坊

There is a bakery near my home. 在我家附近有家烘焙坊。

---

bank
KK [bæŋk]
DJ [bæŋk]　名 銀行

That bank will be closed today. 那家銀行今天將被關閉。

小提醒 到銀行會做什麼事呢？

| 開戶 | open an account | 存錢 | deposit | 提款 | withdraw |
| 匯款 | wire | 轉帳 | transfer | | |

---

bookstore
KK [`bʊkˌstor]
DJ [`bukstɔ:]　名 書店

Amy loves to spend her afternoons in the bookstore.
艾咪喜歡在書店消磨午後時光。

---

bus stop
KK [bʌs] [stɑp]
DJ [bʌs] [stɔp]　名 公車站

There are a lot of bus stops near the Taipei Main Station.
在台北車站附近有非常多公車站。

---

castle
KK [`kæsḷ]
DJ [`kɑ:səl]　名 城堡

Some people believe that the castle is haunted.
有些人相信這座城堡鬧鬼。

例句單字 haunted 形 鬧鬼的

---

church
KK [tʃɝtʃ]
DJ [tʃə:tʃ]　名 教堂

My teacher goes to church every Sunday.
我的老師每個禮拜天都去教堂。

232

city

KK [`sɪtɪ]
DJ [`siti]
名 城市

The crime rate of the city is very high.
那座城市的犯罪率非常高。

例句單字 crime rate 名 犯罪率

---

club

KK [klʌb]
DJ [klʌb]
名 俱樂部

This is a golf club for rich people.
這是一個專門給有錢人加入的高爾夫球俱樂部。

小提醒 club 這個字指的是給有共同興趣或從事共同活動的人加入的團體，常看到的 club 有 golf club（高爾夫球俱樂部）、horse riding club（馬術俱樂部）、tennis club（網球俱樂部）等。

---

convenience store

KK [kən`vinjəns] [stor]
DJ [kən`vi:njəns] [stɔ:]
名 便利商店

You can use the toilet in the convenience store if you want.
如果你想的話，你可以使用便利商店的廁所。

---

country

KK [`kʌntrɪ]
DJ [`kʌntrɪ]
名 國家

The country is famous for natural resources.
這個國家以自然資源聞名。

例句單字 natural resources 名 自然資源

---

crosswalk

KK [`krɔs‚wɔk]
DJ [`krɔswɔ:k]
名 行人穿越道

Please use the crosswalk.
請使用行人穿越道。

---

department store

KK [dɪ`partmənt] [stor]
DJ [di`pa:tmənt] [stɔ:]
名 百貨公司

There is a big sale in the department store.
那家百貨公司有大特賣。

drugstore
KK [`drʌgˌstor]
DJ [`drʌgstɔ:]　名 藥妝店

Her father works in the drugstore.
她的爸爸在藥妝店工作。

小提醒 drugstore 是由「drug（藥）＋store（店）」所組合起來的，所以如果照字面來看會以為是賣藥的地方，但其實它指的是像屈臣氏、康是美那樣的藥妝店，如果是看完病要拿藥，不能去 drug store，要去 pharmacy（藥局）喔！

factory
KK [`fæktərɪ]
DJ [`fæktəri]　名 工廠

Due to recession, many factories were shut down.
因為不景氣，很多工廠關閉。

例句單字 recession 名 （經濟）不景氣　shut down 關閉

farm
KK [farm]
DJ [fɑ:m]　名 農場

Carol lives near a farm.
凱蘿住在一個農場的附近。

fire station
KK [faɪr] [`steʃən]
DJ [faiə] [`steiʃən]　名 消防局

The fire station is across from the police station.
消防局在警察局的對面。

例句單字 across from 在～的對面

flower shop
KK [`flauɚ] [ʃɑp]
DJ [`flauə] [ʃɔp]　名 花店

One of my classmates opened her own flower shop.
我的一個同學開了她自己的花店。

小提醒 在花店裡會看到什麼植物呢？

| 仙人掌 | **cactus** | 蒲公英 | **dandelion** | 康乃馨 | **carnation** |
| 茉莉 | **jasmine** | 鬱金香 | **tulip** | 向日葵 | **sunflower** |

---

gallery
KK [`gælərɪ]
DJ [`gæləri]　名 藝廊

My friend works in a gallery.
我的朋友在一個藝廊裡工作。

---

gas station
KK [gæs] [`steʃən]
DJ [gæs][`steiʃən]　名 加油站

Working in a gas station is bad for your health.
在加油站工作對你的健康不好。

---

hospital
KK [`hɑspɪtl]
DJ [`hɔspitəl]　名 醫院

My mother is a doctor; she works in the hospital.
我的媽媽是個醫生，她在醫院工作。

---

museum
KK [mju`zɪəm]
DJ [mju:`ziəm]　名 博物館

Today you can visit the museum for free.
今天你可以免費參觀博物館。

例句單字 for free 免費

---

park
KK [pɑrk]
DJ [pɑ:k]　名 公園

My father walks our dog in the park every afternoon.
我爸爸每天下午都在公園遛我家的狗。

place
KK [ples]
DJ [pleis]
名 地點

I can show you the place.
我可以告訴你那個地方在哪裡。

小提醒 I can show you the place. 不只可以用在別人問你路的時候，也可以用來回答對方對場地配置的疑問，例如：

A：Where can I drop my bag? 我的包包可以放在哪裡？

B：In the guest room, I can show you the place.
放在貴賓室，我可以告訴你在哪裡。

下次有人問你什麼地方在哪裡的時候，你就可以這樣回答他，然後再告訴他要怎麼去喔！

---

police station
KK [pə`lis] [`steʃən]
DJ [pə`li:s][`steiʃən]
名 警察局

This is the biggest police station in the city.
這是這座城市裡最大的警察局。

---

post office
KK [post] [`ɔfɪs]
DJ [pəust][`ɔ:fɪs]
名 郵局

I need to go to the post office today.
我今天必須去郵局一趟。

---

restaurant
KK [`rɛstərənt]
DJ [`restərənt]
名 餐廳

Can you make a reservation at the restaurant for me?
你能幫我預約這間餐廳嗎？

例句單字 make a reservation 預約

---

shop
KK [ʃɑp]
DJ [ʃɔp]
名 商店

My mom always buys food in the shop near my house.
我媽媽總是在我家附近的商店買食物。

store
KK [stor]
DJ [stɔ:]
名 商店

The candy store is really popular among kids.
這家糖果店非常受到孩子們的喜愛。

小提醒 shop 和 store 的意思雖然都是商店，但是 **shop** 通常規模較小，也不會是連鎖店，而 **store** 則大小不拘，是最常見的「商店」的說法喔！

---

supermarket
KK [`supəˌmɑrkɪt]
DJ [`sju:pəˌmɑ:kit]
名 超級市場

I usually buy milk at the supermarket.
我通常在超市裡買牛奶。

---

temple
KK [`tɛmpl]
DJ [`tempəl]
名 寺廟

My mother goes to the temple twice a month.
我媽媽一個月去那間寺廟兩次。

---

theater
KK [`θɪətə]
DJ [`θiətə]
名 劇院；電影院

I think we can meet at the theater tonight.
我覺得我們今天晚上可以在劇院見面。

小提醒 theater 可以指看電影的電影院，或是看舞台劇的劇院，所以如果想要清楚說明，可以在前面加上 **movie**（電影）來讓意思更清楚喔！

---

town
KK [taʊn]
DJ [taun]
名 城鎮

The town is so small that many people never heard of it.
這個城鎮太小了，以致於很多人從來沒聽過它。

---

zoo
KK [zu]
DJ [zu:]
名 動物園

Susan doesn't like to go to the zoo because she hates to walk a lot in the sun.
蘇珊不喜歡去動物園，因為她討厭在太陽下走很多路。

east
東方

top
上方

backward
向後

left
左方的

here
這裡

middle
中間的

central
中央的

west
西方

south
南方

north
北方

forward
向前

front
前方

right
右方的

turn
轉彎

there
那裡

back
後方

31.MP3

back KK [bæk] DJ [bæk] 名 後方

I've got your back.
我支持你。

 如果直接翻譯 I've got your back. 的話就是「我
拿了你的後方。」，但其實這句話的意思是「我幫你
注意你看不到的後方，放心吧。」，也就是「我支持
你。」的意思。

---

backward KK [`bækwɚd] DJ [`bækwəd] 副 向後

Emily took a step backward in fear.
艾蜜莉因恐懼而向後退了一步。

---

central KK [`sɛntrəl] DJ [`sɛntrəl] 形 中央的

The rent in central London is really expensive.
倫敦市中心的房租真的很貴。

---

east KK [ist] DJ [i:st] 名 東方

The sun rises in the east.
太陽從東方升起。

例句單字 rise 動 升起

---

forward KK [`fɔrwɚd] DJ [`fɔ:wəd] 副 向前

Sam walked forward to greet his friends.
山姆向前走去接待他的朋友們。

例句單字 greet 動 接待；打招呼

240

front
KK [frʌnt]
DJ [frʌnt]
名 前方

Jenny sits in front of me.
珍妮坐在我的前方。

---

here
KK [hɪr]
DJ [hiə]
副 這裡

Please put your bag here.
請把你的包包放在這裡。

---

left
KK [lɛft]
DJ [left]
形 左方的

The girl wears a bracelet on her left hand.
這個女孩在左手戴了一條手鍊。

---

middle
KK [`mɪdl]
DJ [`midəl]
形 中間的

He is the middle child of our family.
他在我們家排行第二。

小提醒 middle 這個字也可以當作名詞，當成名詞的時候就是「中間」的意思。

---

north
KK [nɔrθ]
DJ [nɔ:θ]
名 北方

The North Star is shining in the sky.
北極星在天空中閃耀。

例句單字 North Star 名 北極星

---

right
KK [raɪt]
DJ [rait]
形 右方的

Just turn to your right, then you will see me.
只要往右轉你就會看到我。

south
KK [sauθ]
DJ [sauθ]
名 南方

There is a waterfall in the south.
在南方有一座瀑布。

例句單字 waterfall 名 瀑布

---

there
KK [ðɛr]
DJ [ðɛə]
副 那裡

There is a man over there.
那裡有一名男子。

---

top
KK [tɑp]
DJ [tɔp]
名 上方

Hanson lives at the top of the hill.
韓森住在山丘的最上方。

例句單字 hill 名 山丘

---

turn
KK [tɝn]
DJ [tə:n]
動 轉彎

Turn around and close your eyes for me; I want to give you a surprise.
轉過身然後閉上眼睛,我想給你一個驚喜。

---

west
KK [wɛst]
DJ [west]
名 西方

That ship is sailing to the west.
那艘船向著西方航行。

The sooner, the better. 愈快愈好。

　　這句話就像是它的字面意義「愈快，愈好」。如果有人問你 When should I come over?（我什麼時候過去好呢？），你就可以回答「The sooner, the better.（愈快愈好。）」類似的說法另外還有一句 **As soon as possible.** 表示「盡可能地快。」一般在正式的商業書信文件上，可以省略而寫成 **ASAP**。

Vocabulary 一起看！

★allow [ə`laʊ] 動 允許，准許

★computer game 名 電腦遊戲

★e-mail box 名 電子信箱

★home page 名 首頁

★Internet [`ɪntə͵nɛt] 名 網路

★keyboard [`ki͵bord] 名 鍵盤

★messenger [`mɛsn̩dʒɚ] 名 信差

★more [mor] 形 更多的

★mouse [maʊs] 名 （電腦）滑鼠

★online game 名 網路遊戲

★printer [`prɪntɚ] 名 印表機

★toolbar [`tul͵bar] 名 工具列

★video game 名 電動玩具

★website [`wɛb͵saɪt] 名 網站

243

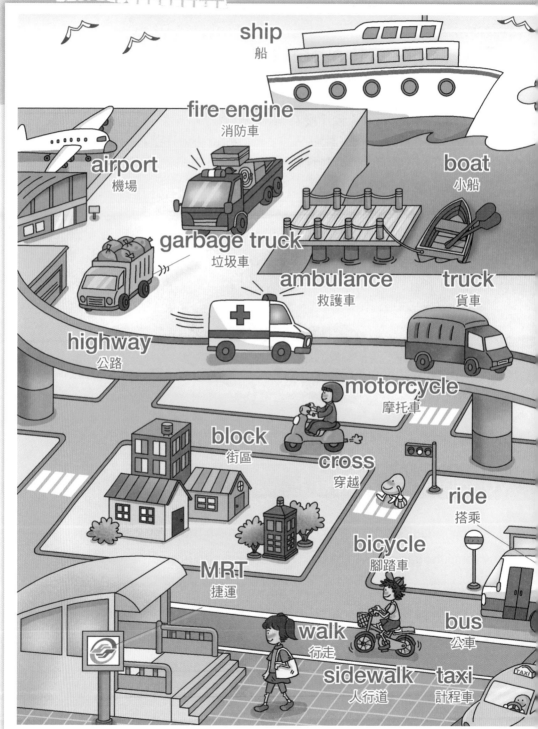

ship 船
fire-engine 消防車
airport 機場
boat 小船
garbage truck 垃圾車
ambulance 救護車
truck 貨車
highway 公路
motorcycle 摩托車
block 街區
cross 穿越
ride 搭乘
bicycle 腳踏車
MRT 捷運
walk 行走
bus 公車
sidewalk 人行道
taxi 計程車

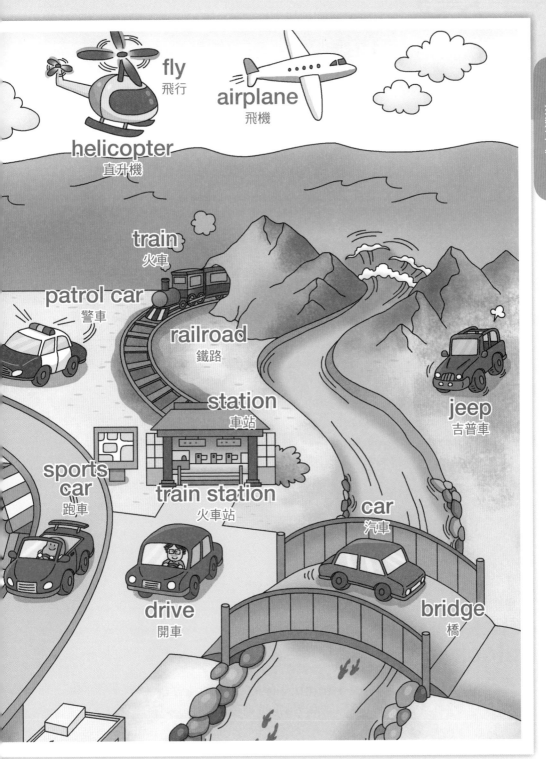

fly
飛行

airplane
飛機

helicopter
直升機

train
火車

patrol car
警車

railroad
鐵路

jeep
吉普車

station
車站

sports
car
跑車

train station
火車站

car
汽車

drive
開車

bridge
橋

主題單字

32.MP3

airplane KK [ˋɛrˌplen] DJ [ˋɛəplein] 名 飛機

Jerry is so fat that he needs two seats on the airplane.
傑瑞太胖了，以致於他在飛機上需要兩個位子。

例句單字 seat 名 位子

小提醒 airplane 有的時候可以簡稱為 **plane**，而說到飛機，你知道飛機上的頭等艙、商務艙跟經濟艙的英文是什麼嗎？

頭等艙 **first class** 商務艙 **business class** 經濟艙 **economy class**

---

airport KK [ˋɛrˌport] DJ [ˋɛəpːt] 名 機場

I went to the airport by taxi because I was in a hurry.
因為我趕時間，所以坐了計程車去機場。

例句單字 in a hurry 趕時間

---

ambulance KK [ˋæmbjələns] DJ [ˋæmbjuləns] 名 救護車

Are you okay? Should I call an ambulance?
你還好嗎？我應該叫救護車嗎？

---

bicycle KK [ˋbaɪsɪkl] DJ [ˋbaisikəl] 名 腳踏車

Jenny has a red bicycle.
珍妮有一輛紅色的腳踏車。

同義字 bike 名 腳踏車

---

block KK [blɑk] DJ [blɔk] 名 街區

I'm almost there! I'm only two blocks away.
我快到了！我離那裡只有兩個街區的距離。

boat
KK [bot]
DJ [bəut]
名 小船

I enjoy the boat rides on the river.
我喜歡搭小船遊河。

例句單字 ride 名 乘坐；行程

bridge
KK [brɪdʒ]
DJ [brɪdʒ]
名 橋

How long is the bridge?
這座橋有多長？

bus
KK [bʌs]
DJ [bʌs]
名 公車

I take a bus to school every day.
我每天搭公車上學。

小提醒 搭公車的「搭」在英文裡用 take，如果要說「上」公車，則要用 get on，「下」公車的時候則是用 get off，下次就用這些字說說看吧～

car
KK [kɑr]
DJ [kɑ:]
名 汽車

You need a driver's license to drive a car.
你需要有汽車駕照才能開車。

例句單字 driver's license 名 汽車駕照

cross
KK [krɔs]
DJ [krɔ:s]
動 穿越

Some people cross roads without looking; it's so dangerous.
有些人穿越馬路不看路，真的很危險。

例句單字 dangerous 形 危險的

drive
KK [draɪv]
DJ [draɪv]
動 開車

Please drive carefully; it's pouring outside.
請小心開車，外面雨下得很大。

例句單字 pouring 形 傾盆的

---

fire engine
KK [faɪr] [ˋɛndʒən]
DJ [faiə] [ˋendʒin] 名 消防車

There was a fire nearby, so I saw several fire engines driving by.
附近發生火災，所以我看到好幾輛消防車開過去。

例句單字 nearby 副 附近　several 形 幾個的

同義字 fire truck 名 消防車

---

fly
KK [flaɪ]
DJ [flai] 動 飛行

I will fly back to Taiwan next week.
我下周會飛回台灣。

小提醒 上面例句裡提到的 fly，不是指這個人真的有一對翅膀可以「飛」回台灣，而是他將會「搭飛機」回台灣，下次要搭飛機的時候，你也可以用 fly 這個字來說說看喔！

---

garbage truck
KK [ˋgɑrbɪdʒ] [trʌk]
DJ [ˋgɑ:bidʒ] [trʌk] 名 垃圾車

Everyone knows a garbage truck is coming because of its unique music.
因為垃圾車獨特的音樂，大家都知道垃圾車要來了。

例句單字 unique 形 獨特的

---

helicopter
KK [ˋhɛlɪkɑptɚ]
DJ [ˋhelikɔptə] 名 直升機

Adam makes up his mind to be a helicopter pilot.
亞當下定決心要當一名直升機飛行員。

例句單字 make up one's mind （某人）下定決心　pilot 名 飛行員

highway
KK [`haɪˌwe]
DJ [`haiwei]
名 公路

There is a severe car accident on the highway.
公路上有一場嚴重的車禍。

例句單字 severe 形 嚴重的

jeep
KK [dʒip]
DJ [dʒi:p]
名 吉普車

Jenny got back in her jeep and started the engine.
珍妮坐回她的吉普車裡並發動引擎。

例句單字 start the engine 發動引擎

motorcycle
KK [`motɚˌsaɪk!]
DJ [`məutəˌsaikəl]
名 摩托車

The motorcycle license test is much more difficult now.
摩托車駕照考試現在難很多。

同義字 scooter 名 （輕型）機車

MRT
名 捷運

I take the MRT every day.
我每天都坐捷運。

小提醒 MRT 其實是 Mass Rapid Transit（KK [mæs] [`ræpɪd] [`trænsɪt] DJ [mæs] [`ræpɪd] [`trænsit]），翻譯成中文就是「大眾快速運輸系統」，但是因為實在太長了，所以現在大家都直接說 MRT 囉！

patrol car
KK [pə`trol] [kɑr]
DJ [pə`trəul] [kɑ:]
名 警車

There is a patrol car parked next to my house.
在我家旁邊停著一輛警車。

小提醒 patrol car 裡面的 patrol 的意思是「巡邏」，所以 patrol car 的意思就是「用來巡邏的車子」，也就是警車，是不是很好記呢？

railroad
KK [ˋrelˌrod]
DJ [ˋreilrəud]
名 鐵路

Do you know the total length of the railroads in Taiwan?
你知道台灣的鐵路總長是多少嗎？

例句單字 railway 名 鐵路

ride
KK [raɪd]
DJ [raid]
動 搭乘

My classmates and I ride a bus to school every morning.
我和同學每天早上搭公車去學校。

ship
KK [ʃɪp]
DJ [ʃɪp]
名 船

There is a ship floating on the beautiful lake.
有一艘船浮在這座美麗的湖泊上。

例句單字 float 動 漂浮

小提醒 ship 和前面看到的 boat 都是船的意思，但是 boat 指的是「小船」，而 ship 則是「大船」，不要搞錯囉！

sidewalk
KK [ˋsaɪdˌwɔk]
DJ [ˋsaidˌwɔːk]
名 人行道

It is safer to walk on the sidewalk.
走人行道比較安全。

sports car
KK [spɔrts] [kɑr]
DJ [spɔːts] [kɑː]
名 跑車

Sports cars are cool; I want to buy one in the future.
跑車很酷，我未來想買一輛。

station
KK [ˋsteʃən]
DJ [ˋsteiʃən]
名 車站

I walked to the station from home.
我從家裡走到車站。

taxi
KK [ˋtæksɪ]
DJ [ˋtæksi]
名 計程車

There are a lot of taxis in front of the train station.
在火車站前有很多計程車。

---

train station
KK [tren] [ˋsteʃən]
DJ [trein] [ˋsteiʃən]
名 火車站

I will meet you at the train station tomorrow.
我明天會和你在火車站碰面。

---

train
KK [tren]
DJ [trein]
名 火車

We decided to take a train to Tainan.
我們決定要坐火車去台南。

---

truck
KK [trʌk]
DJ [trʌk]
名 貨車

The truck driver was driving so fast that he ran several red lights.
這名卡車司機開得太快了，以致於他闖了好幾個紅燈。

---

walk
KK [wɔk]
DJ [wɔːk]
動 行走

The school is really close to his house, so Adam walks home every day.
亞當的學校離他家真的很近，所以他每天都走路回家。

Sizes & Measurements 大小&度量衡

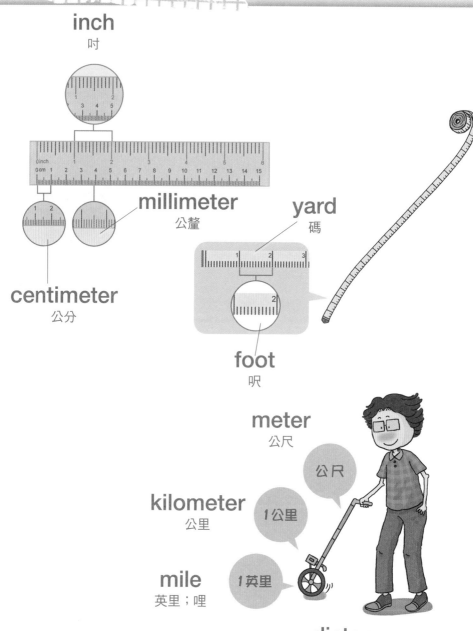

inch
吋

millimeter
公釐

centimeter
公分

yard
碼

foot
呎

meter
公尺

公尺

kilometer
公里

1公里

mile
英里；哩

1英里

distance
距離

kilogram
公斤

pound
磅

gram
克

weight
重量

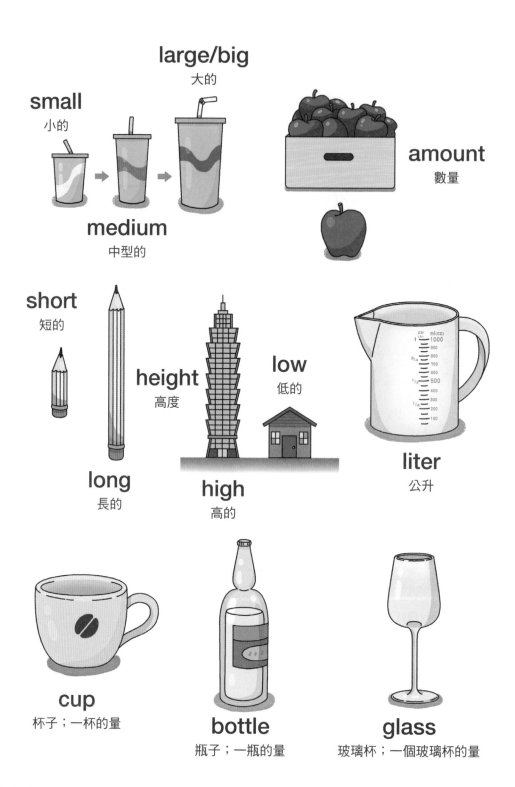

large/big
大的

small
小的

medium
中型的

amount
數量

short
短的

height
高度

long
長的

low
低的

high
高的

liter
公升

cup
杯子；一杯的量

bottle
瓶子；一瓶的量

glass
玻璃杯；一個玻璃杯的量

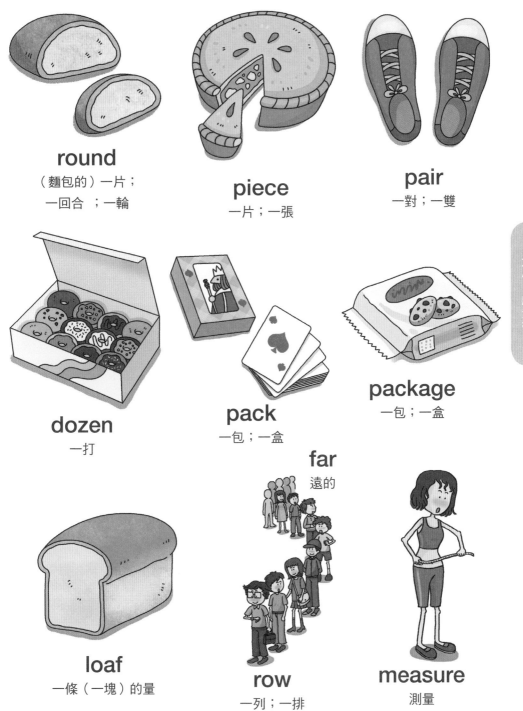

round
（麵包的）一片；
一回合 ；一輪

piece
一片；一張

pair
一對；一雙

dozen
一打

pack
一包；一盒

package
一包；一盒

far
遠的

loaf
一條（一塊）的量

row
一列；一排

measure
測量

 主題單字

33.MP3

amount
KK [ə`maʊnt]
DJ [ə`maunt]
名 數量

I am reducing the amount of meat I eat for my health.
我為了健康而少吃肉。

例句單字 reduce 動 減少

---

big
KK [bɪg]
DJ [big]
形 大的

Adam is really tall, and his hands are big.
亞當真的很高，而且他的手掌很大。

---

bottle
KK [`bɑtl]
DJ [`bɔtl]
名 瓶子；一瓶的量

He put a bottle of water on my desk.
他在我桌上放了一瓶水。

小提醒 bottle 這個字除了當瓶子的意思之外，也常用來當單位表示「**一瓶的量**」，就像上面的例句，**a bottle of** 就是「一瓶的～」，如果是兩瓶以上，就在 bottle 的前面加上數量，並把 bottle 加上表示複數的 s，寫成 **two bottles of**、**three bottles of**…，一起開口說說看吧！

---

centimeter
KK [`sɛntə.mitə]
DJ [`senti.mi:tə]
名 公分

The length of this box is 30 centimeters.
這個箱子的長度是 30 公分。

例句單字 length 名 長度

---

cup
KK [kʌp]
DJ [kʌp]
名 杯子；一杯的量

I usually drink a cup of milk every morning.
我通常每天早上都會喝一杯牛奶。

distance
KK [ˋdɪstəns]
DJ [ˋdistəns]
名 距離

The park is a long distance from my house.
那個公園和我家之間有一段很長的距離。

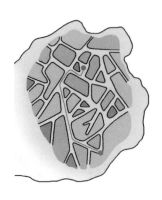

 distance 所表達的距離，除了像上面例句說的從公園到家裡有一段路的**物理距離**，也可以用來表示**心理距離**，例如你和某個同學很不熟，你就可以說：**There is a distance between us.**（我們之間有著距離。）。

---

dozen
KK [ˋdʌzən]
DJ [ˋdʌzən]
名 一打

I bought a dozen eggs for my mom.
我幫媽媽買了一打蛋。

 「一打」是個數量單位，就是 **12** 個的意思，所以 **a dozen eggs** 就是 **12** 個蛋，**dozen** 的用法就和 **million**、**thousand** 一樣，不需要在後面加上 **of**，除非要表達的是「好幾打」，那就要寫成 **dozens of**。

---

far
KK [fɑr]
DJ [fɑ:]
形 遠的

Is your school far from your home?
你的學校離你家很遠嗎？

---

foot
KK [fʊt]
DJ [fut]
名 呎

A foot is 30.48 centimeters.
一呎是 30.48 公分。

 在美國講身高的時候用呎和吋（**1**吋＝**2.54**公分），而不是用公分，所以在看 **NBA** 的時候常會聽到「**Stephen Curry** 的身高六呎三吋」之類的話，如果把六呎三吋換算成我們常用的公分數大約就是 **191** 公分。

glass
KK [glæs]
DJ [glɑːs]
名 玻璃杯；一個玻璃杯的量

Don't touch the glass.
不要碰那個玻璃杯。

小提醒 如果把 glass 加上表示複數的 es，那就變成**眼鏡**的意思囉！

gram
KK [græm]
DJ [græm]
名 克

A bowl of rice is about 180 grams.
一碗飯大約 180 克。

例句單字 bowl 名 碗

height
KK [haɪt]
DJ [hait]
名 高度

Tom and Mary are almost the same height.
湯姆跟瑪莉差不多高。

high
KK [haɪ]
DJ [hai]
形 高的

The oil prices are high recently.
最近的油價很高。

inch
KK [ɪntʃ]
DJ [intʃ]
名 吋

Jerry is three inches taller than his wife is.
傑瑞比他的老婆高三吋。

小提醒 前面有說過一吋就等於 **2.54** 公分，你的身高是幾尺幾吋呢？

kilogram
KK ['kɪləˌgræm]
DJ ['kiləgræm]
名 公斤

My mother wants to lose five kilograms.
我的媽媽想要瘦五公斤。

kilometer

KK [`kɪlə,mitɚ]
DJ [`kilə,mi:tə] 名 公里

Chandler can run ten kilometers a day.
錢德勒一天可以跑 10 公里。

large

KK [lardʒ]
DJ [lɑ:dʒ] 形 大的

Monica lives in a large house alone.
莫妮卡獨自一人住在大房子裡。

小提醒 big 和 large 的意思很接近，雖然 big 比 large 更口語、更常出現在生活對話中，但是它們也很常互相替換使用，這兩個字都可以用來表達尺寸、數量、重量的大小。另外，big 除了大之外，也可以**表示年長的意思**，例如你可以叫哥哥 big brother，而如果是要表示「**數量很大**」，則通常是**用 large 再加上數量詞**，例如 a large amount of money（大量的錢）。但是要注意 big 跟 large 都有自己的固定用法，遇到這種情形的時候，這兩個字就不能互換，例如上面提到的 big brother 就不能寫成 large brother 喔！

liter

KK [`litɚ]
DJ [`li:tə] 名 公升

Could you buy me a liter of milk?
你能幫我買一公升的牛奶嗎？

loaf

KK [lof]
DJ [ləuf] 名 一條（一塊）的量

Aunt Mary buys a loaf of bread for breakfast every Sunday.
瑪麗阿姨每個星期天都會買一條麵包當早餐。

小提醒 loaf 指的是做成**一整塊或是一整條**、而且要吃的時候**通常都會切片**的麵包的量，像是一根法國麵包、一條土司等，都可以用 loaf 來當單位，還有哪些麵包可以用 loaf 來表示數量呢？

吐司	**toast**	黑麥麵包	**rye bread**
全麥麵包	**whole wheat bread**	燕麥麵包	**oats bread**

long KK [lɔŋ] DJ [lɔŋ] 形 長的

There is a long pencil in my pencil box.
我的鉛筆盒裡有一根長鉛筆。

---

low KK [lo] DJ [ləu] 形 低的

The steel price is really low now.
現在鋼的價格真的很低。

例句單字 steel 名 鋼

---

measure KK [`mɛʒɚ] DJ [`meʒə] 動 測量

Joey measured the length of his bed.
喬伊測量了他的床的長度。

---

medium KK [`midɪəm] DJ [`mi:diəm] 形 中型的

This is a medium bag.
這是個中型的包包。

---

meter KK [`mitɚ] DJ [`mi:tə] 名 公尺

A meter is 100 centimeters.
1 公尺是 100 公分。

---

mile KK [maɪl] DJ [mail] 名 英里；哩

A mile is 1.609 kilometers.
一哩是 1.609 公里。

millimeter
KK [`mɪlə͵mitɚ]
DJ [`mili͵mi:tə]
名 公釐

1 centimeter is 10 millimeters.
1 公分是 10 公釐。

---

pack
KK [pæk]
DJ [pæk]
名 一包；一盒

How many packs of cereal do you want?
你想要幾包穀麥片？

---

package
KK [`pækɪdʒ]
DJ [`pækidʒ]
名 一包；一盒

I received a package of fruits today.
我今天收到了一盒水果。

例句單字 receive 動 收受

小提醒 pack 和 package 的意思很相似，都是一包或一盒的意思，但是 **package 裡面的內容物可能會有差異**，例如例句裡的 **a package of fruits**，就有可能是由蘋果、梨子、芭樂等不同的水果所組成的一盒，而 pack 則是**相同的內容物構成的一盒**，例如 a pack of cereal 的內容物就都是相同的穀麥片。

---

pair
KK [pɛr]
DJ [pɛə]
名 一對；一雙

Miranda buys a pair of shoes every year.
米蘭達每年都會買一雙鞋。

---

piece
KK [pis]
DJ [pi:s]
名 一片；一張

Please give me a piece of paper.
請給我一張紙。

小提醒 因為 paper 是不可數名詞，所以如果要說一張、兩張紙的時候，就需要用 a piece of、two pieces of 來表示，使用的時候要注意，數量**超過 1** 的時候 piece 要加上表示**複數的 s** 喔！

261

pound
KK [paʊnd]
DJ [paund]
名 磅

Monica is a few pounds heavier than Robin.
莫妮卡比羅賓重幾磅。

小提醒 在美國講體重的時候都是用「磅」而不是我們常用的公斤，而一磅是 **0.45** 公斤，你的體重是多少磅呢？另外，除了當重量單位之外，pound 也是「英鎊」的意思，要利用句子整體的意義來判斷單字的意思喔～

---

round
KK [raʊnd]
DJ [raund]
名 （麵包的）一片；一回合；一輪

Please give me a round of bread.
請給我一片麵包。

He beat down his rival and entered the next round.
他打敗了對手並挺進下一輪。

例句單字 beat down 打敗

小提醒 round 這個字用在麵包上的時候，就和 piece、slice 一樣，都是「一片」的意思，如果用在比賽、遊戲的時候，就是「回合、局數、一輪」的意思。

---

row
KK [ro]
DJ [rəu]
名 一列；一排

Please line up in a row.
請排成一列。

---

short
KK [ʃɔrt]
DJ [ʃɔ:t]
形 短的

The cheerleader is wearing a short skirt.
那位啦啦隊員穿著一件短裙。

small KK [smɔl] DJ [smɔ:l] 形 小的

Amy lives in a small town.
艾咪住在一個小城鎮裡。

例句單字 town 名 城鎮

---

weight KK [wet] DJ [weit] 名 重量

You are perfect; you don't have to lose any weight.
你很完美，不需要減肥。

小提醒 weight 用在人身上就是「體重」的意思，如果想要問別人體重多重，就可以說 **What is your weight?**，也可以利用 **weight 的動詞 weigh（量測重量）** 來問：**How much do you weigh?**，下次就用這句來問問看別人吧！

---

yard KK [jɑrd] DJ [jɑ:d] 名 碼

Martin currently holds the school record for the 100-yard dash.
馬汀目前是學校百碼短跑的紀錄保持者。

例句單字 currently 副 目前　record 名 紀錄　dash 名 短跑

小提醒 1 碼 = 0.9144 公尺

SHAPES

circle
圓圈

curve
曲線

line
線

point
點

straight
直的

square
正方形

surface
表面

dot
（斑）點

round
圓形

oval
橢圓形

rectangle
長方形

heart
心形

cone
三角錐

triangle
三角形

pentagon
五角形

diamond
菱形

34.MP3

circle KK [`sɝkl] DJ [`sə:kəl] 名 圓圈

How big is this circle?
這個圓圈有多大？

---

cone KK [kon] DJ [kəun] 名 三角錐

My father put a cone in the back of his car.
我爸爸在車後放了一個三角錐。

小提醒 只要是三角錐狀的東西都是 cone，所以甜筒底下三角錐狀的餅乾就叫做 ice cream cone，是不是很簡單呢？

---

curve KK [kɝv] DJ [kə:v] 名 曲線

Without a ruler, I can only draw curves.
沒有尺，我只能畫出曲線。

---

diamond KK [`daɪəmənd] DJ [`daɪəmənd] 名 菱形

The diamonds on the card are red.
卡片上的菱形是紅色的。

小提醒 diamond 也是「鑽石」的意思喔！

---

dot KK [dɑt] DJ [dɔt] 名 （斑）點

There are a lot of colorful dots on that shirt.
那件襯衫上面有很多色彩繽紛的斑點。

小提醒 dot 這個字指的斑點是小小的圓點，如果是比較大的圓點，則可以用 spot 這個字喔！

266

heart

KK [hɑrt]
DJ [hɑːt] 名 心形

Amy's necklace pendant is a crystal heart.
艾咪的項鍊墜子是一個心形水晶。

例句單字 pendant 名 墜子　crystal 名 水晶

---

line

KK [laɪn]
DJ [lain] 名 線

Please stay behind the white line.
請待在白線後方。

---

oval

KK [`ovl]
DJ [`əuvəl] 名 橢圓形

The mirror in my bedroom is oval.
我房間的鏡子是橢圓形的。

---

pentagon

KK [`pɛntə͵gɑn]
DJ [`pentəgən] 名 五角形

A pentagon has five sides and five angles.
一個五角形有五個邊跟五個角。

---

point

KK [pɔɪnt]
DJ [pɔint] 名 點

Two lines meet at one point.
兩條線在一點相交。

小提醒 point 的「點」和前面看到的 dot 的「點」不一樣，point 的點是線和線相交而出現的「交點」，所以我們也會用 point 來表達位置唷！例如車站裡的「會面點」，英文就叫做 meeting point。

---

rectangle

KK [rɛk`tæŋgl]
DJ [rek`tæŋgəl] 名 長方形

Do you know how to fold a piece of paper into
a rectangle box?
你知道要怎麼把一張紙摺成一個長方形盒子嗎？

例句單字 fold 動 摺

round KK [raʊnd] DJ [raund] 名 圓形

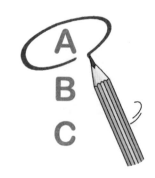

Emily received a round box full of chocolate.
艾蜜莉收到了一個裝滿巧克力的圓盒。

小提醒 circle 是由線所畫成的圓形，指的是**空心的圓**，而 round 則是被填滿的**實心圓**，所以我們在考卷上看到的答題指示會寫 Circle the right answer.（圈出正確答案），而不會寫 Draw a round to the right answer.（把正確答案畫上圓形），不然你考試就得花很多時間在塗滿圓形上囉！

---

square KK [skwɛr] DJ [skwɛə] 名 正方形

Alex's glasses are square.
艾力克斯的眼鏡是正方形的。

---

straight KK [stret] DJ [streit] 形 直的

Some people can draw a straight line without a ruler.
有些人可以不用尺畫出直線。

---

surface KK [ˋsɝfɪs] DJ [ˋsəːfɪs] 名 表面

The surface of the table is smooth.
這張桌子的表面很光滑。

例句單字 smooth 名 光滑的

---

triangle KK [ˋtraɪ͵æŋgl̩] DJ [ˋtraiæŋgəl] 名 三角形

The three-year-old girl is learning how to draw a triangle.
那個三歲小女孩正在學如何畫一個三角形。

What do you want to draw?

你想畫什麼？

What do you want to...? (你想要…什麼？)

在學校上課的時候常常都要畫出各種不同的圖形，這個時候到底是該用 draw 還是 paint 呢？其實 draw 是「描繪；繪畫」的意思，不像 paint 指的大多是「著色」，所以如果我們要畫各式各樣的 shape（形狀），英文要說 draw 而不是 paint。

如果你想問別人要畫什麼，這個時候就可以說 What do you want to draw?（你想畫什麼？），**What do you want to~?** 就是「你想要～什麼？」的意思，只要把 to 後面的動詞換掉，就會變成不同的意思喔！

What do you want to **use**? 你想要用什麼？

What do you want to **buy**? 你想要買什麼？

What do you want to **say**? 你想要說什麼？

Occupations 職業

actor
演員

actress
女演員

boss
老闆

businessperson
商人

clerk
店員

cook
廚師

dentist
牙醫

driver
司機

engineer
工程師

farmer
農夫

fisherman
漁夫

housewife
家庭主婦

lawyer
律師

mailman
郵差

police officer
警察

reporter
記者；播報員

salesman
業務員

secretary
祕書

shopkeeper
店主

singer
歌手

soldier
士兵

waitress
女服務生

worker
工人；員工

writer
作家

general
將軍

vet
獸醫

work
工作（成果）

doctor
醫師

waiter

男服務生

nurse

護士

artist

藝術家

hairdresser

髮型設計師

magician

魔術師

musician

音樂家

president

總統

judge
法官

scientist
科學家

priest
牧師；神父

painter
畫家

sailor
水手

model
模特兒

vendor
小販

actor
KK [`æktɚ]
DJ [`æktə]
名 演員

I have a photo of the famous actor.
我有一張這位知名演員的照片。

---

actress
KK [`æktrɪs]
DJ [`æktris]
名 女演員

The actress is memorizing the script.
這位女演員正在背劇本。

例句單字 memorize 動 背誦　script 名 劇本

---

artist
KK [`artɪst]
DJ [`a:tist]
名 藝術家

Alice's boyfriend is an artist.
愛麗絲的男朋友是個藝術家。

---

boss
KK [bɔs]
DJ [bɔs]
名 老闆

Our boss is a very kind person.
我們的老闆是個很善良的人。

---

businessperson
KK [`bɪznɪs͵pɝsn̩]
DJ [`biznis͵pə:sən]
名 商人

My friend is a successful businessperson.
我的朋友是個成功的商人。

小提醒 businessperson 沒有限定性別，不論是男是女，只要是商人都可以用 businessperson 來稱呼，如果要特別說是**男性商人**就用 **businessman**，**女性**則是 **businesswoman**。

clerk
KK [klɜˋk]
DJ [klɑːk]
名 店員

April is the clerk of the convenience store.
艾波是那間便利商店的店員。

小提醒 到便利商店除了買東西，還會做什麼事呢？
到店取貨　**pick up online orders**
帳單繳費　**pay bills**
貨到付款　**paid on delivery**

---

cook
KK [kʊk]
DJ [kuk]
名 廚師

My wife is a good cook so I go home for dinner every day.
我老婆是個好廚師，所以我每天回家吃晚餐。

---

dentist
KK [ˋdɛntɪst]
DJ [ˋdentist]
名 牙醫

I am really afraid of going to the dentist.
我真的很怕去看牙醫。

小提醒 去看牙醫的時候會做什麼呢？
洗牙　**teeth cleaning**　　拔牙　**tooth extraction**

---

doctor
KK [ˋdɑktɚ]
DJ [ˋdɔktə]
名 醫師

I had a sore throat so I went to see the doctor.
我的喉嚨痛，所以我去看了醫生。

---

driver
KK [ˋdraɪvɚ]
DJ [ˋdraivə]
名 司機

The school bus driver is a nice man and is always smiling.
校車司機是一位好人且總是在微笑。

engineer
KK [ˌɛndʒəˋnɪr]
DJ [ˌendʒiˋniə]
名 工程師

My best friend is an engineer.
我最好的朋友是個工程師。

---

farmer
KK [ˋfɑrmɚ]
DJ [ˋfɑːmə]
名 農夫

My grandfather is a farmer who grows vegetables.
我的爺爺是種蔬菜的農夫。

---

fisherman
KK [ˋfɪʃɚmən]
DJ [ˋfɪʃəmən]
名 漁夫

Monica's husband is a fisherman; he spends most of his time on the ship.
莫妮卡的丈夫是個漁夫，他多半都待在船上。

---

general
KK [ˋdʒɛnərəl]
DJ [ˋdʒenərəl]
名 將軍

Eric's grandfather works in the army; he is a general.
艾瑞克的爺爺在軍隊工作，他是名將軍。

小提醒 軍官官階由高至低可以分成將、校、尉，不論是上將、中將還是少將，都可以稱作 general。general 是軍官中地位最高的。「校」的英文則是 senior officer，senior 是資歷較深、地位較高的意思，所以 senior officer 指的就是地位較高、資歷較深的「校」，「尉」則叫作 junior officer，junior 是資歷較淺、地位較低的意思，所以 junior officer 指的就是資歷較淺、地位較低的「尉」。

---

hairdresser
KK [ˋhɛrˌdrɛsɚ]
DJ [ˋhɛəˌdrɛsə]
名 髮型設計師

My dream is to be a hairdresser.
我的夢想是成為一位髮型設計師。

housewife

KK [ˋhaʊsˌwaɪf]
DJ [ˋhauswaif]
名 家庭主婦

This famous actress decides to be a housewife.
這位知名女演員決定成為家庭主婦。

---

judge

KK [dʒʌdʒ]
DJ [dʒʌdʒ]
名 法官

A judge should judge independently.
一位法官應該獨立審判。

例句單字 independently 副 獨立地

小提醒 judge 也可以當作動詞「**審判；判斷**」的意思。

---

lawyer

KK [ˋlɔjɚ]
DJ [ˋlɔːjə]
名 律師

If you want to be a lawyer, you have to pass the bar exam.
如果你想要成為一名律師，你必須通過律師考試。

例句單字 bar exam 名 律師考試

---

magician

KK [məˋdʒɪʃən]
DJ [məˋdʒiʃən]
名 魔術師

How many tricks should a magician know?
一個魔術師應該要知道多少把戲？

例句單字 trick 名 把戲

---

mailman

KK [ˋmelˌmæn]
DJ [ˋmeilmæn]
名 郵差

The mailman works really hard to deliver all the letters.
這名郵差真的很努力把所有的信送完。

例句單字 deliver 動 遞送

同義字 mail carrier 名 郵差

model
KK [`madl]
DJ [`mɔdəl]
名 模特兒

Laura finally bacame a model.
蘿拉終於成為一名模特兒。

---

musician
KK [mju`zɪʃən]
DJ [mju:`ziʃən]
名 音樂家

How many famous musicians do you know?
你知道幾位有名的音樂家呢？

---

nurse
KK [nɝs]
DJ [nə:s]
名 護士

Susan is a nurse, not a doctor.
蘇珊是位護士而不是醫師。

小提醒 現在台灣在醫院裡看到的幾乎都是「護理師」而不是護士，而護理師的英文是 **registered nurse**，要注意別用錯囉！

---

painter
KK [`pentɚ]
DJ [`peintə]
名 畫家

The painter is really famous, so his paintings are expensive.
這個畫家真的很有名，所以他的畫很貴。

---

police officer
KK [pə`lis] [`ɔfəsɚ]
DJ [pə`li:s] [`ɔ:fisə]
名 警察

The police officer should also obey the law.
警察也應該遵守法律。

例句單字 obey 動 遵守

---

president
KK [`prɛzədənt]
DJ [`prezidənt]
名 總統

Our president loves cats; she has two.
我們總統愛貓，她養了兩隻貓。

priest
KK [prist]
DJ [pri:st]
名 （基督教）牧師；（天主教）神父

The priest stays in the church every day.
神父每天都在教堂裡。

reporter
KK [rɪˋpɔrtɚ]
DJ [riˋpɔ:tə]
名 記者；播報員

The reporter is also a famous writer.
這名記者也是位有名的作家。

sailor
KK [ˋselɚ]
DJ [ˋseilə]
名 水手

He finally became a captain after he worked as a sailor for ten years.
在當了十年水手之後，他終於成為了船長。

例句單字 captain 名 船長

salesman
KK [ˋselzmən]
DJ [ˋseilzmən]
名 業務員

Nobody likes an impolite salesman.
沒人喜歡沒禮貌的業務員。

例句單字 impolite 形 沒禮貌的

scientist
KK [ˋsaɪəntɪst]
DJ [ˋsaiəntist]
名 科學家

These scientists are working on a new experiment.
這些科學家正在進行一個新實驗。

secretary
KK [ˋsɛkrəˌtɛrɪ]
DJ [ˋsekrətri]
名 祕書

Mike hired a new secretary to take care of his schedules.
麥可雇用了一位新祕書來打理他的行程。

例句單字 hire 動 雇用

Occupations
職業

281

shopkeeper

KK [`ʃɑpˌkipə˞]
DJ [`ʃɔpˌkiːpə]
名 店主

David is the shopkeeper of the shop around the corner.
大衛是轉角那家店的店主。

---

singer

KK [`sɪŋə]
DJ [`siŋə]
名 歌手

Emily is a well-known singer.
艾蜜莉是一位知名歌手。

例句單字 well-known 形 知名的

---

soldier

KK [`soldʒə˞]
DJ [`səuldʒə]
名 士兵

The soldiers are hiding in the bush.
那些士兵們正躲在灌木叢中。

例句單字 hide 動 躲藏　bush 名 灌木叢

---

vendor

KK [`vɛndə˞]
DJ [`vɛndə]
名 小販

There are a lot of vendors in the night market.
在夜市中有很多小販。

---

vet

KK [vɛt]
DJ [vɛt]
名 獸醫

If there is anything wrong with your cat, you should take it to the vet immediately.
如果你的貓有什麼不對勁，你應該要立刻帶牠去看獸醫。

例句單字 immediately 副 立刻

小提醒 vet 這個字是 veterinarian（KK [ˌvɛtərə`nɛrɪən] DJ [ˌvetəri`nɛərɪən]）的簡寫，因為 veterinarian 這個字實在太長了，在日常生活中通常只會用 vet 來表示獸醫喔！

waiter
KK [ˋwetɚ]
DJ [ˋweitə]
名 男服務生

I asked the waiter to give me more napkins.
我要求男服務生給我多一點餐巾紙。

---

waitress
KK [ˋwetrɪs]
DJ [ˋweitris]
名 女服務生

The waitress is busy taking orders.
那位女服務生正忙著接受點餐。

例句單字 take order 接受點餐

---

work
KK [wɝk]
DJ [wə:k]
名 工作（成果）

Show me your work.
讓我看看你的工作成果。

小提醒 work 當作動詞就是「工作」的意思。

---

worker
KK [ˋwɝkɚ]
DJ [ˋwə:kə]
名 工人；員工

My mother is a bakery worker.
我媽媽是一家烘焙坊的員工。

---

writer
KK [ˋraɪtɚ]
DJ [ˋraitə]
名 作家

Emily is a writer of eight novels.
艾蜜莉是一位出了八本小說的作家。

rain
下雨

rainy
下雨的

temperature
溫度；氣溫

東京 30℃

blow
颱風

北京 30℃

foggy
起霧的

台北 32℃

cloudy
多雲的

wet
濕的

雅加達 32℃

humid
潮濕的

shower
陣雨

南極洲 -58℃

freezing
非常寒冷的

cool
涼爽的

雪梨 15℃

clear
晴朗無雲的

snowy
下雪的

285

36.MP3

blow
KK [blo]
DJ [bləu] 動 颳風

The wind blows my hat away.
那陣風颳走了我的帽子。

clear
KK [klɪr]
DJ [kliə] 形 晴朗無雲的

Today's sky is very clear.
今天的天空很晴朗無雲。

climate
KK [`klaɪmɪt]
DJ [`klaimit] 名 氣候

The climate of summers in Taiwan is hot and humid.
台灣的夏日氣候高溫又潮濕。

小提醒 因為每年都有夏天，所以合起來有很多個夏天，這個時候 summer 就要加上表示複數的 s，所以如果想要說冬天的氣候，就要在 winter 的後面加上 s 喔！

cloudy
KK [`klaʊdɪ]
DJ [`klaudi] 形 多雲的

The sky is so dark; it is really cloudy today.
天空好暗，今天真的非常多雲。

cold
KK [kold]
DJ [kəuld] 形 冷的

Today is so cold that I have to wear two pairs of pants.
今天真的太冷，以致於我必須要穿兩件長褲。

286

cool
KK [kul]
DJ [ku:l]
形 涼爽的

Even in summer, it is still cool in the mountains.
即使在夏天,山裡面仍然很涼爽。

小提醒 cool 除了在形容天氣之外,也常會被用來形容一個人的**態度很冷淡或冷靜**,或者是用來**形容某件事物很厲害或是很棒**,例如:

Sally is cool about being late for school.
莎莉對於上學遲到這件事很冷靜。

My new cellphone is really cool!
我的新手機真的好酷!

degree
KK [dɪˋgri]
DJ [diˋgri:]
名 (氣溫的)度

Today's highest temperature was 35 degrees.
今天的最高氣溫是 35 度。

小提醒 還有哪些跟氣溫相關的字呢?

最低氣溫	**lowest temperature**	攝氏	**Celsius**
平均氣溫	**average temperature**	華氏	**Fahrenheit**

dry
KK [draɪ]
DJ [drai]
形 乾燥的

It is very dry in the desert.
在沙漠中非常乾燥。

foggy
KK [ˋfɑgɪ]
DJ [ˋfɔgi]
形 起霧的

When it's foggy, Alicia hates driving to work.
當起霧的時候,艾莉西雅討厭開車去上班。

小提醒 foggy 這個字其實就是由 fog(霧)而來的,一起把它們記住吧!

freezing
KK [`friziŋ]
DJ [`fri:ziŋ]
形 非常寒冷的

It is freezing cold outside. Put on your coat and earmuffs.
外面非常寒冷。把你的大衣穿上、耳罩戴上。

小提醒 freezing 是由 freeze（結冰）這個字衍生出來的，所以 freezing 就是「冷到結冰」的意思，下次有寒流來的時候，不要只會說 cold，也用用看 freezing 吧！

---

heat
KK [hit]
DJ [hi:t]
名 熱度；高溫

We are sweating because of the heat.
我們因為高溫而流汗。

例句單字 sweat 動 流汗

---

hot
KK [hɑt]
DJ [hɔt]
形 熱的

I can't walk my dog this afternoon because it is too hot.
我今天下午不能遛狗，因為太熱了。

---

humid
KK [`hjumɪd]
DJ [`hju:mid]
形 潮濕的

It is very hot and humid in the rainforest.
雨林是非常熱且潮濕的。

例句單字 rainforest 名 雨林

---

lightning
KK [`laɪtnɪŋ]
DJ [`laitniŋ]
名 閃電

You should stay indoors when lightning strikes.
當在閃電時，你應該待在室內。

例句單字 indoors 副 在室內

不要待在室外　do not stay outdoors
遠離窗戶及門　stay away from windows and doors
避免碰觸連接電源的裝置　avoid contact with equipment connected to electrical power

---

rain
KK [ren]
DJ [rein] 動 下雨

You should take an umbrella with you because it is raining outside.
因為外面下著雨，你應該帶把雨傘。

---

rainy
KK [`renɪ]
DJ [`reini] 形 下雨的

It was cold and rainy on my birthday, so we could only stay at home.
我生日那天又冷又下雨，所以我們只能待在家裡。

---

scorching
KK [`skɔrtʃɪŋ]
DJ [`skɔ:tʃiŋ] 形 非常炎熱的

It is scorching at noon in summer; you should stay indoors.
夏天的中午非常炎熱，你應該待在室內。

小提醒 scorching 的意思就是「熱到燒焦般」的炎熱，除了用來形容天氣很熱外，也可以用來表示東西「燙到燒焦似的」，例如 a scorching iron（一塊很燙的鐵）。另外，scorching 也可以當副詞，像 scorching hot（要燒焦般的炎熱）就是很常見的表達方式唷！

---

shine
KK [ʃaɪn]
DJ [ʃain] 動 照耀

The sun is shining on the grass.
太陽正照耀草坪。

小提醒 shine 的前面如果加上 sun（太陽），就變成 sunshine（陽光）囉！

shower KK [`ʃaʊɚ] DJ [`ʃauə] 名 陣雨

There are often showers in summer afternoons.
夏天的下午常有陣雨。

---

snowy KK [snoɪ] DJ [snəui] 形 下雪的

It is seldom snowy in Taiwan.
在台灣很少下雪。

例句單字 seldom 副 很少；不常有

---

storm KK [stɔrm] DJ [stɔ:m] 名 暴風雨

I hope the storm will be over quickly.
我希望這場暴風雨可以快點結束。

---

stormy KK [`stɔrmɪ] DJ [`stɔ:mi] 形 暴風雨的

My mother always tells me not to go out on such a stormy day.
我媽媽總是告訴我不要在這樣的暴風雨天出門。

---

sunny KK [`sʌnɪ] DJ [`sʌni] 形 晴朗的

It is a sunny day today; we can go on a picnic!
今天天氣晴朗，我們可以去野餐！

---

temperature KK [`tɛmprətʃɚ] DJ [`tempritʃə] 名 溫度；氣溫

The temperature is too hot for me; I need to drink more water.
氣溫對我來說太熱了，我需要喝更多水。

thunder
KK [`θʌndɚ]
DJ [`θʌndə]
名 雷；雷聲

The kitten is staying under the sofa, because of the thunder.
那隻小貓咪因為雷聲而待在沙發底下。

---

warm
KK [wɔrm]
DJ [wɔ:m]
形 溫暖的

I put on a coat to keep warm.
我穿上了一件大衣來保持溫暖。

---

wet
KK [wɛt]
DJ [wet]
形 濕的

You should hang your wet towel outside.
你應該把你的濕毛巾掛在外面。

例句單字 hang 動 懸掛

小提醒 wet 和 humid 雖然都是「濕」，但 humid 指的是「**空氣中的水蒸氣含量很高**」的潮濕，而 wet 則是「**吸飽了水或液體**」的潮濕，所以濕毛巾要用 wet，而覺得濕氣很重的時候要說 humid，別搞混了喔！

---

windy
KK [`wɪndɪ]
DJ [`windi]
形 颱風的；風大的

It is a windy day today; my hair is a mess.
今天風很大，我的頭髮一團糟。

例句單字 mess 名 一團糟

snow 雪

star 星星

sun 太陽

tree 樹

mountain 山

moon 月亮

woods 樹林；森林

hill 山丘

valley 山谷

plain 平原

forest 森林

environment 環境

pond 池塘

ocean 海洋

flower 花朵

grass 草

pool 小水塘；小水池

lake 湖

land 陸地

rock 岩石

river 河

37.MP3

air
KK [ɛr]
DJ [ɛə]
名 空氣

You can't live without air.
你沒有空氣就無法存活。

---

beach
KK [bitʃ]
DJ [bi:tʃ]
名 沙灘

When he is sad, he always goes to a beach and watches the waves.
當他難過的時候，他總是去沙灘上看海浪。

---

cloud
KK [klaʊd]
DJ [klaud]
名 雲

Those white clouds are so beautiful.
那些白色的雲好美。

---

desert
KK [ˋdɛzɚt]
DJ [ˋdezət]
名 沙漠

Do you know how to survive in the desert?
你知道如何在沙漠中生存嗎？

例句單字 survive 動 生存

Earth
KK [ɝθ]
DJ [ə:θ]
名 地球

We only have one Earth, so we have to take care of the environment.
地球只有一個，所以我們必須要照顧我們的環境。

earthquake
KK [`ɝθ‚kwek]
DJ [`ə:θkweik] 名 地震

Jason is afraid of earthquakes.
傑森很害怕地震。

---

environment
KK [ɪn`vaɪrənmənt]
DJ [in`vaiərənmənt] 名 環境

We have to take care of our environment.
我們必須照顧我們的環境。

---

fire
KK [faɪr]
DJ [faiə] 名 火

My dad doesn't allow me to start a fire on my own.
我爸爸不准我自己生火。

---

flower
KK [`flaʊɚ]
DJ [`flauə] 名 花朵

There is a bee staying on a flower.
有一隻蜜蜂停在一朵花上。

---

fog
KK [fɑg]
DJ [fɔg] 名 霧

The fog was so thick that we got lost.
霧濃到我們迷路了。

例句單字 thick 形 厚的 get lost 迷路

---

forest
KK [`fɔrɪst]
DJ [`fɔrist] 名 森林

They played hide-and-seek in the forest.
他們在森林裡玩捉迷藏。

例句單字 hide-and-seek 名 捉迷藏

fossil oil
KK [`fɑsl̩] [ɔɪl]
DJ [`fɔsəl] [ɔil]
名 石油

There is a great amount of fossil oil in the Middle East.
在中東有大量的石油。

 a great amount of 大量的～ Middle East 名 中東

 fossil oil 裡的 fossil 是「化石」的意思，所以從石油的英文名字就可以看出石油是來自地底下被高溫高壓逐漸轉化的化石，從石油可以提煉出各種不同的油品，你知道哪些呢？

原油	crude oil	汽油	gasoline
石油	petroleum	柴油	diesel

---

gas
KK [gæs]
DJ [gæs]
名 瓦斯

There is a gas leak in that house.
那棟房子的瓦斯外洩。

 leak 名 （水、瓦斯等的）漏出

---

grass
KK [græs]
DJ [grɑ:s]
名 草

Let's sit on the grass.
讓我們坐在草地上。

---

hill
KK [hɪl]
DJ [hil]
名 山丘

There is a castle on the hill.
在山丘上有一棟城堡。

---

hot spring
KK [hɑt] [sprɪŋ]
DJ [hɔt] [spriŋ]
名 溫泉

There are many famous hot springs in Japan.
日本有很多有名的溫泉。

 famous 形 有名的

hurricane
KK [ˈhɝɪˌken]
DJ [ˈhʌrikən]
名 颶風

Hurricanes are very destructive so you have to be careful.
颶風有很強的破壞力，所以你必須小心。

例句單字 destructive 形 破壞的、毀滅性的

小提醒 hurricane 和 typhoon（颱風）一樣都是「熱帶氣旋」，但熱帶氣旋出現在不同海洋上就會有不同的名稱，在北太平洋西部出現的熱帶氣旋叫做 typhoon（颱風），而在北大西洋出現的就是 hurricane（颶風）。

---

island
KK [ˈaɪlənd]
DJ [ˈailənd]
名 島嶼

Taiwan is a small island in the Pacific Ocean.
台灣是太平洋上的一個小島。

例句單字 Pacific Ocean 名 太平洋

小提醒 全世界的海洋被劃分成了五大洋，除了太平洋之外，你還知道哪些呢？

大西洋	Atlantic Ocean	北冰洋	Arctic Ocean
印度洋	Indian Ocean	南冰洋	Antarctic Ocean

---

lake
KK [lek]
DJ [leik]
名 湖

We will stay at a hotel by the lake.
我們會住在湖邊的飯店。

---

land
KK [lænd]
DJ [lænd]
名 陸地

After 10 months at sea, the sailors now finally see land.
在 10 個月的航行之後，水手們現在終於看到陸地了。

---

moon
KK [mun]
DJ [muːn]
名 月亮

Tides are caused by the gravitation of the moon.
潮汐是因月亮的引力而造成的。

例句單字 tide 名 潮汐 gravitation 名 重力；引力

mountain
KK [`maʊntən] DJ [`mauntin] 名 山

How high is this mountain?
這座山有多高？

---

ocean
KK [`oʃən] DJ [`əuʃən] 名 海洋

This river flows into the Pacific Ocean.
這條河流流進太平洋。

---

plain
KK [plen] DJ [plein] 名 平原

There are three wide plains in my country.
在我的國家裡有三個寬廣的平原。

---

planet
KK [`plænɪt] DJ [`plænit] 名 行星；地球

We have to recycle to save our planet.
我們必須做回收來拯救我們的地球。

小提醒 planet 指的是繞著太陽轉的「行星」，但因為我們居住的地球也是行星的一分子，所以 planet 這個字常常被當成「地球」的意思，但其實每個行星都有自己的名字喔！

| 水星 Mercury | 木星 Jupiter | 金星 Venus | 土星 Saturn |
| 地球 Earth | 天王星 Uranus | 火星 Mars | 海王星 Neptune |

---

pond
KK [pɑnd] DJ [pɔnd] 名 池塘

There is a pond in the middle of the park.
在這座公園的中間有一個池塘。

pool
KK [pul]
DJ [pu:l]
名 小水塘；小水池

Miranda always goes to the swimming pool during summer vacation.
米蘭達總是在暑假的時候去游泳池。

rainbow
KK [`ren͵bo]
DJ [`reinbəu]
名 彩虹

A rainbow is a natural phenomenon.
彩虹是一種自然現象。

例句單字 phenomenon 名 現象

river
KK [`rɪvɚ]
DJ [`rivə]
名 河

How can I cross this river?
我要怎麼渡過這條河？

rock
KK [rɑk]
DJ [rɔk]
名 岩石

The rock is too big for me to climb.
這塊岩石對我來說大到爬不上去。

sea
KK [si]
DJ [si:]
名 海

Our house faces the sea.
我們的房子面海。

小提醒 我們常說的「海洋」其實是「sea（海）」和「ocean（洋）」的意思。一般來說，我們會將在**陸地邊緣**的水域稱為 sea，而把**遠離陸地**的水域稱為 ocean。

sky
KK [skaɪ]
DJ [skai]
名 天空

A bird is flying in the sky.
一隻鳥正在天空中飛。

snow
KK [sno]
DJ [snəu]
名 雪

The little girl has never seen snow before.
這個小女孩之前從來沒有看過雪。

spring
KK [sprɪŋ]
DJ [sprɪŋ]
名 噴泉

"Old Faithful" is a famous spring in the U.S.
「老忠實」是一座在美國的有名噴泉。

star
KK [stɑr]
DJ [stɑ:]
名 星星

The clear sky and shining stars are so beautiful.
晴朗的天空和閃耀的星星非常美麗。

sun
KK [sʌn]
DJ [sʌn]
名 太陽

The sun is going down.
太陽正在下沉。

tree
KK [tri]
DJ [tri:]
名 樹

To slow down global warming, we should protect trees.
為了減緩全球暖化，我們應該要保護樹。

typhoon
KK [taɪˋfun]
DJ [taiˋfu:n]
名 颱風

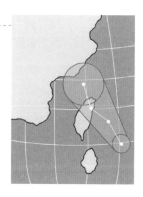

How many typhoons does Taiwan have every year?
台灣一年會有幾個颱風？

小提醒 說到颱風，你知道哪些跟颱風相關的英文呢？

海上颱風警報	sea warning	發布警報	issue the warning
陸上颱風警報	land warning	颱風眼	the eye of typhoon
解除警報	lift the warning	暴風半徑	radius

---

valley
KK [`vælɪ] DJ [`væli] 名 山谷

My grandparents live in a small valley.
我的爺爺奶奶居住在一個小山谷中。

---

volcano
KK [vɒl`keno] DJ [vɒl`keinəu] 名 火山

There are many volcanoes in my country.
在我的國家裡有很多火山。

---

waterfall
KK [`wɔtɚˌfɔl] DJ [`wɔːtəfɔːl] 名 瀑布

A lot of people climb all the way up to see this famous waterfall.
很多人為了要看這座有名的瀑布而一路爬了上來。

---

wind
KK [wɪnd] DJ [wɪnd] 名 風

The wind is so strong that I can barely stand.
這陣風強到我快要站不住。

例句單字 barely 副 幾乎不

---

woods
KK [wʊdz] DJ [wudz] 名 樹林；森林

Don't leave any garbage in the woods.
不要在樹林裡留下任何垃圾。

小提醒 wood（木材）這個字的複數就變成了 woods（樹林；森林）的意思。

eagle
老鷹

whale
鯨魚

dragon
龍

shark
鯊魚

dolphin
海豚

koala
無尾熊

crab
螃蟹

fish
魚

shrimp
蝦子

bat
蝙蝠

fox
狐狸

zebra
斑馬

horse
馬

elephant
大象

mosquito
蚊子

lion
獅子

snake
蛇

kangaroo
袋鼠

snail
蝸牛

hippo
河馬

swan
天鵝

worm
蟲

38.MP3

ant
KK [ænt]
DJ [ænt]　名 螞蟻

Ants have their own society.
螞蟻有牠們自己的社會。

---

bat
KK [bæt]
DJ [bæt]　名 蝙蝠

Although bats can fly, they are not birds.
儘管蝙蝠能飛，但是牠們不是鳥。

---

bear
KK [bɛr]
DJ [bɛə]　名 熊

The hunter met a bear in the woods.
獵人在樹林裡遇到一隻熊。

---

bee
KK [bi]
DJ [bi:]　名 蜜蜂

Bees dance in the air to warn other bees.
蜜蜂在空中跳舞以警告其他的蜜蜂。

例句單字 warn 動 警告

---

bird
KK [bɝd]
DJ [bə:d]　名 鳥

There is a bird standing on the roof.
有一隻鳥站在屋頂上。

---

bug
KK [bʌg]
DJ [bʌg]　名 蟲

There are a lot of annoying bugs in summer.
夏天有很多討厭的蟲。

例句單字 annoying 形 討人厭的

bull
KK [bʊl]
DJ [bul]
名 公牛

The bull pushed the fence down and ran away.
那隻公牛撞倒圍欄跑了。

---

butterfly
KK [ˋbʌtəˏflaɪ]
DJ [ˋbʌtəflai]
名 蝴蝶

The life of a butterfly is short.
蝴蝶的壽命很短。

---

cat
KK [kæt]
DJ [kæt]
名 貓

Although cats are cute, Emily is still scared of cats.
儘管貓很可愛，艾蜜莉還是很怕貓。

小提醒 在英文裡，有些動物的小時候和長大之後的名稱不一樣，你知道哪些呢？

小熊	**cub**	小雞	**chick**	小貓	**kitten**
小牛	**calf**	小狗	**puppy**	小豬	**piglet**

---

chicken
KK [ˋtʃɪkɪn]
DJ [ˋtʃikin]
名 雞

I want to have a hot bowl of chicken soup on a cold night.
在寒冷的晚上我想要喝一碗熱雞湯。

小提醒 chicken 還有雞肉的意思，我們常吃的雞肉部位該怎麼說呢？

雞胸肉 **chicken breast**
棒棒腿 **chicken drumsticks**
雞大腿 **chicken thigh**　　　　雞翅膀 **chicken wings**

---

cockroach
KK [ˋkɑkˏrotʃ]
DJ [ˋkɔkrəutʃ]
名 蟑螂

My mom screams every time she sees cockroaches.
我媽媽每次看到蟑螂就會尖叫。

例句單字 scream 動 尖叫

cow KK [kaʊ] DJ [kau] 名 乳牛

The little girl is feeding a cow grass.
那個小女孩正在用草餵一頭乳牛。

---

crab KK [kræb] DJ [kræb] 名 螃蟹

Can you teach me how to cook this crab?
你能教我怎麼煮這隻螃蟹嗎？

---

deer KK [dɪr] DJ [diə] 名 鹿

The deer ran so fast that lions couldn't catch it.
那隻鹿跑得非常快，讓獅子抓不到牠。

---

dog KK [dɔg] DJ [dɔg] 名 狗

My dog always looks forward to going out with me.
我的狗總是期待和我一起出去。

---

dolphin KK [`dɔlfɪn] DJ [`dɔlfɪn] 名 海豚

I gave a dolphin toy to my little brother.
我給了弟弟一個海豚玩具。

---

donkey KK [`dɑŋkɪ] DJ [`dɔŋki] 名 驢子

The donkeys in the zoo are eating apples.
動物園裡的驢子正在吃蘋果。

dragon
KK [ˈdrægən]
DJ [ˈdrægən]
名 龍

The dragon is a mysterious creature in stories.
龍是一種故事裡的神祕生物。

例句單字 mysterious 形 神祕的　creature 名 生物

小提醒 我們在神話故事和小說裡看到的「龍」，用英文說就是
dragon，不能用 dinosaur（恐龍）喔！

duck
KK [dʌk]
DJ [dʌk]
名 鴨子

The duck is swimming in the pond near my house.
那隻鴨子正在我家附近的池子裡游泳。

eagle
KK [ˈigl̩]
DJ [ˈiːgəl]
名 老鷹

Eagles can fly really high in the sky.
老鷹可以在天空中飛得非常高。

elephant
KK [ˈɛləfənt]
DJ [ˈelifənt]
名 大象

We torture elephants when we ride them.
騎大象就是虐待大象。

例句單字 torture 名 虐待

fish
KK [fɪʃ]
DJ [fɪʃ]
名 魚

A fish is a beautiful creature.
魚是美麗的生物。

例句單字 fish tank 名 水族箱　relaxed 形 放鬆的

小提醒 fish 如果是指「**種類不同的魚**」的時候就是**可數名詞**，例如 There are
several kinds of fishes in the fish tank.（水族
箱裡有好幾種魚。），但如果是想要說「**魚肉**」、「**魚
這種生物**」，那就是**不可數名詞**，後面**不能再加上表示
複數的 es**，如 Fish is a beautiful creature.（魚
是一種美麗的生物。）、I like to eat fish a lot.
（我非常喜歡吃魚。），要注意喔！

fox
KK [fɑks]
DJ [fɔks]
名 狐狸

There are two little foxes hiding in the hollow tree.
有兩隻狐狸躲在中空的樹中。

例句單字 hollow 形 中空的

---

frog
KK [frɑg]
DJ [frɔg]
名 青蛙

There are a lot of frogs living near the lake.
有很多青蛙住在那個湖的附近。

---

goat
KK [got]
DJ [gəut]
名 山羊

Can I feed those goats, please?
可以拜託你讓我去餵那些山羊嗎？

---

goose
KK [gus]
DJ [gu:s]
名 鵝

There are a group of geese over there trying to cross the road.
那邊有一群鵝想過馬路。

小提醒 goose 的複數是不規則變化的 geese，不要寫錯囉！

---

hen
KK [hɛn]
DJ [hen]
名 母雞

In the story, the fox tries really hard to catch the hen and her babies.
在故事裡，這隻狐狸很努力地想抓到母雞和她的寶寶們。

---

hippo
KK [`hɪpo]
DJ [`hipəu]
名 河馬

There is a hippo bathing in the pond.
有隻河馬正泡在池塘裡。

小提醒 hippo 是 hippopotamus（KK [ˌhɪpə`patəməs], DJ[ˌhipə`potəməs]）的簡稱，因為 hippopotamus 實在太長了，所以我們通常只用 hippo 來稱呼河馬喔～

horse
KK [hɔrs]
DJ [hɔ:s] 名 馬

Do you know how to ride a horse?
你知道怎麼騎馬嗎？

---

insect
KK [ˋɪnsɛkt]
DJ [ˋinsekt] 名 昆蟲

One of Maggie's hobbies is collecting insects.
梅姬的興趣之一是蒐集昆蟲。

例句單字 collect 動 蒐集

---

kangaroo
KK [ˌkæŋgəˋru]
DJ [ˌkæŋgəˋru:] 名 袋鼠

The kangaroo is the most famous animal in Australia.
袋鼠是澳洲最有名的動物。

---

koala
KK [koˋɑlə]
DJ [kəuˋɑ:lə] 名 無尾熊

Amy wants to take pictures with a koala.
艾美想要跟無尾熊一起拍照。

---

lion
KK [ˋlaɪən]
DJ [ˋlaiən] 名 獅子

Male lions have furry hair around their necks.
雄性的獅子脖子上環繞著毛茸茸的鬃毛。

例句單字 male 形 雄性的　furry 形 毛茸茸的

---

monkey
KK [ˋmʌŋkɪ]
DJ [ˋmʌŋki] 名 猴子

Even monkeys fall from trees.
就算是猴子也會從樹上掉下來。

309

mosquito KK [məsˋkito] DJ [məsˋkiːtəu] 名 蚊子

The mosquito keeps flying around me.
蚊子一直繞著我飛來飛去。

---

mouse KK [maʊs] DJ [maus] 名 老鼠

My classmate keeps a mouse as his pet.
我同學養了一隻老鼠當寵物。

小提醒 mouse 的複數是不規則的 **mice**。

---

panda KK [ˋpændə] DJ [ˋpændə] 名 熊貓

The panda is an endangered animal.
熊貓是瀕臨絕種的動物之一。

例句單字 endangered 形 瀕臨絕種的

---

parrot KK [ˋpærət] DJ [ˋpærət] 名 鸚鵡

My parrot is repeating my words.
我的鸚鵡正在重複我說的話。

例句單字 repeat 動 重複做～

---

pig KK [pɪg] DJ [pig] 名 豬

Every part of a pig is useful.
豬身上的所有部位都有用途。

例句單字 useful 形 有用的

---

pigeon KK [ˋpɪdʒɪn] DJ [ˋpidʒin] 名 鴿子

You can't feed pigeons in this park.
在這個公園裡你不能餵食鴿子。

rabbit
KK [`ræbɪt]
DJ [`ræbit]　名　兔子

Rabbits have long ears and short tails.
兔子有長耳朵跟短尾巴。

---

rooster
KK [`rustɚ]
DJ [`ru:stə]　名　公雞

The girl is holding a bag with a rooster logo on it.
那個女孩拿著一個上面有公雞圖案的袋子。

---

shark
KK [ʃɑrk]
DJ [ʃɑ:k]　名　鯊魚

Sharks have a lot of sharp teeth.
鯊魚有很多銳利的牙齒。

例句單字 sharp 形 銳利的

---

sheep
KK [ʃip]
DJ [ʃi:p]　名　綿羊

My mom took me to a farm to feed sheep.
媽媽帶我到農場餵綿羊。

小提醒 sheep 的複數和單數長得一樣喔！

---

shrimp
KK [ʃrɪmp]
DJ [ʃrimp]　名　蝦子

My mom always peels shrimps for me.
媽媽總是幫我剝蝦殼。

---

snail
KK [snel]
DJ [sneil]　名　蝸牛

I saw a snail crawling slowly on the tree.
我看到一隻蝸牛緩慢的在樹上爬行。

例句單字 crawl 動 爬行

snake KK [snek] DJ [sneik] 名 蛇

Some snakes are poisonous, but not all of them.
有些蛇有毒，但不是全部。

例句單字 poisonous 形 有毒的

---

spider KK [`spaɪdɚ] DJ [`spaɪdə] 名 蜘蛛

Spiders are not insects.
蜘蛛不是昆蟲。

小提醒 雖然蜘蛛也是屬於節肢動物門，是昆蟲的親戚，但是蜘蛛有八隻腳，而且身體可以分成頭胸部和軀幹部，這些都和昆蟲的特徵不同，所以蜘蛛當然不是昆蟲囉！

---

swallow KK [`swɑlo] DJ [`swɔləu] 名 燕子

You can see swallows making their nests there.
你可以看到那邊有燕子在築巢。

例句單字 nest 名 鳥巢

---

swan KK [swɑn] DJ [swɔn] 名 天鵝

Swans are swimming gracefully in the lake.
天鵝們正在湖裡優雅地游泳。

---

tiger KK [`taɪgɚ] DJ [`taigə] 名 老虎

Do tigers purr like cats?
老虎會像貓一樣發出呼嚕聲嗎？

例句單字 purr 動 （貓等）發出呼嚕聲

turkey
KK [ˈtɝkɪ]
DJ [ˈtəːki]
名 火雞

Do you want to have a turkey sandwich?
你想吃個火雞三明治嗎？

---

turtle
KK [ˈtɝtl̩]
DJ [ˈtəːtəl]
名 烏龜；海龜

Turtles lay eggs on the beach.
烏龜在沙灘上下蛋。

---

whale
KK [hwel]
DJ [hweil]
名 鯨魚

The whale is a kind of smart and huge animal.
鯨魚是一種聰明且巨大的動物。

---

wolf
KK [wʊlf]
DJ [wulf]
名 狼

Wolves and dogs sometimes look alike, but they are in fact very different.
狼和狗有的時候看起來很像，但是牠們其實非常不同。

---

worm
KK [wɝm]
DJ [wəːm]
名 蟲

It is really disgusting that there is a worm in this apple.
這個蘋果裡面有一條蟲，這真的很噁心。

---

zebra
KK [ˈzibrə]
DJ [ˈziːbrə]
名 斑馬

Zebras have beautiful stripes.
斑馬有美麗的條紋。

例句單字 stripe 名 條紋

instrument

樂器

flute

長笛；橫笛

piano

鋼琴

trumpet

小喇叭

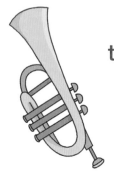

guitar

吉他

violin

小提琴

drum
鼓

harmonica
口琴

recorder
直笛

electric guitar
電吉他

play
演奏

voice
嗓音

cello
大提琴

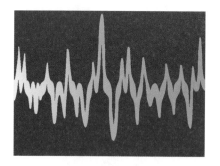

frequency
頻率

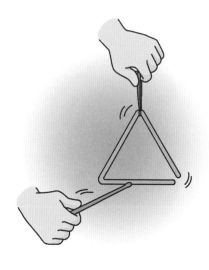

triangle
三角鐵

pitch
音調；音高

bass
貝斯

saxophone
薩克斯風

song
歌曲

jazz
爵士樂

pop music
流行音樂

39.MP3

bass
KK [`bes]
DJ [`beis]
名 貝斯

I play bass in a jazz band.
我在爵士樂團裡擔任貝斯手。

---

cello
KK [`tʃɛlo]
DJ [`tʃeləu]
名 大提琴

Cello is a kind of expensive instrument.
大提琴是一種昂貴的樂器。

---

drum
KK [drʌm]
DJ [drʌm]
名 鼓

Do you like playing the drums?
你喜歡打鼓嗎？

小提醒 如果不是只有一個鼓，而是像爵士鼓那樣「一整組的鼓」，英文叫做 drum set 或 drum kit。

---

electric guitar
KK [ɪ`lɛktrɪk] [gɪ`tɑr]
DJ [i`lektrik] [gɪ`tɑ:]
名 電吉他

Is playing an electric guitar harder than playing an acoustic guitar?
彈電吉他比彈原聲吉他困難嗎？

---

flute
KK [flut]
DJ [flu:t]
名 長笛；橫笛

Monica learned how to play the flute from her mother.
莫妮卡從媽媽那裡學會吹長笛。

frequency

KK [`frikwənsɪ]
DJ [`fri:kwənsi]
名 頻率

Do you know the frequency of this radio station?
你知道這家電台的頻率是多少嗎？

例句單字 radio station 名 電台

小提醒 frequency 除了是聲音波動的頻率之外，也代表**做某事的頻率**，在英文裡有一些常用來表示頻率的副詞，一起來學吧！

總是	always	有時候	sometimes	通常	usually
偶爾	occasionally	經常	often	很少	seldom
頻繁	frequently	幾乎不	hardly		

---

guitar

KK [gɪ`tɑr]
DJ [gi`tɑ:]
名 吉他

I want to buy a guitar for my nephew.
我想要買把吉他給我的姪子。

例句單字 nephew 名 姪子；外甥

---

harmonica

KK [har`mɑnɪkə]
DJ [hɑ:`mɔnikə]
名 口琴

Playing someone else's harmonica makes me feel weird.
吹別人的口琴讓我覺得很奇怪。

例句單字 weird 形 怪異的

Music 音樂

---

instrument

KK [`ɪnstrəmənt]
DJ [`instrumənt]
名 樂器

How many instruments can you play?
你能演奏幾種樂器呢？

---

jazz

KK [dʒæz]
DJ [dʒæz]
名 爵士樂

Adam is so crazy about jazz that he goes to jazz restaurants every night.
亞當對爵士樂非常瘋狂，所以他每天晚上都去爵士餐廳。

piano
KK [pɪˋæno]
DJ [piˋænəu]
名 鋼琴

The pianist plays the piano seven hours a day.
這位鋼琴家每天彈奏鋼琴七小時。

---

pitch
KK [pɪtʃ]
DJ [pitʃ]
名 音調；音高

Lisa has absolute pitch.
麗莎擁有絕對音感。

小提醒 absolute pitch（絕對音感）也可以稱做 perfect pitch，擁有絕對音感的人，能夠在沒有其他參考音高的狀況之下，聽到一個音就準確地辨認出這個聲音的音高。

---

play
KK [ple]
DJ [plei]
動 演奏

Rita can play the piano beautifully.
麗塔能夠優美地彈奏鋼琴。

---

pop music
KK [pɑp] [ˋmjuzɪk]
DJ [pɔp] [ˋmju:zik]
名 流行音樂

Sam likes pop music very much; he has a long playlist.
山姆非常喜歡流行音樂，他有一張很長的播放清單。

例句單字 playlist 名 播放清單

小提醒 pop music 裡的 pop，就是 popular（流行的）的簡寫。

---

recorder
KK [rɪˋkɔrdɚ]
DJ [riˋkɔ:də]
名 直笛

Everyone in elementary schools should learn how to play the recorder.
小學裡的每個人都應該學如何吹直笛。

---

saxophone
KK [ˋsæksəˏfon]
DJ [ˋsæksəfəun]
名 薩克斯風

I saved all my money to buy a new saxophone for my dad.
我把所有的錢都存起來去買一隻新的薩克斯風給爸爸。

song
KK [sɔŋ]
DJ [sɒŋ]
名 歌曲

This is my favorite song.
這是我最愛的歌曲。

---

triangle
KK [ˋtraɪˏæŋgl̩]
DJ [ˋtraiæŋgəl]
名 三角鐵

Who wants to play the triangle?
誰想敲三角鐵？

小提醒 triangle 是「percussion instrument（打擊樂器）」的一種，你還知道哪些打擊樂器呢？

| 高音木琴 | xylophone | 鈴鼓 | tambourine |
| 鐵琴 | glockenspiel | 響板 | castanet |

---

trumpet
KK [ˋtrʌmpɪt]
DJ [ˋtrʌmpɪt]
名 小喇叭

You can't play the trumpet in the middle of the night; it's too noisy.
你不能在半夜吹小喇叭，太吵了。

---

violin
KK [ˏvaɪəˋlɪn]
DJ [ˏvaiəˋlin]
名 小提琴

I won't touch my brother's violin because it is really expensive.
我不會去碰我弟的小提琴，因為它非常昂貴。

---

voice
KK [vɔɪs]
DJ [vɔis]
名 嗓音

Alice has a beautiful voice, so she joins the school choir.
愛麗絲有美麗的嗓音，所以她參加了學校合唱團。

例句單字 choir 名 合唱團

Emotions 情緒

bored
無聊的

interested
對～有興趣的

happy
快樂的

unhappy
不高興的

sad
難過的；悲傷的

excited
興奮的

afraid／scared
害怕的

excellent
極好的

angry
生氣的

mad
憤怒的；瘋狂的

bad
壞的

good
好的

favorite
最愛的

wonderful
很棒的

surprised
驚訝的

323

glad

開心的

sorry

抱歉的；遺憾的

serious

嚴肅的

pleasure

愉快

joy

愉快；高興

lucky

幸運的

fine
很好的

busy
忙碌的

relaxed
放鬆的

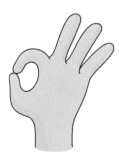

sure
確定的

strange
奇怪的

fantastic
很棒的

lonely
孤單的

40.MP3

afraid KK [ə`fred] DJ [ə`freid] 形 害怕的

My six-year-old cousin is really afraid of my neighbor's dog.
我六歲的表弟很怕我鄰居家的狗。

angry KK [`æŋgrɪ] DJ [`æŋgri] 形 生氣的

Why are you angry at me?
你為什麼生我的氣？

bad KK [bæd] DJ [bæd] 形 壞的

Today is a bad day because my mom doesn't let me go out with my friend.
今天是很糟的一天，因為媽媽不讓我和朋友出去。

bored KK [bord] DJ [bɔ:d] 形 無聊的

This lesson is so boring that I am really bored in class.
這堂課非常無趣，讓我在上課的時候覺得非常無聊。

 bored 是用來形容「**人覺得無聊**」，如果我們覺得「**某件事或東西**很無趣、無聊」，這個時候要用 boring（令人無聊的），在使用的時候要多注意喔！

busy KK [`bɪzɪ] DJ [`bizi] 形 忙碌的

Alicia's mother is a busy lawyer.
艾莉西亞的媽媽是一位忙碌的律師。

excellent
KK [ˈɛksḷənt]
DJ [ˈeksələnt]
形 極好的

I feel excellent today because my friends and I are going to celebrate my birthday!
我今天心情非常好，因為我要和朋友一起慶祝我的生日！

---

excited
KK [ɪkˈsaɪtɪd]
DJ [ikˈsaitid]
形 興奮的

The children are excited because they are going to the amusement park.
小孩們很興奮，因為他們要去遊樂園玩。

小提醒 當人覺得興奮的時候，要用 excited 來表達，如果是什麼**事情或東西**讓你覺得興奮的話，那就要使用 exciting（令人興奮的）。有沒有注意到這個用法很眼熟？沒錯，和 bored、boring 的用法是一樣的喔！**ed 結尾**的 excited 是用來形容人，而 **ing 結尾**的則是**用在事物上**，別忘記囉！

---

fantastic
KK [fænˈtæstɪk]
DJ [fænˈtæstik]
形 很棒的

After eating a lot of chocolate, Alice feels fantastic.
在吃了很多巧克力之後，愛麗絲覺得心情很棒。

---

favorite
KK [ˈfevərɪt]
DJ [ˈfeivərit]
形 最愛的

My favorite food is pizza.
我最愛的食物是披薩。

---

fine
KK [faɪn]
DJ [fain]
形 很好的

Everything will be fine, so stop worrying.
一切都會很好，所以不要再擔心了。

glad
KK [glæd]
DJ [glæd]
形 開心的

I am glad to help people in need.
我很開心去幫助需要幫助的人。

---

good
KK [gʊd]
DJ [gud]
形 好的

I feel good after taking a shower.
在沖過澡之後,我覺得很舒服。

小提醒 good 這個字的意思很多,可以用來形容「心情愉快」,也可以表示某事物「令人滿意」,用在人的身體狀況時則是「舒服」的意思,總之,看到 good 就知道和「好」脫不了關係啦!

---

happy
KK [ˋhæpɪ]
DJ [ˋhæpi]
形 快樂的

Spotty is a happy dog; she is lucky to have a nice owner.
斑斑是一隻快樂的狗,她很幸運有個好主人。

小提醒 有注意到上面這個例句裡的狗,主詞用了 she 而不是動物應該要用的 it 嗎?這是因為現在寵物常會被視為家人之一,所以越來越多人會用擬人化的 he / she 來稱呼寵物,但如果不是已經建立感情的動物,則仍然使用 it。

---

interested
KK [ˋɪntərɪstɪd]
DJ [ˋintəristid]
形 對～有興趣的

I am interested in math.
我對數學有興趣。

小提醒 interested 如果把字尾換成 ing,就會變成 interesting(令人有興趣的),也就是「有趣的」的意思,這個變化和前面看到的 bored、boring 及 excited、exciting 很相似喔!

joy
KK [dʒɔɪ]
DJ [dʒɔi]
名 愉快；高興

The boy is dancing with joy.
那個男孩愉快地跳著舞。

lonely
KK [ˋlonlɪ]
DJ [ˋləunli]
形 孤單的

Mosby doesn't have a girlfriend; he feels lonely.
莫斯比沒有女朋友，他覺得很孤單。

lucky
KK [ˋlʌkɪ]
DJ [ˋlʌki]
形 幸運的

Wendy is a lucky girl; she often wins the lottery.
溫蒂是個幸運的女孩，因為她常常中樂透。

例句單字 lottery 名 樂透；彩券

mad
KK [mæd]
DJ [mæd]
形 憤怒的；瘋狂的

Our teacher is mad at us because we don't like to prepare for the class.
因為我們不喜歡預習，我們的老師對我們感到很憤怒。

The mad man is trying to blow up the building.
這個瘋狂的人試圖要炸毀大樓。

小提醒 mad 比前面提到的 angry（生氣的）的生氣程度更高，就是「**氣到要發瘋**」的感覺，所以如果你覺得 angry 已經沒辦法表現你的憤怒，就可以用 mad 這個字喔～另外，mad 還有「**失去理智**」的意思，所以 mad scientist 是「瘋狂科學家」而不是憤怒的科學家喔！

Emotions
情緒

pleasure
KK [ˋplɛʒɚ]
DJ [ˋpleʒə]
名 愉快

It is a pleasure to see you again.
再見到你讓我很愉快。

relaxed

KK [rɪˋlækst]
DJ [riˋlækst]
形 放鬆的

I feel relaxed in this comfortable armchair.
在這張舒服的扶手椅上我覺得很放鬆。

---

sad

KK [sæd]
DJ [sæd]
形 難過的；悲傷的

Romeo and Juliet is a sad love story.
羅密歐與茱麗葉是一個悲傷的愛情故事。

---

scared

KK [skɛrd]
DJ [skɛəd]
形 害怕的

I am scared of heights; I can't walk on the balcony.
我很怕高，我沒辦法在這個陽台上走。

小提醒 一般來說 scared 和 afraid 都是形容「恐懼」且常常互相替代使用，但是 scared 的害怕程度比前面提到的 afraid 更高，而且這種害怕是帶著「驚慌」的害怕，像例句裡的 scared of heights（怕高）就是會因為高度而怕到驚慌失措的意思。

---

serious

KK [ˋsɪrɪəs]
DJ [ˋsiəriəs]
形 嚴肅的

My teacher is very serious about everything.
我的老師對所有事情都很嚴肅。

---

sorry

KK [ˋsɔrɪ]
DJ [ˋsɔri]
形 抱歉的；遺憾的

I am so sorry for being late.
對於遲到我真的很抱歉。

I am really sorry for your loss.
我對你的損失感到很遺憾。

---

strange
KK [strendʒ]
DJ [streindʒ]
形 奇怪的

Amy's voice sounds strange through my cellphone.
艾咪的聲音透過我的手機聽起來很奇怪。

---

sure
KK [ʃʊr]
DJ [ʃuə]
形 確定的

I am very sure that Susan will come to the party.
我非常確定蘇珊會來派對。

---

surprised
KK [sə`praɪzd]
DJ [sə`praɪzd]
形 驚訝的

I am very surprised that there is a bouquet on my desk.
我很驚訝我桌上有一束花。

例句單字 bouquet 名 花束

---

unhappy
KK [ʌn`hæpɪ]
DJ [ʌn`hæpi]
形 不高興的

My parents are unhappy about my mid-term grades.
我的父母對我的期中考成績感到不高興。

---

wonderful
KK [`wʌndɚfəl]
DJ [`wʌndəfəl]
形 很棒的

I hope you have a wonderful weekend.
祝你有個很棒的週末。

同義字 amazing 形 令人驚嘆的　fabulous 形 很棒的
miraculous 形 奇蹟般的；驚奇的　stunning 形 令人驚嘆的

情緒 Emotions

Describing Words – Opposite Words

bright 明亮的

dark 黑暗的

right 正確的　wrong 錯誤的

dangerous 危險的

different 不同的

safe 安全的

same 一樣的

easy
簡單的

difficult
困難的

public
公開的

private
私人的

loud
大聲的

quiet
安靜的

alive
活的；有活力的

dead
死的；無生氣的

terrible
糟糕的

great
很好的

special
特別的

common
一般的；普通的

clean
乾淨的

dirty
髒的

modern
現代的

traditional
傳統的

national
全國性的；國家的

foreign
國外的

present
出席的

absent
未出席的

positive
正面的

negative
負面的

true
真的

false
假的

41.MP3

absent
KK [`æbsn̩t]
DJ [`æbsənt]
形 未出席的

Jason doesn't feel well today, so he is absent from school.
傑森今天覺得不舒服，所以沒有去學校。

---

alive
KK [ə`laɪv]
DJ [ə`laiv]
形 活的；有活力的

Gary is almost 80, but he is still alive and energetic.
蓋瑞快 80 歲了，但他仍然很有活力且精力旺盛。

例句單字 energetic 形 精力旺盛的

---

bright
KK [braɪt]
DJ [brait]
形 明亮的

There is always a bright side, so don't be so sad.
總是會有光明的一面，所以不要這麼難過。

小提醒 There is always a bright side. 是一句很常用來安慰別人，要別人往好處想的一句話，下次如果想要安慰沮喪的朋友，也可以試著這樣說說看喔～

---

clean
KK [klin]
DJ [kli:n]
形 乾淨的

Please keep your bedroom clean.
請保持你的房間乾淨。

---

common
KK [`kɑmən]
DJ [`kɔmən]
形 一般的；普通的

It is important to have common sense.
擁有常識是很重要的。

小提醒 common sense 一般都會翻譯成「普通常識」，但這種「常識」和我們念書所學會的例如「1＋1＝2」、「水在零度會結冰」等常識不一樣，上面這種叫做 general knowledge，而不是 common sense。common sense 指的是「**大家都有的認知**」，所以像是「颱風天不能去海邊」、「買東西要付錢」，這種才是 common sense，不要搞混囉！

dangerous
KK [ˋdɛndʒərəs]
DJ [ˋdeindʒərəs]
形 危險的

Fire is useful but also dangerous.
火很有用但也很危險。

---

dark
KK [dɑrk]
DJ [dɑ:k]
形 黑暗的

Cats have great sight even in the dark.
貓在黑暗中仍擁有極佳的視力。

---

dead
KK [dɛd]
DJ [ded]
形 死的；無生氣的

Alice's dog is dead and that breaks her heart.
愛麗絲的狗死掉了，而這傷透了她的心。

---

different
KK [ˋdɪfərənt]
DJ [ˋdifərənt]
形 不同的

Are these two pictures different?
這兩張照片不同嗎？

---

difficult
KK [ˋdɪfəˌkəlt]
DJ [ˋdifikəlt]
形 困難的

The English exam was very difficult for me.
這場英文考試對我來講非常困難。

---

dirty
KK [ˋdɝtɪ]
DJ [ˋdə:ti]
形 髒的

My hands are dirty; can you hold my bag for me?
我的手很髒，你能幫我拿著我的袋子嗎？

---

easy
KK [ˋizɪ]
DJ [ˋi:zi]
形 簡單的

There is no easy way to success, so keep working.
成功沒有簡單的道路，所以繼續努力吧。

false
KK [fɔls] DJ [fɔːls] 形 假的

There are a lot of false rumors on the Internet.
網路上有很多假謠言。

例句單字 rumor 名 謠言

同義字 untrue 形 非真實的；錯誤的　fake 形 假的

---

foreign
KK [ˈfɔrɪn] DJ [ˈfɔrin] 形 國外的

How many foreign languages can you speak?
你能夠說幾種外國語言呢？

---

great
KK [gret] DJ [greit] 形 很好的

Adam has great command of English; he can talk in English fluently.
亞當的英文能力很好，他可以用英文流利地說話。

例句單字 have great command of~ 對～的能力很好　fluently 副 流利地

---

loud
KK [laʊd] DJ [laud] 形 大聲的

Don't make loud noises at night.
晚上不要發出大聲的噪音。

例句單字 noise 名 噪音

---

modern
KK [ˈmɑdən] DJ [ˈmɔdən] 形 現代的

Monica is really interested in modern literature.
莫妮卡對於現代文學很有興趣。

例句單字 literature 名 文學

national
KK [ˈnæʃn̩l]
DJ [ˈnæʃənəl]
形 全國性的；國家的

There was a national celebration because the baseball team won the championship.
因為棒球隊贏得冠軍而全國慶祝。

There are a lot of national treasures in museums.
博物館裡面有很多國家珍寶。

 championship 名 冠軍（身分）
treasure 名 珍寶

---

negative
KK [ˈnɛgətɪv]
DJ [ˈnegətiv]
形 負面的

Jack's negative attitude toward life makes his mother really worried.
傑克對人生的負面態度讓他媽媽很擔心。

 pessimistic 形 悲觀的

---

positive
KK [ˈpɑzətɪv]
DJ [ˈpɔzitiv]
形 正面的

Let's look on the positive side.
讓我們正面思考。

 optimistic 形 樂觀的

---

present
KK [ˈprɛzn̩t]
DJ [ˈprezənt]
形 出席的

My teacher will be present at tomorrow's party.
我的老師會出席明天的派對。

---

private
KK [ˈpraɪvɪt]
DJ [ˈpraivit]
形 私人的

This is a private party.
這是一個私人派對。

public KK [`pʌblɪk] DJ [`pʌblik] 形 公開的

The president of the company will make a public speech.

那家公司的總裁將會進行一場公開演講。

quiet KK [`kwaɪət] DJ [`kwaiət] 形 安靜的

You are so quiet today; are you alright?

你今天好安靜，你還好嗎？

right KK [raɪt] DJ [rait] 形 正確的

It is not right to cheat on exams.

考試作弊是不對的。

同義字 correct 形 正確的 proper 形 適當的

safe KK [sef] DJ [seif] 形 安全的

Is it safe for kids to swim in this pool?

小孩子在這個池子裡游泳安全嗎？

same KK [sem] DJ [seim] 形 一樣的

Karen and I are in the same class.

凱倫和我在同一個班級。

special KK [`spɛʃəl] DJ [`speʃəl] 形 特別的

I want to give a special gift to my best friend.

我想要給我最好的朋友一份特別的禮物。

terrible
KK [`tɛrəbl̩]
DJ [`terəbəl]
形 糟糕的

It was a terrible idea to stay up all night; I feel sick now.
熬夜熬整晚是個糟糕的主意，我現在覺得很不舒服。

例句單字 **stay up** 熬夜

---

traditional
KK [trə`dɪʃən!]
DJ [trə`diʃənəl]
形 傳統的

It is a traditional ceremony in their tribe.
那是他們部落的傳統儀式。

例句單字 **ceremony** 名 儀式　**tribe** 名 部落

---

true
KK [tru]
DJ [tru:]
形 真的

Dreams do come true if you go after them.
如果你追尋夢想，那麼它們將會成真。

例句單字 **go after** 追求，追逐

---

wrong
KK [rɔŋ]
DJ [rɔːŋ]
形 錯誤的

You should apologize once you know you are wrong.
當你知道自己錯的時候應該馬上道歉。

例句單字 **apologize** 動 道歉

同義字 **incorrect** 形 不正確的　**improper** 形 不適當的

Describing Words – Similar Words

else
其他；另外

other
其他的；
（兩者中的）另一個

unique
獨特的

only
唯一的

primary/main
主要的

own
自己的

personal
個人的；私人的

terrific
很棒的；了不起的

marvelous
令人驚嘆的；非凡的

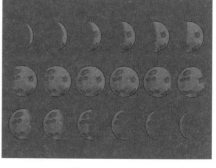

usual
平常的；通常的

regular
一般的；普通的

new
新的

latest
最新的;最近的

likely
很可能的

possible
可能的

alike
相似的;相像的

similar
相似的;相像的

available
可獲得的;可利用的

ready
準備好的

ordinary
普通的;平凡的

general
普遍的;一般的

valuable
珍貴的

precious
珍貴的

42.MP3

alike
KK [ə`laɪk]
DJ [ə`laik]
形 相似的；相像的

The twins look alike; even their mother has a hard time telling them apart.
這對雙胞胎看起來很相像，就連他們的母親都很難區別他們。

例句單字 **have a hard time ~** 做～有困難　**tell apart** 區別

---

available
KK [ə`veləbl]
DJ [ə`veiləbəl]
形 可獲得的；可利用的

The new album is now available in record stores.
新專輯現在可以在唱片行買到。

I don't have the available material to make a robot.
我沒有可利用的材料來做機器人。

例句單字 **record store** 名 唱片行

---

else
KK [ɛls]
DJ [els]
副 其他；另外

There are so many people in this restaurant; let's go somewhere else!
這間餐廳裡人超多，我們去別的地方吧！

Who else wants to join us?
還有誰想加入我們？

小提醒 **else** 是個要放在**疑問詞（who、when、what、how、where）**和不**指定代名詞（代替不特定對象的代名詞，如 something、anything、somewhere 等）**之後的**副詞**，使用的時候要小心別放錯囉！

general KK [ˋdʒɛnərəl] DJ [ˋdʒenərəl] 形 普遍的；一般的

It is general knowledge that water freezes at zero degrees Celsius.
水會在攝氏零度結冰是個普遍的知識。

例句單字 freeze 動 結冰

---

latest KK [ˋletɪst] DJ [ˋleitist] 形 最新的；最近的

My dad bought me the latest cellphone.
我爸買給我最新的手機。

---

likely KK [ˋlaɪklɪ] DJ [ˋlaikli] 形 很可能的

It is likely my dog is a mix of Golden Retriever and Corgi.
我的狗很可能是黃金獵犬和柯基的混種。

---

main KK [men] DJ [mein] 形 主要的

The main actors of the movie are really famous.
這部電影的主要演員們都很有名。

---

marvelous KK [ˋmɑrvələs] DJ [ˋmɑ:viləs] 形 令人驚嘆的；非凡的

The food in that Thai restaurant is marvelous.
那家泰國餐廳裡的食物令人驚嘆。

---

new KK [nju] DJ [nju:] 形 新的

My friends and I go to the new bookstore near our school.
我和朋友一起去學校附近新開的書店。

only
KK [`onlɪ]
DJ [`əunli]　形　唯一的

Sam is the only child in his family.
山姆是他家唯一的孩子。

小提醒 可以用 **only** 後面加上 **son**（兒子）或 **daughter**（女兒）來表示獨生子或獨生女。

---

ordinary
KK [`ɔrdn͵ɛrɪ]
DJ [`ɔ:dənri]　形　普通的；平凡的

I'm not a genius; I'm just an ordinary person.
我不是天才，我只是個普通人。

例句單字 genius 名 天才

---

other
KK [`ʌðɚ]
DJ [`ʌðə]　形　其他的；（兩者中的）另一個

I have other things to do, so I can't go to the party.
我有其他事要做，所以我不能去派對。

I have two pens; one is blue and
the other is red.
我有兩支筆，一支是藍的；而另一支是紅的。

小提醒 other 如果要用來指「兩個東西之中的另一個」，因為有指定的對象，所以**在 other 前面一定要加上 the** 喔！

---

own
KK [on]
DJ [əun]　形　自己的

I finished the puzzle with my own hands.
我用自己的雙手完成了這幅拼圖。

personal
KK [`pɝsənḷ]
DJ [`pəːsənəl]
形 個人的;私人的

It is my personal information; please keep it safe.
這是我的個人資訊,請好好保管。

---

possible
KK [`pɑsəbḷ]
DJ [`pɔsəbəl]
形 可能的

I will walk my dog in the park, if possible.
如果可能的話,我會去公園遛狗。

---

precious
KK [`prɛʃəs]
DJ [`prɛʃəs]
形 珍貴的

My mom gave me a precious ring.
我媽媽給了我一個珍貴的戒指。

---

primary
KK [`praɪˌmɛrɪ]
DJ [`praiməri]
形 主要的

The primary lesson of this story is that you shouldn't take food from a stranger.
這個故事的主要教訓就是你不該拿陌生人給的食物。

---

ready
KK [`rɛdɪ]
DJ [`redi]
形 準備好的

I am ready for the trip!
我準備好去旅行了!

---

regular
KK [`rɛgjələ]
DJ [`regjulə]
形 一般的;普通的

Do you need a bit larger than the regular size?
你需要比普通尺寸再大一點的嗎?

similar KK [ˋsɪmələ] DJ [ˋsimilə] 形 相似的；相像的

Bob and his brothers have similar hobbies.
鮑伯和他的兄弟們有著相似的嗜好。

---

terrific KK [təˋrɪfɪk] DJ [təˋrifik] 形 很棒的；了不起的

Hanson has terrific taste in clothes.
韓森在衣服上有著很棒的品味。

---

unique KK [juˋnik] DJ [ju:ˋni:k] 形 獨特的

It is their unique family tradition.
這是他們獨特的家族傳統。

例句單字 tradition 名 傳統

---

usual KK [ˋjuʒʊəl] DJ [ˋju:ʒuəl] 形 平常的；通常的

As usual, I walk to work.
和平常一樣，我走路去上班。

---

valuable KK [ˋvæljʊəbl] DJ [ˋvæljuəbəl] 形 珍貴的

Those pictures are valuable to me.
那些照片對我來說很珍貴。

It's worth a try. 值得一試。

 worth 是表示「有價值」或是「值得」的意思，而 **try** 這邊是當作名詞「嘗試」，所以整句話直接翻成中文就是「這個值得一次的嘗試」。所以這句話就是指「也許可以很順利，也或許很困難，但是值得一試」喔！

It's worth a try!

Vocabulary 一起看！

★age [edʒ] 名 年齡

★doctor [`dɑktɚ] 名 醫生

★flute [flut] 名 長笛；橫笛

★graduate [`grædʒuˌet] 動 畢業

★harmonica [hɑr`mɑnɪkə] 名 口琴

★hobby [`hɑbɪ] 名 嗜好

★interest [`ɪntərɪst] 名 興趣；愛好

★leap [lip] 動 跳，跳躍

★musician [mju`zɪʃən] 名 音樂家

★pianist [pɪ`ænɪst] 名
 鋼琴家；鋼琴演奏者

★policeman [pə`lismən] 名 警察

★rich man 片 有錢人

★think [θɪŋk] 動 想，思考；認為

★violin [ˌvaɪə`lɪn] 名 小提琴

★young [jʌŋ] 形 年輕的，幼小的

349

blow
吹

bow
鞠躬

move
移動

clap
拍（手）；輕拍

wave
揮動

brush
刷

dig
挖掘

hit
打；打擊

jump 跳躍

kick
踢

knock
敲；敲打

kiss
親吻

laugh
大笑

nod
點頭

sleep
睡覺

smile
微笑

throw
丟；投擲

wake
喚醒

stand
站；站立

share
分享

raise
舉起

sit
坐；坐著

follow
跟隨

catch
抓住

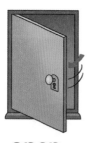

open
打開

close
關閉

make
製作

go
去；離去

come
來；去

pick
撿；挑選

push
推

pull
拉

touch
觸摸；接觸

put
放置

take
拿取

give
給予

43.MP3

blow
KK [blo]
DJ [bləu] 動 吹

Can you blow out the candles?
你能把蠟燭吹熄嗎？

---

bow
KK [baʊ]
DJ [baʊ] 動 鞠躬

Peter bows to the old lady.
彼得跟那位老太太鞠躬。

---

brush
KK [brʌʃ]
DJ [brʌʃ] 動 刷

You should brush your teeth every day.
你應該每天刷牙。

小提醒 刷牙之前需要用 floss（牙線）來清理一下牙
齒，刷牙的時候你需要 toothbrush（牙刷）和
toothpaste（牙膏），一起把這些單字記下來吧～

---

catch
KK [kætʃ]
DJ [kætʃ] 動 抓住

Lions are trying to catch the goats.
獅子正試圖抓住山羊。

---

clap
KK [klæp]
DJ [klæp] 動 拍（手）；輕拍

Let's clap our hands.
讓我們一起拍手。

My teacher clapped me on my shoulder and told me it's okay.
我的老師輕拍我的肩膀，告訴我這沒關係。

close KK [kloz] DJ [kləuz] 動 關閉

You should close the door after you enter the room.
你進房間之後應該要關門。

---

come KK [kʌm] DJ [kʌm] 動 來；去

The bus is coming!
公車來了！

Do you want to come to the party with me?
你想跟我一起去這個派對嗎？

小提醒 come 這個字是指「**往說話的人的方向前進**」，所以「來」是「往說話者的方向前來」，而「去」是「來到說話者身邊一起去」的意思。所以像上面的例句裡的 **bus** 就是往說話者的方向前進，而 **come to the party** 則是說話者本人會去派對，而詢問對方要不要來到自己身邊一起去的意思。

---

dig KK [dɪg] DJ [dig] 動 挖掘

Adam's dog is digging holes happily on the beach.
亞當的狗正開心地在沙灘上挖洞。

反義詞 bury 動 埋

---

follow KK [ˋfɑlo] DJ [ˋfɔləu] 動 跟隨

Amy's cat likes to follow her.
艾咪的貓喜歡跟著她。

---

give KK [gɪv] DJ [giv] 動 給予

I want to give you a gift.
我想給你一個禮物。

同義詞 present 動 贈送　offer 動 提供；給予　provide 動 提供

go KK [go] DJ [gəu] 動 去；離去

I want to go to the library.
我想去圖書館。

小提醒 go 的意思是「**離開現在所在的地方，去另一個地方**」，所以和前面提到的 **come** 不一樣，例如我們要回家的時候會說 **go home** 而不會說 **come home**，因為我們現在不在家裡，而是要「離開目前所在的地點，然後回到家裡」，所以不能用有「往說話的人的方向前進」意思的 **come**。

---

hit KK [hɪt] DJ [hit] 動 打；打擊

The baseball player hits the ball with a bat.
棒球員用球棒打球。

---

jump KK [dʒʌmp] DJ [dʒʌmp] 動 跳躍

How high can you jump?
你能跳多高？

---

kick KK [kɪk] DJ [kik] 動 踢

I can feel her baby kicking inside her belly.
我可以感覺到她的寶寶在她肚子裡踢腳。

---

kiss KK [kɪs] DJ [kis] 動 親吻

Kelly's father kisses her forehead before she goes to bed every night.
凱莉的爸爸每天晚上在她睡覺前都會親吻她的額頭。

knock
KK [nɑk]
DJ [nɔk]
動 敲；敲打

Alicia knocked on the door before entering.
艾莉西雅在進去之前先敲了門。

laugh
KK [læf]
DJ [lɑ:f]
動 大笑

Laughing is good for health.
大笑有益健康。

make
KK [mek]
DJ [meik]
動 製作

Can you teach me how to make a cake?
你能教我怎麼做蛋糕嗎？

move
KK [muv]
DJ [mu:v]
動 移動

Can you move the box to there for me?
你可以幫我把這個箱子移動到那邊嗎？

nod
KK [nɑd]
DJ [nɔd]
動 點頭

The little girl is nodding her head.
這個小女孩正在點頭。

open
KK [`opən]
DJ [`əupən]
動 打開

Can you open the door for me?
你可以幫我開門嗎？

反義詞 shut 動 關閉　close 動 關閉

pick
KK [pɪk]
DJ [pik]
動 撿；挑選

Can you pick up the knife?
你能把刀子撿起來嗎？

I picked one person to go with me, and left the others.
我挑了一個人跟我走，留下了其他人。

小提醒 如果你聽到有人對你說 Can you pick me up?，
這句話可不是叫你把他「撿起來」，而是問你「能
不能去接他」的意思喔！因為 pick up 有「（用
車子）接送」的意思，可以想成是把人從路邊「撿
到」自己車上，這樣是不是好記多了呢？

pull
KK [pʊl]
DJ [pul]
動 拉

Miranda pulled the door.
米蘭達拉開了門。

push
KK [pʊʃ]
DJ [puʃ]
動 推

I pushed the button.
我按下了這個按鈕。

例句單字 button 名 按鈕；鈕扣

put
KK [pʊt]
DJ [put]
動 放置

I put my pen in the pencil box.
我把我的筆放進鉛筆盒裡。

raise
KK [rez]
DJ [reiz]
動 舉起

Sam raised his hand to answer the question.
山姆舉手作答。

share
KK [ʃɛr]
DJ [ʃɛə]
動 分享

My best friend always shares her class notes with me.
我最好的朋友總是跟我分享她的課堂筆記。

---

sit
KK [sɪt]
DJ [sit]
動 坐；坐著

Ricky is trying to teach his dog to sit and wait.
瑞奇正試著教他的狗坐下等待。

動作 Actions

---

sleep
KK [slip]
DJ [sli:p]
動 睡覺

It's late; go to sleep now.
現在很晚了，馬上去睡覺。

---

smile
KK [smaɪl]
DJ [smail]
動 微笑

This joke makes my serious teacher smile.
這個笑話讓我嚴肅的老師微笑了。

小提醒 smile 和 laugh 雖然都是笑，但是笑的程度不一樣，smile 是嘴角上揚的微笑，而 laugh 則是笑出聲音的大笑。

---

stand
KK [stænd]
DJ [stænd]
動 站；站立

Amy stands there waiting for her mother.
艾咪站在那裡等她的媽媽。

take KK [tek] DJ [teik] 動 拿取

Please don't take shells away from the beach.
請不要從沙灘上拿走貝殼。

---

throw KK [θro] DJ [θrəu] 動 丟；投擲

The boy is throwing the ball to his dog.
這個男孩正在把球丟給他的狗。

---

touch KK [tʌtʃ] DJ [tʌtʃ] 動 觸摸；接觸

No one can touch you without your permission.
沒有人可以在沒有你的允許下觸碰你。

例句單字 permission 名 允許

小提醒 touch 是「觸摸；接觸」的意思，如果把 touch 加上 ing 變成 touching 就會變成「**感人的；動人的**」的意思喔！這個字可以用來形容像是故事、戲劇或是音樂等事物，你可以想像如果有一個故事能夠「觸摸、接觸」到你的內心，那這個故事是不是很動人、很感人呢？

---

wake KK [wek] DJ [weik] 動 喚醒

Please wake me up at six o'clock tomorrow morning.
請在明天早上六點叫我起床。

---

wave KK [wev] DJ [weiv] 動 揮動

I wave goodbye to my friends.
我跟我的朋友揮手說再見。

Take care.
小心。

　　不管是出門去上學或是外出去玩耍，爸媽都會讓擔心我們在外面的安全，這個時候他們就可以對我們說 take care，「take care」可以解釋為「小心」，或是「保重」的意思。如果想要說的更仔細，可以說 Take care of yourself. 這句話的意思是「好好照顧自己。」

　　另外我們有的時候會聽到的 Watch out!，則是要引起別人注意的「小心!」，通常是用來提醒別人有需要注意的情況，也可以解釋為「危險!」及「注意!」的意思喔！除了 Watch out! 之外，也可以說「Look out!」或是「Be careful!」來提醒別人。

Take care. 小心。
Take care of yourself. 好好照顧自己。
Watch your step! 小心腳步！
Mind your step! 留心腳步！

Senses 感官

feel
感覺

hear
聽；聽見

listen
聆聽

sound
聽起來

see
看；看見

look
注視；看

watch
觀看

smell
聞

taste
嚐起來

think

想；思考

want

想要

love

喜愛

remember

記得

believe

相信

guess

猜測

need

需要

hope

希望

know

知道

like

喜歡

wish

希望

care

在乎；照顧

enjoy

享受

thank

感謝

welcome

歡迎

believe
KK [bɪˋliv]
DJ [biˋliːv] 動 相信

44.MP3

Do you believe there are ghosts in that castle?
你相信那座城堡裡有鬼嗎？

care
KK [kɛr]
DJ [kɛə] 動 在乎；照顧

Amy doesn't care about being late for school.
艾咪不在乎上學遲到。

Sherry is responsible for caring for our dog.
雪莉負責照顧我們的狗。

 responsible for~ 負責～

enjoy
KK [ɪnˋdʒɔɪ]
DJ [inˋdʒɔi] 動 享受

I hope all of you can enjoy your summer vacation.
我希望你們都可以享受暑假。

feel
KK [fil]
DJ [fiːl] 動 感覺

I don't feel right after eating those shrimp.
我在吃完那些蝦子後感覺不太對勁。

guess
KK [gɛs]
DJ [ges] 動 猜測

It is hard to guess what he is thinking.
很難去猜測他在想什麼。

感官 Senses

365

hear
KK [hɪr]
DJ [hɪə]
動 聽；聽見

Can you hear me?
你可以聽見我說的話嗎？

小提醒 **Can you hear me?** 是一句在測試音量或設備的時候很常用的話，通常是在無法看到對方的情況下使用，例如在接電話的時候聽到的聲音斷斷續續，你就可以說這句話喔！

---

hope
KK [hop]
DJ [həup]
動 希望

Karen hopes her mother buys her a new dress.
凱倫希望她的母親買一件新的洋裝給她。

---

know
KK [no]
DJ [nəu]
動 知道

If you know the answer to the question, you can nod your head.
如果你知道這個問題的答案，你可以點點頭。

---

like
KK [laɪk]
DJ [laik]
動 喜歡

I like my job.
我喜歡我的工作。

---

listen
KK [ˋlɪsn̩]
DJ [ˋlisn̩]
動 聆聽

Please listen to me carefully.
請仔細聽我說。

小提醒 listen 和 hear 雖然都是聽，但是 listen 是「**專注地聽**」，而 hear 則只是單純地「**聽見**」而已，所以如果有人跟你說：I hear you.，很可能他只是隨便聽聽而已，其實根本沒聽進去。但如果他對你說：I listen to you.，那你可以確認他真的有在聽你說話，而且很可能會照你說的去做，因為 I listen to you. 也有「我聽你的。」的意思喔！

---

look
KK [lʊk]
DJ [luk]
動 注視；看

I look at myself in the mirror.
我注視著鏡子裡的自己。

---

love
KK [lʌv]
DJ [lʌv]
動 喜愛

Alan loves his cat with all his heart.
亞倫全心全意地愛著他的貓。

---

need
KK [nid]
DJ [ni:d]
動 需要

What you need is different from what you want.
需要跟想要是不同的。

小提醒 就像例句裡說的，need 和 want 的意思不一樣，want 是「**因為欲望而產生的要求**」，其實不一定真的需要，而 need 則是「**因為需要所產生的要求**」，舉個例子來說，你的午餐是 need，而飯後甜點是 want，這樣是不是很清楚呢？

---

remember
KK [rɪˋmɛmbɚ]
DJ [riˋmembə]
動 記得

Please remember the password of your account.
請記得你帳號的密碼。

see KK [si] DJ [si:] 動 看；看見

I saw you walking into the library.
我看到你走進圖書館。

---

smell KK [smɛl] DJ [smel] 動 聞

How does this perfume smell?
這個香水聞起來怎麼樣？

例句單字 perfume 名 香水

小提醒 smell 如果當名詞的時候是「氣味」的意思，但也有「臭味」的意思，如果你想要特別指出是「香味」，可以用 fragrance 或 aroma 喔！

---

sound KK [saʊnd] DJ [saund] 動 聽起來

It sounds like there is a dog barking in front of our house.
聽起來好像有一隻狗在我們家前面叫。

---

taste KK [test] DJ [teist] 動 嚐起來

How does this cake taste?
這個蛋糕嚐起來怎麼樣？

---

thank KK [θæŋk] DJ [θæŋk] 動 感謝

I thank her for helping me.
我感謝她幫助我。

---

think KK [θɪŋk] DJ [θiŋk] 動 想；思考

We should think how to fix the problem.
我們應該思考要怎麼解決這個問題。

例句單字 fix 動 修理；解決

368

want
KK [wɑnt]
DJ [wɔnt]
動 想要

Emily wants to travel around the world.
艾蜜莉想要環遊世界。

---

watch
KK [wɑtʃ]
DJ [wɔtʃ]
動 觀看

Peter was watching TV all day long.
彼得一整天都在看電視。

例句單字 all day long 一整天

---

welcome
KK [`wɛlkəm]
DJ [`welkəm]
動 歡迎

Mary welcomed me with a big warm hug.
瑪莉用一個大大的溫暖擁抱來歡迎我。

---

wish
KK [wɪʃ]
DJ [wiʃ]
動 希望

I wished for all my dreams to come true.
我希望我所有的夢想都成真。

小提醒 wish 和 hope 的中文都是希望，但 hope 是「**有可能達成的希望**」，而 wish 是「**達成的可能性很低的希望**」，所以如果你想請媽媽買新的遊戲給你，你該用 hope 還是 wish 呢？一起想想看吧！

附錄

人稱代名詞

所謂的代名詞，是指**代替人或事物**的用詞。
人稱代名詞依在句子中的作用不同，會有下列的變化喔！

- 主格：「～是」的意思，做為句子的主詞。
- 所有格：「～的」的意思，置於名詞前方，代表所有者（持有物品的人）。
- 受格：「把～」的意思，置於動詞後方，指接受動作的對象（被～的人）。
- 所有代名詞：「屬於～的」的意思，是所有格加上名詞的形態。

＜單數＞

人稱／所有格	主格 （～是）	所有格 （～的）	受格 （把～）	所有代名詞 （屬於～的）
第一人稱	I	my	me	mine
第二人稱	you	your	you	yours
第三人稱	he she it	his her its	him her it	his hers -

<複數>

人稱／ 所有格	主格 （～是）	所有格 （～的）	受格 （把～）	所有代名詞 （屬於～的）
第一人稱	we	our	us	ours
第二人稱	you	your	you	yours
第三人稱	they	their	them	theirs

反身代名詞

用來表示「～自己」的意思，

這種代名詞會以 **-self [-selves]** 來呈現。

單數		複數	
I	myself	we	ourselves
you	yourself	you	yourselves
he she it	himself herself itself	they	themselves

主要的動詞不規則變化

　　許多動詞的過去式、過去分詞都是在字尾加 ed 來規則變化（規則動詞）。但這些動詞卻不同，不依照一定的規則，而是不規則變化的動詞（不規則動詞）。在此整理出不規則動詞的形態變化。

①原形、過去式、過去分詞皆相同
②原形和過去分詞相同
③過去式和過去分詞相同
④原形、過去式、過去分詞皆不同

①原形、過去式、過去分詞皆相同

原形	主要字義	過去式	過去分詞	ing形
burst	爆發	burst	burst	bursting
cost	花費	cost	cost	costing
cut	切	cut	cut	cutting
hit	打	hit	hit	hitting
hurt	弄傷	hurt	hurt	hurting
let	讓～	let	let	letting
put	放	put	put	putting

quit	退出	quit	quit	quitting
set	設置	set	set	setting
shut	關閉	shut	shut	shutting
spread	伸展、散布	spread	spread	spreading
upset	使心煩意亂	upset	upset	upsetting

②原形和過去分詞相同

原形	主要字義	過去式	過去分詞	ing形
become	變成～	became	become	becoming
come	來	came	come	coming
overcome	克服	overcame	overcome	overcoming
run	跑	ran	run	running

③過去式和過去分詞相同

原形	主要字義	過去式	過去分詞	ing形
bend	彎曲	bent	bent	bending
bring	帶來	brought	brought	bringing
broadcast	廣播	broadcast(ed)	broadcast(ed)	broadcasting
build	興建	built	built	building
buy	購買	bought	bought	buying
catch	捕捉	caught	caught	catching
deal	處理	dealt	dealt	dealing

dig	挖掘	dug	dug	digging
feed	餵養	fed	fed	feeding
feel	感覺	felt	felt	feeling
fight	戰鬥	fought	fought	fighting
find	發現	found	found	finding
have	擁有	had	had	having
hear	聽見	heard	heard	hearing
hold	抓住、舉辦	held	held	holding
keep	保持	kept	kept	keeping
lay	放置	laid	laid	laying
leave	離開	left	left	leaving
lend	借（出）	lent	lent	lending
lose	失去、失敗	lost	lost	losing
make	製作、讓～	made	made	making
mean	意指	meant	meant	meaning
meet	見面	met	met	meeting
pay	支付	paid	paid	paying
read	閱讀	read[rɛd]	read[rɛd]	reading
say	說	said	said	saying
seek	尋求	sought	sought	seeking
sell	賣	sold	sold	selling
send	傳送	sent	sent	sending

shine	發光	shone	shone	shining
shoot	射擊	shot	shot	shooting
sit	坐	sat	sat	sitting
sleep	睡覺	slept	slept	sleeping
slide	滑動	slid	slid	sliding
spend	花費	spent	spent	spending
stand	站立	stood	stood	standing
strike	打擊	struck	struck	striking
swing	搖擺、動搖	swung	swung	swinging
teach	教導	taught	taught	teaching
tell	告訴	told	told	telling
think	思考	thought	thought	thinking
understand	理解	understood	understood	understanding
win	贏	won	won	winning

④原形、過去式、過去分詞皆不同

原形	主要字義	過去式	過去分詞	ing形
be	是～	was, were	been	being
bear	生產、承受	bore	borne/born	bearing
begin	開始	began	begun	beginning
blow	吹	blew	blown	blowing
break	破壞	broke	broken	breaking

choose	選擇	chose	chosen	choosing
do	做	did	done	doing
draw	畫	drew	drawn	drawing
drink	喝	drank	drunk	drinking
drive	駕駛	drove	driven	driving
eat	吃	ate	eaten	eating
fall	掉落	fell	fallen	falling
fly	飛翔	flew	flown	flying
forget	忘記	forgot	forgotten/forgot	forgetting
forgive	原諒	forgave	forgiven	forgiving
freeze	凍結	froze	frozen	freezing
get	得到	got	gotten/got	getting
give	給	gave	given	giving
go	去	went	gone	going
grow	成長	grew	grown	growing
hide	隱藏	hid	hidden	hiding
know	知道	knew	known	knowing
lie	躺	lay	lain	lying
mistake	弄錯	mistook	mistaken	mistaking
ride	乘坐	rode	ridden	riding
ring	響	rang	rung	ringing

rise	上升	rose	risen	rising
see	看	saw	seen	seeing
shake	震動	shook	shaken	shaking
show	展示	showed	shown	showing
sing	唱	sang	sung	singing
sink	沉沒	sank	sunk	sinking
speak	說話	spoke	spoken	speaking
steal	偷竊	stole	stolen	stealing
swim	游泳	swam	swum	swimming
take	拿	took	taken	taking
tear	撕扯	tore	torn	tearing
throw	丟	threw	thrown	throwing
wake	醒來、叫醒	woke	woken	waking
wear	附著、穿戴	wore	worn	wearing
write	書寫	wrote	written	writing

數字的基數與序數

在英文裡面 one、two、three… 等數字的意思是「1、2、3…」，這些數字被稱作「**基數**」，本身**不帶有順序的意思**。但是如果我們想要**表達出「順序」的意思**，例如「第1、第2…」的時候，這個時候我們就必須使用「**序數**」，也就是「first、second、third…」。

一起來看看基數和序數有什麼不同吧！

基數	
1	one
2	two
3	three
4	four
5	five
6	six
7	seven
8	eight
9	nine
10	ten
11	eleven
12	twelve
13	thirteen
14	fourteen
15	fifteen
16	sixteen
17	seventeen
18	eighteen
19	nineteen
20	twenty

序數	
第1	first
第2	second
第3	third
第4	fourth
第5	fifth
第6	sixth
第7	seventh
第8	eighth
第9	ninth
第10	tenth
第11	eleventh
第12	twelfth
第13	thirteenth
第14	fourteenth
第15	fifteenth
第16	sixteenth
第17	seventeenth
第18	eighteenth
第19	nineteenth
第20	twentieth

21	twenty-one	第21	twenty-first
30	thirty	第30	thirtieth
40	forty	第40	fortieth
50	fifty	第50	fiftieth
60	sixty	第60	sixtieth
70	seventy	第70	seventieth
80	eighty	第80	eightieth
90	ninety	第90	ninetieth
100	one hundred	第100	one hundredth
1,000	one thousand	第1,000	one thousandth
10,000	ten thousand	第10,000	ten thousandth
100,000	one hundred thousand	第100,000	one hundred thousandth
1,000,000	one million	第1,000,000	one millionth
1,000,000,000	one billion	第1,000,000,000	one billionth

● 基數在 21 之後，十位數（twenty ~ ninety）和個位數（one ~ nine）中以（-）來連接。

例 ・21 → twenty-one　・22 → twenty-two
　　・23 → twenty-three

● 序數在 21 之後，十位數（twenty ~ ninety）之後的個位數要使用序數（first ~ ninth），中間以（-）連接。

例 ・21 → twenty-first　・22 → twenty-second
　　・23 → twenty-third

● 百位數使用 hundred 來表示。

例 ・101 → one hundred (and) one
　　・250 → two hundred (and) fifty

● 千位數使用 thousand，百萬單位使用 million，十億單位用 billion 來表示。

數字的讀法

①小數點

小數點唸為 point，小數點以下的數字都以基數來唸。

> 例　3.14 ＝ three point one four

②分數

分子以基數，分母以序數來唸。分子若為 2 以上時，分母的序數
則使用複數形。

> 例　・三分之一（1/3）＝ one third
>
> 　　・四分之三（3/4）＝ three fourths
>
> 　　・一百分之一（1/100）＝ one hundredth

※ 二分之一以 half 來表示。

　另外，四分之一（1/4）除了用 one fourth，也可以用 a
quarter 表示。

③時刻

基本上是以「時」→「分」的順序，以基數來唸。

> 例　・7:50 → seven fifty
>
> 　　・8:55 → eight fifty-five

④月日

在一般的情況下，「日」會以序數來唸（但也有以基數來唸的情況）。另外在序數的前面可以選擇加上或不加上 the。

例　· January 21 → January (the) twenty-first /

January twenty-one

⑤年

百位數和十位數分開，各分成兩位數以基數來念。

例　· 1492 → fourteen ninety-two

· 1984 → nineteen eighty-four

但 21 世紀（2000 ～ 2099 年）的情況，被念成 two thousand (and)~ 的比較多。

例　· 2001 → two thousand (and) one

· 2017 → two thousand (and) seventeen

1本就通 國中英文文法

作者：長澤壽夫

附 QR碼線上音檔

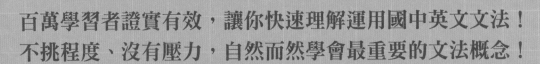

百萬學習者證實有效，讓你快速理解運用國中英文文法！
不挑程度、沒有壓力，自然而然學會最重要的文法概念！

★ 6大句型法則＋87個句型＋實戰練習，國中文法只要87個句型就搞定！

★ 超過300萬名學生見證、結合補教名師多年教學經驗，最實用、最有效！

★ 無論在學還是上班族都適用！學生課外加強、上班族重新打基礎，都好用！

★ 徹底學好重要句型，只要替換關鍵字和時態，就能運用自如、不出錯！

台灣廣廈 國際出版集團
Taiwan Mansion International Group

國家圖書館出版品預行編目（CIP）資料

1本就通！小學生必備單字2000/李宗玥著.
-- 初版. -- 新北市：國際學村出版社，2024.02
　　面；　公分
　　ISBN 978-986-454-338-0(平裝)
　　1.CST: 英語教學 2.CST: 詞彙 3.CST: 初等教育

523.318　　　　　　　　　　　　　　　112022807

 國際學村

1本就通！小學生必備單字2000

作　　　者／李宗玥	編輯中心編輯長／伍峻宏
	編輯／徐淳輔
	封面設計／林珈仔・內頁排版／東豪
	製版・印刷・裝訂／東豪・弼聖・明和

行企研發中心總監／陳冠蒨　　　線上學習中心總監／陳冠蒨
媒體公關組／陳柔彣　　　　　　數位營運組／顏佑婷
綜合業務組／何欣穎　　　　　　企製開發組／江季珊、張哲剛

發　行　人／江媛珍
法 律 顧 問／第一國際法律事務所 余淑杏律師・北辰著作權事務所 蕭雄淋律師
出　　　版／國際學村
發　　　行／台灣廣廈有聲圖書有限公司
　　　　　　地址：新北市235中和區中山路二段359巷7號2樓
　　　　　　電話：（886）2-2225-5777・傳真：（886）2-2225-8052
讀者服務信箱／cs@booknews.com.tw

代理印務・全球總經銷／知遠文化事業有限公司
　　　　　　地址：新北市222深坑區北深路三段155巷25號5樓
　　　　　　電話：（886）2-2664-8800・傳真：（886）2-2664-8801
郵 政 劃 撥／劃撥帳號：18836722
　　　　　　劃撥戶名：知遠文化事業有限公司（※單次購書金額未達1000元，請另付70元郵資。）

■出版日期：2024年02月　　　ISBN：978-986-454-338-0
　　　　　　2024年07月3刷　　版權所有，未經同意不得重製、轉載、翻印。